5/13/03

To Mark —

From Moonshine to Madison Avenue

From one Mark to
another! A fan of
Mark Martin is a
true friend of mine....
Best wishes for a
happy birthday!

From Moonshine to Madison Avenue:
A Cultural History
of the NASCAR Winston Cup Series

Mark D. Howell

with a Foreword by

Brett Bodine

Bowling Green State University Popular Press
Bowling Green, OH 43403

Sports and Culture

General Editors
Douglas Noverr
Lawrence Ziewacz

Other books in the series:

The Wonder Team:
The True Story of the Incomparable 1927 New York Yankees
Leo Trachtenberg

The Sports Immortals: Deifying the American Athlete
Peter Williams

Hunting and Fishing for Sport: Commerce, Controversy, Popular Culture
Richard Hummel

Cricket for Americans: Playing and Understanding the Game
Tom Melville

Baseball in 1889: Players vs. Owners
Daniel M. Pearson

The Kid on the Sandlot: Congress and Professional Sports, 1910-1992
Stephen R. Lowe

Copyright © 1997 Bowling Green State University Popular Press

Library of Congress Cataloging-in-Publication Data
Howell, Mark D.
    From moonshine to Madison Avenue : a cultural history of the
NASCAR Winston Cup series / Mark D. Howell.
        p.   cm.
    Includes bibliographical references and index.
    ISBN 0-87972-739-X (clothbound). -- ISBN 0-87972-740-3 (pbk.)
    1. NASCAR (Association)--History.   2. Stock car racing--United
States--History.   3. Stock car racing--Economic aspects--United
States.   I. Title.
GV1029.9.S74H68   1997
796.72'0973--dc21   97-4215
                                                                  CIP

Cover design by Dumm Art

This project is dedicated to my father and mother, who introduced me to the sport of stock car racing, and to all those who lost their lives chasing the checkered flag.

All my heartfelt gratitude to my wife, Bonnie, and to our daughter, Corrie Love. Their unconditional love is what sustains me and makes me appreciate every day.

Contents

Foreword, by Brett Bodine   ix

Acknowledgments   xiv

1. Looking Ahead, Looking Within: An Introduction   1

2. The Show Goes On: NASCAR, Control,
   and the Winston Cup Series   13

3. A Fight to the Finish: NASCAR Versus Organized Labor   29

4. A High-Banked Learning Curve: Acculturation
   and Stock Car Racing   49

   Photos   70

5. Changing Identities in American Culture:
   Sponsorship and Drivers' Roles in NASCAR's
   Winston Cup Series   81

   Photos   98

6. Made in America: Ritual, Folklore,
   and Cultural Mythology of the NASCAR
   Winston Cup Series   109

   Photos   136

7. Seeing is Believing: A Personal Ethnography
   of NASCAR's Winston Cup Series
   and Stock Car Racing in America   147

8. Is Bigger Always Better? The Future of the NASCAR
   Winston Cup Series   179

Appendices
  A: 1997 Winston Cup Schedule   199
  B: Winston Cup Tracks and Locations   200
  C: 1997 Winston Cup Team Listing   203
  D: NASCAR Winston Cup Champions, 1949-1996   205
  E: Manufacturers' Champions, 1949–1996   206

F: Outstanding NASCAR Winston Cup Career Victories   207
G: NASCAR Winston Cup Series' Most Popular Drivers   209
H: NASCAR Rookies of the Year, 1996–1958   210
I: How Points Are Distributed in the Winston Cup Series   211
J: NASCAR Winston Cup Series Race Shops   213
K: Fifty Current NASCAR-Related Web Sites   221
L: Restaurants with Racing Themes   225
M: Stock Car Driving Schools   227

Notes   229

Glossary   231

Bibliography   235

Index   257

Foreword, by Brett Bodine

The title of the book by Dr. Howell says it all—"From Moonshine to Madison Avenue."

That is how far the NASCAR Winston Cup Series has come in the last 40 years.

Yes, the sport's roots go back to the days when "hauling moonshine" was an everyday occurrence in as they say in North Carolina—"the hills."

And the natural evolution was for the "boys" doing the hauling to feel that their car was faster than the next one. After all, speed was essential if you were going to outrun the "feds."

At first, the racing was through those "hills." But then they turned to the local race tracks. And this was the real beginning of what we know today as the NASCAR Winston Cup Series.

If it wasn't for a man named Bill France Sr. or "Big Bill" as was affectionately called, there would be no NASCAR—the National Association for Stock Car Auto Racing.

But Mr. France was a man of vision. And because of his vision, the fastest-growing sport in the country today is NASCAR Winston Cup racing.

And today, Madison Avenue is as much a part of the sport as the cars themselves. For if it wasn't for those Fortune 500 companies and the news media, in particular television, the sport wouldn't have taken off like a rocket being launched from Cape Kennedy.

NASCAR Winston Cup racing really started running wide open in the late 1970s and 1980s. And the main reason was companies like R.J. Reynolds Tobacco Company.

RJR was the first non-automotive company to be involved in the sport, and when it threw its marketing, promotional and public relations muscle at the marketplace the big winner was NASCAR and the sport of NASCAR Winston Cup racing.

The Winston brand began sponsoring NASCAR's premier series in 1971.

Before the 1970s had come to an end, Winston and RJR had proven to Madison Avenue that stock car racing was one of the great untapped marketing tools in the world.

And when other Fortune 500 companies saw what a great marketing tool the sport was, they jumped on the bandwagon.

And then in 1979, CBS televised the Daytona 500 live.

The race had everything that makes NASCAR Winston Cup racing great—side-by-side racing, lots of lead changes, a great battle for the win, a memorable finish and controversy.

CBS couldn't have picked a better race to broadcast live from start to finish. And what a finish!

The last lap came down to a duel between Donnie Allison and Cale Yarborough. The two literally tangled on the backstretch at Daytona International Speedway with both cars spinning off the track. Both drivers were quite upset by the turn of events and they expressed their unhappiness like boys will do sometimes by getting into a fight that also included Bobby Allison, Donnie's brother. Bobby had stopped his race car and got out to see what was going on, and before too long, he was right in the middle of the fight. CBS caught every minute of the dispute.

While the Allisons and Yarborough were battling each other, the King, Richard Petty, was battling Darrell Waltrip, the new up-and-coming star, for the win. King Richard held off Darrell to score his seventh Daytona 500 triumph. No one else has won more than three Daytona 500s—the Super Bowl of stock car racing.

I'll remember that race forever. I was sitting at home in Chemung, New York, watching it.

And so will the history books. As that television broadcast and the unbelievable finish along with the marketing expertise of RJR and others played the major role in speeding up—and I do mean speeding up—the growth and popularity of NASCAR Winston Cup racing.

We did a lot of growing in the 1980s. But it has been nothing like the '90s.

The sport has been running faster than the sound barrier in the '90s. And who knows how fast we will be running when we hit the 21st century.

We are riding a rocketship that seems to be picking up speed almost on a daily basis.

And for those of us on the inside, it seems to be running faster off the track than we are running on it.

For those of us who have been part of the sport of racing for all our lives, it is just amazing how far we have come.

We always knew it was the greatest sport in the world. But for the general public and Madison Avenue to feel the same way makes us feel really proud that we are part of this rocketship.

For Brett and Diane Bodine, it has been a pretty wild ride of our own. We moved south early in the 1980s as we knew we needed to do that to speed up our chances of becoming a part of the Winston Cup racing.

We made our Winston Cup debut in 1986, driving for Rick Hendrick in the World 600 at Charlotte, North Carolina, Motor Speedway.

And then in 1987, I ran 14 races for Hoss Ellington. But my big break came when Junior Johnson asked me to be the relief driver for Terry Labonte during the 1987 season after Terry was injured. Driving for a legend like Junior Johnson was like a dream come true.

I didn't know it at the time, but Junior would later play an even bigger role in my career.

Driving for Junior twice in 1987 helped me land a full-time ride with another of the sport's legends—Bud Moore. Bud is a war hero, and he has been part of the sport for almost 30 years.

My two years with Bud were a real learning experience. Like I said, he has been around the sport forever, and he was a great teacher. And we had two real good years together.

In 1990, I moved to the Kenny Bernstein team. And what a great year it was. I won my first Winston Cup race at North Wilkesboro, North Carolina. I won my first pole position at Charlotte. And we finished 12th in the race for the national championship. It was just a great year.

Larry McReynolds was our crew chief. Larry is one of the best in the business. Early in 1991, Larry moved to the Robert Yates team, and immediately the 28 car become a big winner with Davey Allison.

I ended up spending five years with Bernstein. The last three years, Donnie Richeson, my brother-in-law, was the crew chief. Donnie is married to Donna, Diane's twin sister.

It was a good five years, and again I learned a lot—especially the side of how to run a race team since Kenny was gone a lot running his other racing teams. As a result, I was heavily involved in running the team. And it was during this time that I first began thinking about owning my own team.

In 1994, I began seriously investigating the possibility of owning my own team. Because of the huge cost to run a Winston Cup team, you have to have a major company sponsoring your operation.

All of us want to win races. And to be competitive in this very competitive business, it takes cubic dollars. Today, you need at least $4 million to run a Winston Cup team. And many of the top teams are spending much more than that.

While Madison Avenue and many of the top Fortune 500 companies are sponsoring race cars, it is still a difficult and time-consuming process to find a sponsor for a new race team. And that's what we would have been in 1995.

When you talk to companies about spending the kind of money we are talking about, it is a very long process, especially if you are talking with companies that are new to the sport.

We had several good leads, and if we had more time, we probably would have secured that all-important sponsor. But as we got closer and closer to the start of the 1995 season, we decided the best approach would be to put off the idea of being both owner and driver.

About the same time we decided we better start reexamining our plans for 1995, Junior Johnson popped back in the picture. He asked us to become the driver of the No. 11 Ford Thunderbird. He had landed a new sponsor—Lowe's Home Improvement Warehouse.

This was Lowe's first venture into the world of sport sponsorship.

Diane and I decided the best thing to do was go with Junior. We decided we'd look at owning our team down the road.

As we got into the 1995 season, we started talking to Junior about buying his race team. Junior had been part of the sport for almost 40 years, and he felt it was time to retire, if that's the right word.

In between races, we began negotiating with Junior to buy the team. The deal wasn't finalized until after the last race at Atlanta.

As a result, that put us way behind in getting ready for the 1996 season. And 1996 was a very trying year because of the late start we got.

But owning our own race team has been a dream for Diane and me. This is something we have wanted to do for years. And we feel the future is quite bright for BDR Motorsports. We believe there are a lot of good days ahead.

This is especially true now that we have signed a three-year contract with Catalyst Communications and Frontier Communications. They are the people who have put together the Close Call Phone Card and Sweepstakes program that will back our team in 1997 and for the next two years.

Lowe's decided they wanted to move elsewhere in 1997, and that meant we had to go back in the sponsor-hunting mold.

As I said, sponsor hunting is a very time-consuming process. When you are trying to run a race team and find a sponsor, you are under a lot of pressure. But thanks to the great people at Sports Marketing Enterprises (SME), we landed that all-important sponsor. They are the ones that secured the sponsor for our team.

For both Catalyst and Frontier, motorsports sponsorship is new to them. But they and SME have come with a very unique program—a promotion that I think will be a big hit on and off the race track.

First, they have decided to sponsor five other teams in addition to our Winston Cup operation. It has to be the largest motorsports sponsorship package in the history of motorsports.

The other teams include Jim Head's Top Fuel Dragster on the NHRA Winston drag racing circuit, the Pro Stock Motorcycle drag racing team with John Myers and Angelle Seeling, Mark Tate's Unlimited Hydroplane and the Late Model Stock car of Toby Robertson.

The Close Call Phone Card is a prepaid phone card. Every cardholder gets 15 minutes of prepaid phone time. In addition, each card carries a "scratch and win" section in which the cardholder will be able to tell immediately if he or she has won one of the more than six million prizes. More than $60 million will be given away as part of the sweepstakes. It's hard to believe, but $60 million will be given away. There will be 16 grand prizes of $250,000 and a new car. One out of every 15 cards will be a winner in this promotion.

It is one great promotion, and it shows again what a great marketing tool NASCAR Winston Cup racing is.

As you will see as you read Dr. Howell's book, the sport of NASCAR Winston Cup racing has come a long way. It is a very interesting story, and one Dr. Howell has done a great job in telling.

I know you are going to enjoy the story of the sport that I love so much.

Acknowledgments

As I cross the finish line of this project, I would like to thank my "team," the many people who worked behind the scenes and believed in this long overlooked subject and me. This project would never have become reality if not for the help, guidance, and support of some very important people. A mere mention within the following pages will never match the kindness and assistance I received during the course of my work.

First, I want to thank the many people in and around Winston Cup racing who gave of their time and energy to help me. I would like to thank Alex Beam of Davidson, North Carolina, for all of his assistance and friendship. He took me in as an intern, and the opportunity turned into the book before you. Alex led me to others in the NASCAR family, people like Billy Biscoe, whose interest in restoring old stock cars made us fast friends, and an unassuming gentleman by the name of Robert Glenn Johnson—although most folks around Wilkes County call him Junior. Alex also introduced me to Deb Williams, a warm and friendly woman who is editor of *Winston Cup Scene,* one of America's great racing trade papers. Deb helped me very much in the early days of my research, despite her busy schedule following the NASCAR circuit.

Many thanks to Brett Bodine for his help, especially with the foreword he wrote. Thanks also to Jimmy Spencer for the visit we had at the Motorsports Hall of Fame in Novi, Michigan. It is always nice to talk with drivers away from the hustle and bustle of the speedway, and these two men were friendly, open, and gracious right from the start.

I received assistance from many of the fine people at Sports Marketing Enterprises in Winston-Salem, North Carolina—especially the information provided to me by Dean Kessel when Brett Bodine was with Team Lowe's and by Jim Bowling. My gratitude runs deep for all of the help he and his associates gave me. Thanks also to Bob Moore for his time and consideration.

I am grateful to Andy Macvicar, who worked for the Smokin' Joe's Ford Thunderbird, owned by Travis Carter and driven by Jimmy Spencer. Andy made it possible for me to travel with the Smokin' Joe's team to the AC-Delco 500 at Rockingham in October of 1994, the event where Dale Earnhardt wrapped up his record-tying seventh Winston Cup championship. Thanks to Travis and his team for their kindness and hospitality.

Other Winston Cup teams have helped me as well, including: Joe Gibbs Racing, Bobby Allison Motorsports, Alan Kulwicki Racing, Bahari Racing, Junior Johnson and Associates, Penske South Racing, Rudd Performance Motorsports, Kranefuss-Haas Racing, Radius Motorsports, Morgan-McClure Racing, Billy Hagan Racing, and Larry Hedrick Racing. These teams supplied me with media kits and information regarding sponsorship, personal appearances, and other areas pertinent to campaigning in the Winston Cup Series.

I also want to thank the individuals who answered my call for assistance. This list includes Stephen Brown, director of public relations at Michigan International Speedway; Chuck Martin, vice president of public relations at Martinsville Speedway; and Jim Freeman, director of public relations at Talladega Superspeedway. These men helped me with pit passes and information when others in the racing business turned away. All my gratitude to George Issacs and everyone at Pocono International Raceway for the opportunity to do research there while the Winston Cup Series was in town. I found assistance at NASCAR by talking with Competition Administrator Jerry Cook and the former Winston Cup Media Coordinator, Richard "Chip" Williams. To them I am grateful.

Some sponsors' representatives were also willing to take part in my project, including people from Anheuser-Busch, Kodak, Miller Brewing, and GM Goodwrench. Thanks also to the people at the Ford Motor Company, McDonald's Corporation, R.J. Reynold's Tobacco Company, Exide Batteries, and Owens-Corning for all of their help. These companies supplied me with everything from press kits to photograph opportunities, things that made my research more detailed and better suited for publication.

I owe a large debt to racing historian Greg Fielden. His five-volume history of NASCAR events made my work much easier. His documentation provided me with fast references and a "safety net" of sorts when I found myself dealing with conflicting names, dates, or statistics. Greg saved me many days, if not weeks, of newspaper research. Thanks also to Jerry Cashman, Dick Berggren, Allen Bestwick, and Sylvia Wilkinson for their guidance and advice.

Some names I cannot miss are those of my family and friends. Linda and Alan Hoke, my sister-in-law and brother-in-law, always provided me with warm hospitality when I was working in Charlotte, and my North Carolina friends always made research more fun than work. Many thanks to Joe Estes, Robert and Denise Shinn, Frank and Susan Guy, and David and Leslie Fox for all of their help.

My parents, Glenn and Virginia Howell, and my in-laws, Bruce and Jane Corrie, have shown me support since the very beginning of my work, and to them I will always be grateful. Special thanks to my father for his teaching me about all things automotive. He has always been, and will always be, my favorite driver and hero. Thanks also to my brother, Roger, and his wonderful family. He is more than just a sibling to me— he is my role model and best friend. I apologize to the people whose names I missed; the oversight was purely accidental.

To my colleagues at Bowling Green State University, who witnessed the beginning of this project, I thank them for their advice, support, and friendship. The following people provided me with guidance and constructive criticism: James Coon, John Dowell, Paul Fischer, Torey King, March McCubrey, Molly Merryman, Diana Montague, Ginny Schwartz, Mary Thompson, Ben Urish, Sharon Vriend, Mitty Wherry, and Shawn Wilbur.

I thank my colleagues and students at Michigan State University for their assistance and emotional support. The fine people in the Department of American Thought and Language asssisted me in the final stages of this book, and the following folks helped me greatly: Gary Hoppenstand, Pat Julius, Chris Felker, Greg Garvey, Hal Bush, Liz Davey, Carl Eby, Lisa Rashley, Leon Jackson, Nora Roberts, Erik Lunde, Phoebe Jackson, Tersh Palmer, Paul Tidwell, and Kathleen McGarvey.

I thank William Grant, Burton Beerman, Trish Cunningham, and Eldon Snyder who were vital to this project at Bowling Green State University for their patience and guidance.

I also want to thank my editors at Popular Press, Doug Noverr and Lawrence Ziewacz, for all their advice and friendship. It was an honor to work with two of the finest sports historians in the business. Much of my gratitude goes to all of the people at the Popular Press for their hard work and assistance. Deepest thanks as well to Ray and Pat Browne for all their faith in this project. I hope the final product does them proud.

Last, but certainly not least, I want to thank my wife, Bonnie, for all of her help and support. She has traveled with me, typed for me, edited my work, given me ideas, and shown me unconditional love. Her strength and warmth inspired me. One last minute helper was someone who came along just as the manuscript was going to press—our baby daughter, Corrie Love Howell. After days and nights of revising, editing, and organizing, her little smile and loving warmth provided me with a welcome escape. No book could ever mean more than the sparkle of happiness I get from my little girl's eyes.

1

Looking Ahead, Looking Within:
An Introduction

... damn foolishness to one person is breath of life to another.
—Junior Jackson's father in the film
The Last American Hero (1973)

The NASCAR Winston Cup Series is unique in the world of professional sports because it provides such an overwhelming sensory experience. It is not that other sports are less sensory-intensive, the difference is that Winston Cup racing swells and expands our senses. The rush and the roar of the race cars—row after row of double-file machines brightly burnished with names, logos, decals, and digits—overwhelm us. Smells of gasoline, burnt rubber, suntan lotion, hot dogs, and beer drift through the air. Waves of men, women, and children move en masse from parking lots to grandstands to restrooms to souvenir trailers; most are decked out in driver-emblazoned attire, all looking sunburned and windblown.

The most prominent attack on the senses comes aurally in the form of engine noise, the low growl of unharnessed horsepower that shakes the ground and rattles our insides. It is a sound that melts the spine, especially as the green flag waves and 40 cars—each one 3,400 pounds of hell on wheels—explode to life. We cheer and shout, we jump and wave. The cars surge forward in a stream of controlled chaos, each one manned by a pilot who aims his mount toward an imaginary spot on the track's surface. If the first corner is tight and flat, the cars will nose down into the turn, brakes applied hard to lower the car and set it on target. If the first corner is high-banked and open, the cars will simply fly off against the wall of asphalt, physics replacing reason as the cars drift and bob through the turbulent air. Gas pedals are glued to the floor as throttles stay wide open—to lift is to lose. Through it all, you thrill at the spectacle whether you are in the grandstands, in the infield, or standing behind the pit wall.

Winston Cup stock car racing is just that—a spectacle of sights, sounds, smells, and emotions. Everything about the sport involves the spectator; you cannot attend a Winston Cup event and remain passive. If you are a seasoned race fan, you know the drivers, their reputations on the track, their cars, and their sponsors. If you are attending a race for the first time, it takes little more than the command to start engines to get your blood and sweat flowing. From the first flip of an ignition switch, as electricity, air, and gasoline blend to create mechanized life, you know this is something different; this is not an ordinary professional sporting event. There is more to this than just prize money and trophies.

Part of the fun of a Winston Cup weekend is people-watching. Race fans, being a silent majority for many years, find solace in the infields and grandstands across America. They share food, drinks, and high fives; they trade stories, gossip, and race analysis. These are the people at the center of the sport—the folks who buy the tickets, the souvenirs, and the sponsors' products. NASCAR recognizes and appreciates the fans who fill the seats. The sanctioning body has been mindful of its fans since the late 1940s when the Strictly Stock and Modified divisions started running races. Stock car racing has always drawn loyal audiences, folks who live for the sights and sounds of cars and drivers battling for supremacy on America's speedways.

I have been following the NASCAR Winston Cup Series my entire life, and have seen this first-time revelation on the faces of many people over the years. Watching people discover the nuances of stock car racing is fun and fascinating, especially when the revelation strikes someone you think of as being an "unlikely" racing fan. I admit, it is an unusual experience to talk about stock cars with a fifteen-year old girl who can recite driver statistics and track specifications. When a teenaged girl can explain qualifying strategy or race day chassis setups as easily as the latest movies or music videos, it is a testimony to the depth of interest and the level of knowledge the Winston Cup Series inspires.

My niece, Melissa, is one of these young women. She follows Jeff Gordon and his Rainbow Warriors religiously, sending me a card (featuring Jeff, naturally) after each of his wins. Missy was familiar with stock car racing, but she had never seen a race in person. Then she attended her first Winston Cup event in June of 1996. Since Pocono was near where we lived, and I was going to do fieldwork there, this was the best opportunity for Missy to experience NASCAR for herself. My mother and my wife, both experienced race-goers, gave Missy suggestions regarding what to wear, what to bring, and what to look for. By the time the race started, Missy was wearing her newly purchased Jeff Gordon rainbow-styled baseball cap, hairbow, and socks, her camera loaded and ready with a roll of Kodak film. By the time the race ended and Gordon climbed from his car in Victory Lane, Melissa was ecstatically looking forward to her next trip to the speedway. A month later, she returned with her grandparents and father and saw Rusty Wallace take the checkered flag.

The great thing about Winston Cup racing is its capacity to convert fans from other sports, especially other types of motorsports. One of my best friends, a man who has attended the Indianapolis 500 for 30 consecutive years, was skeptical of stock cars running at the Brickyard. He cracked jokes about race cars "with doors," about drivers stopping "to put their luggage in their trunks." His brother, a yellow shirt at Indianapolis Motor Speedway, referred to Winston Cup cars running at the Brickyard as "taxi cabs."[1] Their comments were not all that unusual, especially amongst purists who cringed at the thought of full-bodied, production-based cars running at the shrine of open-wheeled action. Both men would be at the Brickyard.

Their opinions changed following the inaugural running of the Brickyard 400 in August of 1994. The altercation between Brett and Geoff Bodine, Ernie Irvan's cut tire during the closing laps, and Jeff Gordon's subsequent victory caused these two men to re-evaluate their take on Winston Cup cars at Indianapolis. Slower lap speeds were countered with nose-to-tail, door-to-door, fender-rubbing action—typical for Winston Cup fans but something new for people familiar with open-wheeled cars at IMS.

Winston Cup racing is a sport of addiction. Once you experience it firsthand, you feel compelled to keep following it. In many cases, you quickly identify with a driver, his sponsor, or the make of car he drives. You watch races on television, you scan the newspaper for articles or photographs, you see people on the street wearing a NASCAR T-shirt or cap, you notice numbered decals on the back windows of cars and trucks, you start to recognize (and buy) products based on which team they sponsor. Once you start, you cannot escape the sport's magnetic pull. Given that Winston Cup racing is currently enjoying a period of rapid and dramatic growth, there is really no limit to the amount of attention the sport demands. To keep informed, you need to keep up with the championship points battle, driver changes, sponsor changes, rule changes, and—within the last year—schedule changes involving new speedways and new countries.

The dramatic growth in Winston Cup racing and the sport's impact on American culture, deserves detailed study. A cultural reading of NASCAR's evolution shows that stock car racing has become part of our national consciousness, both accepted and recognized by corporate America and the media. As a lifelong fan of NASCAR competition, I have found it exciting to watch stock car racing evolve from a sport largely ignored by the mainstream media to a sport worthy of its own television news and information programming. My memories of Winston Cup racing (then called "Grand National" racing) on television come from Saturday afternoons spent watching ABC's *Wide World of Sports,* where NASCAR races would be taped and edited to fit a one or two-hour time slot, usually sandwiched around figure skating or an exhibition by the Harlem Globetrotters. As a boy, my exposure to NASCAR was limited to *Stock Car Racing* magazine, the occasional partial race on television, and regular trips to racetracks with my mother and father.

Times have changed and so has the attention given to stock car racing. With the advent of cable television, Winston Cup races are now a common part of weekend programming. Newspapers once reluctant to print NASCAR coverage now give the sport equal page space with sports like professional golf and tennis. No longer does a race fan have to search for Winston Cup news; today the news comes to the fan via the Internet on a daily basis. Sites on the World Wide Web dedicate themselves to stock car racing; NASCAR has its own online service, and many race teams have their own home pages. Chat groups enable NASCAR fans to have open discussion about the changes they see taking place. No longer do NASCAR fans have to hide their light under a bushel. Stock car racing has entered an exciting era of worldwide growth and international acceptance.

Why has such rapid change and growth taken place within NASCAR Winston Cup racing? Has the sport changed so much over the last ten years that Americans are now willing to give it a closer look? When you consider the millions of people who are attending NASCAR races in person each year—over 10 million during the 1995 season alone—it appears as though something has happened to capture the world's attention. Look at the television ratings for 1995, and you will discover over 120 million people who tuned their sets to NASCAR race broadcasts ("NASCAR Set to Drive").[2] What has caused such significant change?

As a cultural historian, it was only a matter of time before my profession caught up with my obsession. I had watched stock car racing evolve into a major professional sport, but I never considered the factors responsible for this rapid growth. Nothing exists in a vacuum, so I felt there had to be some explanation that would define exactly how NASCAR racing had found such a home within the culture that had, at one time, considered it insignificant—just an excuse for rednecks to get drunk, fight, and watch men smash cars in horrific, and sometimes fatal, accidents.

The success and acceptance of the NASCAR Winston Cup Series comes from its ability to be interpreted on two distinct levels: one tangible and one intangible. It is a sport of numbers and statistics, a sport suited for quantitative analysis: laps led, races won, engine revolutions per minute turned, gear ratios used, seconds needed per pit stop, prize money earned, and championship points awarded. These are the things easily recognized, the stuff of press releases, sponsorship deals, and Victory Lane speeches. These tangible elements make NASCAR racing understandable at a public level. We know about such criteria because these are items we hear about on a regular basis.

The NASCAR Winston Cup Series is also a sport of the intangible: symbols, rituals, and images. It is a sport rooted in cultural mythology— the stereotypes of rural America and the agrarian Southeast, the outlaw nature of folks forced to break the law in order to put food on their tables, and the eventual transition that turned regional folk heroes into national sports heroes. An analysis of American culture presents Winston Cup racing as a phenomenon connected to our romanticism of the West. It is a sport with ties to the rebellious actions of post-Revolutionary frontiersmen. This is an activity with deep roots, the lines that connect the America of today with the America of yesterday. Stock car racing is more than a sport; it represents an important element of our nation's culture.

Our initial reaction to stock car racing is its connection to moonshining—the making, hauling, and selling of corn liquor. This has been the basis for many of the stereotypes tied to the sport. Men like Junior Johnson, Tim Flock, and Curtis Turner started out in the moonshine business not because of its glamour, but for its ability to generate much-needed income. American popular culture romanticizes moonshining, interpreting it through mediums like motion pictures and music. Such interpretation sanitizes the experience, making it palatable for mass audiences who want more fiction than fact.

Popular culture is, according to Jane and Michael Stern, "the closest thing America has to a national faith. . . . pop culture has become the drumbeat of everyday life. . . . [it] is American culture. . . . America's modern mythology" (xi-xii). America's influence on world civilization is not from its fine art or classical music; it comes from our creation and distribution of popular art: our television programs, our rock and country music, our motion pictures, magazines, newspapers, and attention to fads and trends. Popular culture has the greatest impact on the largest number of people in a society, and it often shapes our interpretations and presentations of cultural icons, whether they be historical, physical or material, ritualistic, or symbolic. If people in a society share some common knowledge of a particular person or artistic work, then that person or work is recognized—understood by the culture at large and therefore considered to be "popular." Such a general understanding of cultural issues and artifacts can alter our definition of them, causing us to see them differently than what they were originally.

I saw evidence of this phenomenon at a dinner party I attended in Evanston, Illinois, a few years ago. After dessert, I was sitting at the dining room table with some of the other guests. We were enjoying coffee and conversation when the discussion turned to automobiles, and someone mentioned my research on stock car racing. Several of the people seated at the table began asking me questions; many had heard of NASCAR racing or seen it on television, and they wanted to know more about it. I spoke of the sport's roots in moonshining, and how popular culture had made the dangerous business look glamourous. An older woman, seated directly across the table from me, began to shake her head. "Moonshining wasn't fun," she said, "it was a hard way to make a living and it was anything but glamourous."

I agreed with her and explained that it was American popular culture that had romanticized moonshining, and that such an idealized view simplified the reality of what these people did. It truly was a harsh and dangerous life. I asked the woman why she responded to my initial comment so passionately, and she said, "I grew up in North Wilkesboro, North Carolina, and I had friends at school whose families made and ran corn liquor. They did it because they had to, just to survive."

The other people at the dining room table were stunned. Here, at a quiet dinner party in an upper-middle class suburb of Chicago, was an elegant older woman who had seen firsthand the harsh realities of moonshining. *Thunder Road* was more than just a movie or a song to her; it ran through her town and past her childhood home. It was American popular culture that had redefined the images of her community.

The film *Thunder Road* (1958) presented moonshining in more mythic than realistic terms, emphasizing the self-reliance and rugged individualism of Lucas Doolin (Robert Mitchum). Doolin's violations of federal law were insignificant when compared to his personal struggle against government oppression and organized crime. Lucas Doolin may be seen from a popular culture perspective as an independent man of principle. To achieve such a perspective, attention is placed on Doolin's character, not his actions or his environment. The character traits of self-reliance and individualism are played out on the back roads of Kentucky, where outlaw behavior takes a back seat to principle, dedication to community, and sacrifice for the good of others.

Such attention to character is a major component of American popular culture. The line between reality and what is perceived of as reality are two distinctly different things. Take, for example, the film *Days of Thunder* (1990) in which Tom Cruise played Cole Trickle, a sprint car driver from California who gets a Winston Cup ride in a car owned by a Charlotte-area automobile dealer (played by Randy Quaid). Trickle's crew chief is a NASCAR veteran (played by Robert Duvall) who tries to take the aggressive young driver under his wing. This story, based on the real-life teaming of the late Tim Richmond with car owner Rick Hendrick and crew chief Harry Hyde (who passed away in the fall of 1996) had the potential to illustrate NASCAR's transformation into a major professional sport. Richmond came along at a time when corporate money was being spent on Winston Cup racing in a big way, and Rick Hendrick was ushering in the new era of multi-car "super teams," where drivers had good cars financed with Fortune 500 money. This was a story waiting to be told. All that was needed was a high quality film that utilized a big name cast and a budget of millions.

The premise of the film was to present Winston Cup racing in authentic terms. Great pains were taken to make the movie an accurate and realistic presentation of the sport. In-car cameras were used at a number of actual Winston Cup events, and cars from the film were actually "entered" in Winston Cup races to shoot on-track footage. A number of Winston Cup drivers, including Rusty Wallace and Harry Gant, were used in cameos, and ESPN commentator Dr. Jerry Punch played himself. The stage was set for a major motion picture about Winston Cup racing, and that was where the interpretive powers of popular culture took over.

Whereas a realistic film about the NASCAR Winston Cup Series would show the sport's dedication to competition, safety, and professionalism, *Days of Thunder* showed how popular stereotypes had been used to interpret the world of stock car racing. Drivers in the film drove with reckless abandon, pushing each other into walls and causing accidents on purpose solely for the sake of winning. "'I don't think they did us justice,'" the late Alan Kulwicki was quoted as saying, "'they portrayed us like we're running bumper cars'" (Hager 50).

What ruined the project was Hollywood's insistence that stereotypes are what people want from motion pictures. The late Don Simpson, who co-produced the film with Jerry Bruckheimer, told NASCAR executives, "'We're going to take the image of stock car racing as most of the public perceives it and turn it around. . . . We're going to show them how high tech and professional it really is'" (qtd. in Hager 50). Seeing the finished product, NASCAR and its participants felt betrayed by the production team. The building where Harry Hogge (Duvall's character) builds Trickle's first Winston Cup car is little more than a barn, complete with sunlight streaming through cracks in the wooden walls. This portrayal bothered many NASCAR crew chiefs, including Harry Hyde himself. In an article written for *Entertainment Weekly,* Dave Hager stated:

Hyde did object to the movie's suggestion that champion race cars are put together in tumbledown barns in smoky mountain hollers—the very sort of hick image that stock car racing so desperately wants to shed. "I guess they wanted to show it like it was instead of how it is," he [Hyde] says. (53)

The portrayal of Winston Cup participants as moonshine-swilling rednecks also bothered many in the NASCAR community. Dale Earnhardt, who refused to discuss the film following its release, was "annoyed . . . about the scene of a racing crew chugging moonshine out of mason jars while returning from a race" (Hager 52). Rusty Wallace addressed the moonshine scene—which occurs while the team is celebrating Trickle's first Winston Cup win—by saying " 'There is not that much redneck-ery in the sport these days' " (Hager 53). Even though Harry Hyde admitted that the moonshine episode actually happened during his tenure with Tim Richmond, it refers more to Hyde's history with the sport of stock car racing than it does to the sport in its current state, which is what the movie was supposed to be depicting. When Hyde began working in stock car racing, moonshine was still part of the sport's culture.

Moonshine was a central product in communities along the Western frontier of the 1790s, including mid-Atlantic seaboard states like Pennsylvania, Virginia, and North Carolina. It served many purposes: as currency in barter, as a means of preserving and transporting a perishable crop, and as a way to dull the senses of those who lived each day of their lives with the danger and uncertainty of life in the wilderness. The "Whiskey Rebellion" of 1794 in Pennsylvania helped propel the anti-establishment philosophy that rang throughout the earliest days of stock car racing.

When the federal government forced itself on the rights of these men and women to earn the living they chose, these strong-willed and independent people did what they felt was best for themselves, not their national government. Freedom of the individual is central to life in America. When people migrated from Europe to America during the 17th and 18th centuries, they did so—in part—to escape the oppression of sovereign rule and the limitations of hierarchical life. Part of the ideology that defines the American character is individualism. Because of this, no one should infringe on another person's freedom. To live free, to prosper, and to be self-reliant—these are the basic components of American culture.

These social and cultural qualities: independence, self-reliance, freedom, faith in family, community, and God—these are the threads that have been woven into our traditional national fabric. We need to recognize such qualities and their influence on our lives. These qualities drive our basic understanding of what it means to be American. To recognize these character traits is just, however, a tiny piece of the bigger picture. We need reminders of how and why these traits affect us to reaffirm our foundation as Americans. The spectacle of sports provides us with the necessary reminders that we often fail to recognize.

Sports address life in terms we can understand. On college campuses across America each fall, people reflect on football as being "a metaphor for life." I often use football as an example in my classes on American culture studies, saying that the sport reflects the struggle of the life experience and the influences of living in a country built on militaristic achievement. Some students, especially football players, will question such logic. "How can that be? Football is just a game that teaches respect and discipline," they charge.

To explain myself, I take the class through a cultural "reading" of football as if it were a "text" on American culture. I analyze the field, little more than a piece of the American natural landscape that is shaped, measured, and lined off into sections with stripes of lime. American society has had an impact on the landscape, I tell the students, by taking the "wilderness" of an empty grassy space and "civilizing" it through human agency—a lush, grass-covered pasture does not naturally turn into a football field; it requires contact with humans who manipulate the geography and make nature into a "controlled" environment.[3]

I have the students then consider the metaphorical aspects of football. Football, I explain, resembles warfare with its attention to opposing teams and the need to have both offensive and defensive strategy. We talk about the goal of football: for a team to move across its "enemy's" territory and invade their last holding of land, their end zone. Advances by the offense are defended against, blocked, and stopped by the defense, who tries to move against the offense to reach its holding of land. The idea of the game is to take a material possession (the football) and occupy your opponent's physical space (their half of the field and its end zone). This metaphor was one way to interpret the history of American society.

The NASCAR Winston Cup Series may be read in a similar manner. It can be viewed as a microcosm of contemporary American society. There is competition between corporations, attention drawn to high-performance machines, and an emphasis on mass consumption of material goods. This may be why the sport has gained such increased national interest. Americans love football with little or no consideration of its "meaning." We love the thrill of football's physical contact, speed, strategy, and the group social dynamic. The same is true for the Winston Cup Series. It is a sport that thrills us and draws us by the tens of millions to speedways and television sets each year, yet we have never considered what the sport means to us as a country, as a community of Americans.

Community plays a large part in the sport of stock car racing. The sport itself is a community, one that travels to race tracks all over the country each week. As is the case with transitory social groups, the NASCAR Winston Cup participants look to each other for solidarity. The drivers, mechanics, officials, media people, and families of NASCAR move about the nation as a group with its own rules, ethics, and etiquette. For a group that spends so much time each year away from home, looking within the group to find a communal connection is vital to maintaining stability and sanity. Whether it is a pit road church service on Sunday morning, or a "village" of recreational vehicles where children of drivers and crew chiefs can play together, to be a part of NASCAR is to be a part of a community.

The same is true for stock car fans who gather to watch the cars at Winston Cup events. As the audience for stock car racing grows, speedways try to accommodate the many families who now attend races on a regular basis. Improvements in bathroom facilities have been made at many race tracks, some even including diaper-changing stations for fathers with infants. Infields have also been undergoing change, given an increase of families who camp during race weekends. According to journalist Benny Phillips:

Despite the rise of stock car racing, the infield crowd retains a separate identity, especially at Talladega. There was a time when an event here wasn't complete unless an RV or pickup truck was set afire in the infield, it seemed. But in recent years, management has tried to weed out the rowdies in favor of more family-value behavior among the 40,000 to 50,000 who watch the race from the infield. . . . In some cases, neighborhoods spring up with kids playing ball and riding bikes. ("Feel the Power" 10)

The days of people fighting, playing loud music, and displaying inappropriate signs are not over completely, but as NASCAR's grip on family-entertainment dollars tightens, such improper behavior will be less tolerated. Fans throwing chicken bones, beer bottles, and profanities in the grandstands are steadily being displaced by families and respect. These fans spend money, and lots of it, to the delight of NASCAR and its corporate sponsors.

The economics of the Winston Cup Series are simple—if the sponsors profit, so do the teams and the drivers. Big increases in consumer traffic for sponsors often cause the sponsors to hang around and pump more revenue back into the race team. Bigger money means bigger teams, bigger shops, and bigger purses of prize money. NASCAR's growth is cyclical: if the sponsors make money, the teams make money. If the teams make money, their cars get better. Better cars mean better competition and more exciting races. As the races get more exciting, more fans follow the sport and support their favorite teams, which usually leads to supporting that team's sponsor. This, in turn, begins the cycle all over again.

Because of this cycle, the drivers in Winston Cup racing are often identified by their sponsorship deals more than by their accomplishments. Dale Earnhardt, win or lose, drives the No. 3 GM Goodwrench Chevrolet, and that carries with it a great deal of economic clout. When STP signed on as Richard Petty's sponsor in 1972, the company embarked on a journey that would earn it national recognition and substantial profits, in part because of its automatic identification with one of America's most famous sports figures of the 20th century (Vehorn, *Farewell* 11).

This sense of unification between racers, their sponsors, and the fans is just a part of what has influenced the growth of the NASCAR Winston Cup Series. The sport's connection to American culture has also had an impact on why stock car racing is now one of the most popular spectator sports in America. It is more than colorful cars going in circles around a racetrack; it is a reflection of the character traits we consider essential to our role as Americans. It is a celebration of rugged individualism, freedom, and community. Winston Cup racing is also a celebration of the automobile, that vital piece of technology that carries us through life and provides us with the same sense of mobility that settled the frontier.

The NASCAR Winston Cup Series is part of our nation's popular culture, too. Its roots in rural Southern America have been transformed by the population at large into stereotypes reflecting the outlaw nature of moonshiners and the aggressive nature of men who make their living going fast and turning left. Popular culture often causes us to reinterpret figures, regions, and events central to our heritage, and sometimes these reinterpretations change fact into fiction. When history becomes folklore, there is something greater at work than the mere retelling of a story. Our culture goes out of its way to redefine people, places, and things so they better fit the current needs of our society.

Such was the case with NASCAR's creation as a sanctioning body dedicated to organizing the sport of stock car racing. An outlaw element had been running various types of races, and the lack of structure caused many drivers to be cheated out of money by crooked race promoters. Some kind of controlling force was needed to make stock car racing a professional sport, especially during the postwar era when men and new automobiles returned to the American forefront. Our society was anxious to get back on the road following World War II, and NASCAR was all set to take road cars and race them into the history books. What follows is the story of how—and why—that history was made, and what that history says about American culture.

Chapter 2 looks at how NASCAR has attempted to use institutional control as a means of maintaining authority over the sport of stock car racing. Keeping a tight grip on the rules and how they are interpreted has allowed NASCAR to make big profits while putting on a close and competitive show almost every week.

NASCAR's struggle with competitors is explored in detail in chapter 3, which focuses on attempts by drivers to unionize during the 1960s. The creation of a union seemed to be the best way to fight what drivers considered unfair treatment by the sanctioning body. Two attempts at unionization were struck down by NASCAR with actions that resulted in lifetime suspensions of drivers and a boycott of the first race at Talladega Superspeedway.

The lives and roles of stock car drivers are studied in chapters 4, 5, and 6. Chapter 4 addresses the acculturation of Winston Cup drivers, while chapter 5 explains how these athletes have evolved from lead-footed daredevils to internationally recognized corporate spokesmen. The cultural mythology of Winston Cup racing is the subject of chapter 6, where drivers are analyzed as folk heroes—products of the traits and behaviors admired by most Americans.

The impact of Winston Cup racing on American culture, and my personal observations of that impact, is at the core of chapter 7. Spending time following the NASCAR community was more enlightening than any amount of formal research. In chapter 8, I consider the future of the NASCAR empire. As American culture changes and evolves, so does the subculture of stock car racing. The evolution of a truly American sport is detailed throughout the pages that follow.

2

The Show Goes On:
NASCAR, Control,
and the Winston Cup Series

The highest level of NASCAR—the National Association of Stock Car Automobile Racing—competition is the Winston Cup Series. The cars raced in this division are called "stock," mainly because they resemble production-based American automobiles, even though they are hand-built custom race cars in every way. "Shadetree" ingenuity is part of this sport's heritage—considered more important than high tech assistance from automobile manufacturers.

Perhaps the best way to describe NASCAR and its operational behavior is to use the words of *Winston Cup Scene*'s Steve Waid. He once wrote:

It is a dictatorship, pure and simple. Let's make that a benevolent dictatorship. It makes the rules; calls the shots. As a result, everyone might not agree, but everyone does what they are told—and the positive results have become obvious. ("What the Move Represents" 4)

The "positive results" are ones that other sanctioning bodies in motorsports can only wish to have. This is a series that makes money, has so many dedicated fans that some of its facilities are unable to accommodate all of them, and has no problem maintaining a full nationwide schedule. Winston Cup racing is the darling of major corporations and the national media. Each race on the 1996 NASCAR Winston Cup schedule was televised live, in addition to the regular live radio coverage of each event provided by the Motor Racing Network (MRN).

The greatest "positive result" has been NASCAR's acceptance as a mainstream sport. Winston Cup races are the most attended sporting events in America, while NASCAR drivers are becoming household names through national television and print media coverage. This growth in the sport has attributed to its success. As Steve Waid has written, "NASCAR represents stability and growth," and this is what makes the sport so successful ("What the Move Represents" 4). Part of NASCAR's success is rooted in its emphasis on growth and stability through strong administration. It is a cyclical operation. NASCAR was established by concerned racers who sought organization and equality for their sport. The creation of equality through standardized rules and regulations made NASCAR stock car racing more popular. This, in turn created a need for even greater administrative control on the heels of the division's growth. As NASCAR became more successful, its demands for increased government and control became greater.

With the growth and success of the sport came the need for greater participant reward. Increases in prize money and sponsorship packages followed suit. In 1954, Lee Petty won $21,101.35 for his first NASCAR championship title; in 1994, Dale Earnhardt earned $3,300,733 as the Winston Cup Series' champion (1995 *NASCAR Preview and Press Guide* 38). Kyle Petty finished 25th in the 1994 Brickyard 400 at Indianapolis and won $39,000—more than Herb Thomas, 1954's top money winner, won for that entire season (Snyder, "NASCAR Numerology" 70). Jeff Gordon, the 1995 Winston Cup champion, earned more than $4.3 million setting a record for prize money won in a season (1995 *NASCAR Preview and Press Guide* 86). This accomplishment is just another part of racing success attributed to NASCAR's largeness

Not only did the prize money grow, but so did the manner in which it was presented. On December 3, 1993, Winston Cup driver Ken Schrader took the stage at the Waldorf-Astoria Hotel in New York City. It was the night when NASCAR and its corporate sponsors presented trophies and prize money to the top teams in the Winston Cup Series. Manhattan was a far cry from Daytona Beach, Florida, where the teams originally gathered to receive their accolades. Schrader was given a check for $90,283, his team's award for ninth place in the points championship for the year. T. Wayne Robertson, Senior Vice President of Sports Marketing Enterprises—the R.J. Reynolds Tobacco Company branch that watches over brand sponsorship of better than 1,600 events each year—gave Schrader his check, then stepped aside to allow the driver to make a few comments to the audience of NASCAR participants. Schrader looked down from the podium and said, "Mr. France, you've made a wonderful sport here."

The sport of Winston Cup stock car racing certainly did look wonderful in the Grand Ballroom of the Waldorf-Astoria, all of the series' participants and their spouses dressed in black-tie and formal evening gowns. This was the 45th annual awards banquet, the official conclusion to the 1993 NASCAR Winston Cup season. It was being televised live, as it always is, by ESPN, which had sandwiched it between an hour of original stock car programming and a half-hour "shop-over-the-phone" souvenirs show featuring Darrell Waltrip. Much had changed since 1947, when William H.G. France and several of his friends in stock car racing took the initiative and created an organization that transformed the chaos of a rough-and-tumble sport into a business driven by its attention to safety, equality and honesty.

The path from humble beginnings to "wonderful" was sometimes a difficult one, however. "Big Bill" France and his organization were trying to settle the wilderness of automobile racing, and doing so often meant assuming a position of consummate authority. Such iron rule was not always appreciated, nor was it always fair, but it was always leveled with some positive benefit in mind. The legend of "Big Bill" France is rooted in this, as is the history of NASCAR.

To better understand the "wonderful sport" referred to by Ken Schrader, we must first examine NASCAR's history and evolution. A look into the governing body should provide us with a good look at the sport itself, and exhaustive documentation by racing historian Greg Fielden provides us with hard-to-locate specific information. The NASCAR of today is under the watchful eyes of Bill France, Jr., the "Mr. France" in Schrader's statement. He took control of the organization when Bill France, Sr. retired on January 11, 1972 (Fielden 4: 7). It was the work of "Big Bill" that got the sport of Winston Cup racing underway.

The motivation that resulted in the creation of NASCAR was an ongoing instability within the sport of stock car racing. There was little in the way of formal organization. Promoters sometimes bent the rules, if there were any to bend in the first place. With no sanctioning body to enforce regulations and specifications, the participants were literally at the whim of the promoter. A motor deemed legal at one speedway might not be legal at another, which meant a racer would have to have different engines if he wanted to run different tracks. Racers could also bend the rules, and have little fear of being caught. As Allan Girdler has written:

racing was in chaos and confusion. There were too many conflicts of interest. The rules weren't uniform, they weren't fair and the promoters couldn't be trusted. This wasn't news. Everybody who'd been in racing longer than a week knew about getting cheated out of a win, swindled out of the purse, or tricked in one way or another. (16)

From chaos came a call to arms. France had been all around the sport of automobile racing. He had been a mechanic and a driver, and he had even been a promoter for a while. Racing and its problems were something he wanted to change, but he could not do it alone. "Big Bill" organized a meeting in Daytona Beach, Florida, where others in the automobile racing game could discuss their grievances and plan for the future.

On December 12, 1947, in a conference room at the Streamline Hotel, France addressed an assembly of mechanics, car owners, and drivers who were looking for the same thing out of the sport of stock car racing—safety, fairness, equality, and honest organization (Girdler 16). Because of their like-minded approach to automobile racing, this group in Daytona was ready and willing to try anything if it meant strengthening their sport. Anything, at this time, would have been an improvement.

France and his associates were able to design a total system of rules, regulations, and standards for stock car racing because no other group had attempted to do so. In the years prior to NASCAR's creation, race promoters and governing bodies were greedy, which explained the unfair rules and purses of prize money. France and his colleagues sought to create a sanctioning organization that would look after the interests of two groups: the participants and the spectators. Mechanics and drivers would be given safe conditions and fair competition; race fans would be provided with an exciting show every time they went to the speedway. No one had attempted this kind of organization for stock cars. France wanted to produce a racing series that would achieve superiority nationwide because of its size. No racing division for stock cars was as big as NASCAR would become, at least in the mind of "Big Bill."

What France did, according to racing journalist Brock Yates, was assemble "a dissident collection of dirt-track drivers, independent track promoters, and car owners into joining his new organization. . . . [NASCAR] was based on France's belief that the key to growth in the sport was the establishment of consistent rules, guaranteed purses, and a season-long computation of points to determine a national champion" (*Drivers* 40+).

France reined in the strays and made them stick to the rules, going so far as to disqualify the winner of NASCAR's first Strictly Stock race in 1949 for using a car that had been modified to haul moonshine. Stock car racing was under control, and the man in charge was Bill France.

France, who served as a chairman for the Florida proceedings, had previously founded and operated the National Championship Stock Car Circuit (NCSCC). He had secured control of racing competition because of his willingness to take charge. In the early days of the sport, someone who could organize, promote, and officiate an event could make the rules as he wished. "Big Bill" brought civilization to the untamed sport of stock car racing. France's National Championship Stock Car Circuit had held events and developed somewhat of a following (Fielden 1: 5).

The NCSCC's slogan, "Where the fastest that run, run the fastest," was already promoting the quickest of the quick, an honor that NASCAR would adopt following its incorporation.

Part of NASCAR's appeal is its folklore, and part of NASCAR's folklore concerns the origin of its name. Jerome "Red" Vogt, one of Atlanta's best mechanics, was the individual who suggested the NASCAR name that is used today. Some controversy surrounded the choice, mainly because a few people thought the anagram sounded too much like the phrase "Nash car" (Girdler 17). As history shows, Nash cars are long gone while NASCAR just keeps on growing.

Another point to come from this initial meeting was that those involved with NASCAR from the very beginning were businessmen, not wild moonshiners as popular culture leads us to believe. This stereotype developed because of the sport's southern ties, despite the fact that NASCAR's organizers were from all over America. The rural southern stereotype eased a bit during the 1980s, once ESPN and other television networks began dedicating significant airtime to broadcasts of Winston Cup races, but NASCAR's southern roots continue as a connection to the romantic imagery derived from Southeastern lore.

The National Association for Stock Car Automobile Racing was incorporated on February 21, 1948. For its administration, NASCAR elected William H.G. France as president; E.G. "Cannonball" Baker from Indiana, national commissioner; and a competitive driver, Marshall Teague, treasurer. Baker, a race driver and endurance record-holder, was assigned the task of administering the rules and regulations in competition. He worked as a referee of sorts, with his call being the final and ultimate decision.

What made NASCAR unique within the world of automobile racing was that it operated itself as a business. The idea was to assure all competitors, speedway owners, and fans the best in motorsports competition. Through its club format, NASCAR would accept members on a dues-paying basis. The entire organization, however, was to be controlled by "Big Bill" France and his associates. According to Allan Girdler:

France had created the foundation for a new sport. He'd done it with the help and cooperation of his peers. NASCAR would have memberships and dues, just like a club. But at the same time, it was established as a corporation, a privately held corporation, with the France family, [Bill] Tuthill [a New England promoter] and Ed Otto [co-founder of NASCAR] as the partners and owners. . . . The founders were racers and businessmen and they knew what they were doing. (Girdler 17)

From the absolute beginning, NASCAR was operated on the basis of control by a limited few. Bill France and his family would use this leverage for a variety of reasons, depending on what they saw happening within the sport and what they felt was best for it. There would be no overruling of decisions or judgments, since they came most often from the administrative level.

This is the aspect of NASCAR that has generated the most criticism from teams, drivers, automobile manufacturers, and fans. Much of the sanctioning body's reputation as a dictatorship stems from the fact that whatever the front office says goes. Rule changes that help one make of automobile while, at the same time, hurt the others, are just part of NASCAR's complete control. This power structure dictates everything from sponsor advertisement placement on cars to the flow and pace of the stock car races themselves.

NASCAR functions as a private company under the command of the France family, unlike the CART IndyCar Division—founded in 1978—which operates through its car owners (Byrnes 52).[1] CART is run by a board of directors comprised of IndyCar franchise owners. Franchise ownership means fielding one or more race teams, which opens the division up to multi-car operations, like those of Roger Penske or Dick Simon. Because of this structure, CART "is a private, for-profit organization that divides its revenues equally among the franchises" (Byrnes 52). NASCAR, on the other hand, because of its familial foundation, is allowed to maintain secrecy regarding revenues and their distribution.

Amidst the controversy surrounding the split between CART and the Indy Racing League (IRL) in 1995, most notably with regard to the formation of two Memorial Day events, NASCAR's name was summoned by team owners as an example of what was occurring within the ranks of American open-wheel racing. The point of contention was the creation of the U.S. 500, a CART-sanctioned IndyCar race at Michigan International Speedway. It was designed to accommodate the teams who were not willing to run in the more traditional Indianapolis 500. The Indianapolis 500 had for the first time focused on IRL regulars; only eight of the proposed 33 starting spots at Indy were open to CART teams (Kelly 18). As a result, full-time CART participants wanted a race of their own. A boycott of the Indy 500 was the basis for the Michigan race.

Tony George, who created the IRL and was also president of the Indianapolis Motor Speedway, hoped to swing open-wheel racing back toward its roots—the days when American-born drivers and mechanics would rise from the dirt track ranks and achieve excellence at the Brickyard. Indianapolis-type racing through CART had been taken over by participants with foreign origins and machines with foreign backgrounds. In 1995, the Indy 500 "featured twenty foreign-born competitors among the thirty-three-car starting field, had no American-born rookies and only one driver—Stan Fox—cut from the once-traditional stepping stones of midgets and sprints" (Stilley 78). Several Formula One veterans—experienced drivers like Emerson Fittipaldi—had already made the switch to CART. His success as a two-time Indianapolis 500 winner made the exodus of European drivers from Formula One more enticing.

The Indianapolis 500 was as American as, well, stock car racing. Tony George seemingly looked toward NASCAR's success with sponsors and fans alike, and came up with the idea that would shake automobile racing overall right down to its rafters, a low-cost series centered on American-built race cars run on oval tracks throughout the United States. It would be a place for short track drivers and mechanics—those who campaign sprint cars, midgets, and late model stock cars—to race before a national audience at a venue that was founded on the hard work and sacrifice of American ingenuity, the same quality that could be found in names like Vukovich, Dallenbach, Ruttman, Foyt, and Unser.[2]

These were the same qualities trumpeted by William "Big Bill" France when he founded NASCAR in 1947. His idea was to provide men and women with a division where they could demonstrate their driving and mechanical talents without needing a big financial investment. NASCAR, unlike racing at the Brickyard, had attempted to maintain such a heritage by limiting devices such as computer telemetry. Indianapolis-type racing, however, had leaned toward the high-technology of Formula One. Winning teams were those with big budgets, while lesser-financed teams were relegated to also-ran status.

NASCAR, however, was also guilty of such financial advantages. What attracted Tony George's attention was NASCAR's ability to regulate competition and "create" a better show for spectators. A closer race meant more fans, and more fans meant more attention (and money) from sponsors. NASCAR had embraced corporate America through the use of such traits as loyalty, strict rules, and close finishes. The lack of parity had cost Indianapolis-type racing many of its fans—a parity that existed during the dirt track days of drivers working their way into the 500. Indianapolis had devolved into a battle of foreign-held checkbooks with huge balances, and that was not what America wanted to cheer for on Memorial Day.

NASCAR entered the CART/IRL fray, at least in a referential way, with a comment by CART IndyCar team owner Derrick Walker. Walker, who owned the cars driven by Robby Gordon in 1996, was quoted as saying, "They [the IRL] will have developed a dictatorship, a NASCAR kind of concept, and our people are used to the democratic way" (Woolford, "Brickyard Opens").[3] This comment, albeit meant to explain the CART ideology, raises a more significant issue to be considered. The statement questions the entire cultural mythology of not only NASCAR's Winston Cup Series, but the whole notion of democracy and how Americans view the powers in control of their nation.

Democracy, as a whole, is a central element of American cultural myth. It is the concept that many Americans use to describe the United States and its government, its method of operation, and its function as a symbol to lands throughout the world. Part of an ancient Greek heritage, "democracy" is how people can play a role in the day-to-day workings of our country.

But what of the limitations within a democracy as we know it? Is this country truly a democracy? Do everyday Americans really take part in the democratic process? This is where NASCAR attracts skepticism from the CART owners and drivers—the *image* of NASCAR differs from the *organization* of the sport itself. NASCAR, as we have seen throughout its history, is actually more akin to a dictatorship.

Such a power structure should not be all that foreign to the American people. The United States of America has long been known for its emphasis on democracy—the rule of the people. That plays well within the notions of the public sector. The private sector, on the other hand, is an entirely different game. In this arena, the emphasis is placed on control. Corporate structures assure a heavy amount of pressure from above, giving those below a job without any part in the decision-making process. Do what the company tells you. Do not make waves. If you do make waves, know that there is no guarantee that they will do any good. Make sure you play the game. Be sure you know the rules.

NASCAR has operated under this edict for 50 years, maintaining strict control over its competitors and presenting the closest competition in all of motorsports. Part of this emphasis on strict control may have something to do with the fact NASCAR wanted to run completely stock automobiles in its early Strictly Stock division. What better way to enforce absolute control over race drivers and mechanics than to make them run fully unmodified cars. No modifications means no direct advantage over your competition. These kinds of rules kept everyone on a short leash, and they gave NASCAR the first say in who raced, who went home, and who won.

In the days before NASCAR's Strictly Stock division, most of the events governed by the sanctioning body were Modified races. Modifieds were anything but "stock" cars. Engines could be taken from newer models and put under the hoods of older models, and the engines could be "modified"—bored, stroked, and fitted with high-performance carburetors, camshafts, and cylinder heads—to produce more horsepower and speed (Girdler 17). All of this changed as NASCAR carried stock car racing into 1949. The Strictly Stock division was to be NASCAR's headlining series, with Modified and Roadster classes designated as "support" divisions.[4]

One of the things Bill France could do to guarantee that his organization's champion was the one and only national champion was to promote NASCAR's Strictly Stock division's use of showroom-type automobiles as racing vehicles. France and his associates figured that people would like seeing American-built, production-based cars in racing competition, especially since the cars being used were ones that the fans could actually purchase from a dealership. Racing fully stock automobiles also emphasized a driver's skills, rather than dependence on a special engine configuration or modification. No other sanctioning body had tried such an idea, giving NASCAR a chance to claim its best driver as the true "national" champion (Fielden 1: 6).

The concept of "stock" car racing evolved with the automobile itself. From the origins of American automobile culture, the idea of racing production vehicles has had commercial ties. Alexander Winton, an automobile manufacturer from Cleveland, Ohio, used racing to sell his "Bullet," and Henry Ford turned racing success into business success thanks to Barney Oldfield and the "999" (Nolan 19). The attempt to race cars as they came from the factory, however, seemed doomed from the start.

Early sanctioning bodies, such as the American Automobile Association (AAA), were hindered by the fact that there were forty companies producing automobiles in America, and each manufacturer "wanted to win more than they wanted to be fair" (Girdler 9). As the companies fought over rules, "stock" car racing evolved into events like hill climbs, economy trials, and speed record runs. As production-type racing seemed less likely, given the feuds between manufacturers, "stock" cars became cars with factory-built chassis and bodies fitted with modified engines. These machines were run head-to-head on oval tracks, making them the forefathers of stock car racing in America.

This idea is what has helped secure NASCAR racing within the realm of American culture. Stock car racing—especially as done in the Winston Cup Series—is based, at least in theory, on the notion that the race cars are "stock." In 1949 they were, but by the mid-1950s, NASCAR competitors were already adding safety and performance equipment. This happened because the cars coming from Detroit auto makers were getting faster, easier to handle at speed, and more durable.

Despite the evolution of stock cars into fully-fabricated racing machines, the original idea behind NASCAR has remained part of stock car racing lore. The term "stock car" suggests a production-based model. In reality, today's Winston Cup race cars are completely built by hand from high-performance parts. Today's Winston Cup cars are anything but stock, but the spirit of those early machines is still a part of the sport's popular image.

By 1948, when Bill France decided to hold off the initial Strictly Stock season until Detroit could catch up with its new automobile production, his logic was that people would not want to attend races where brand new cars were being beaten in competition while spectators made do with their worn out pre-war models (Fielden 1: 6). Since the Modifieds thrived on late model bodies and parts, the division could present NASCAR racing while Strictly Stock cars were being "prepared" for their eventual debut. An "experimental" NASCAR Strictly Stock race was run in South Florida at Broward Speedway on February 27, 1949 (Fielden 6). It was used as a support race—being scheduled after a 100-mile National Grand Prix Roadster race and a 25-mile European Sports Car race. The Strictly Stock event, a five-lap sprint around Broward's two-mile paved track, received third billing against the other more recognized divisions. Benny Georgeson, of Fort Lauderdale, won the race in a Buick, with Eddie Mitchell, from Defiance, Ohio, taking second place (Fielden 1: 7). Mitchell's performance at Broward Speedway reflected the national interest in stock car racing, demonstrating that the sport's rural Southern image was not necessarily etched in stone.

Unfortunately, this initial Strictly Stock race went somewhat unrecognized because of its supporting presentation. What NASCAR needed was an event that showcased the production automobiles in a race by themselves. Such a race was scheduled for June 19, 1949. It was to be in Charlotte, North Carolina, where drivers would run 150 laps for a purse of $5,000. A field of 33 cars would take the green flag that day, a number that caused many observers to wonder if France could attract enough cars to fill out his planned grid. Since anyone with a full-sized American passenger car was eligible to enter the event, Bill France seemed sure that the race would go off as planned (Fielden 1: 7).

Bill France was also watching another sanctioning body as it began to go after many of the drivers and car owners being sought by NASCAR. This organization, the National Stock Car Racing Association (NSCRA), was one of several governing bodies competing to regulate stock car events throughout the country. Numerous stock car racing organizations like the National Auto Racing League (NARL), the American Stock Car Racing Association (ASCRA), and the United

Stock Car Racing Association (USCRA) declared their own "national" champions, which confused the general public and made the sport an unorganized mixture of titles, trophies, and events (Fielden 1: 6-7). The NSCRA gave NASCAR added problems because it was trying to attract competitors from the same geographical region. France's race in June 1949 would get NASCAR substantial attention because of its "strictly stock" format, despite any competition attempted by the NSCRA.

The Charlotte, North Carolina facility where history would be made was "a rough three-quarter mile dirt track surrounded by scraggly fences of undressed lumber misappropriating the name 'speedway'" (Fielden 1: 7). Marshall Teague, the treasurer for NASCAR, wanted the sanctioning body to adopt a policy for its Charlotte debut similar to one used by the American Automobile Association (AAA) for its Indianapolis-type race cars. This policy would guarantee NASCAR's drivers 40 percent of the gate receipts, an amount that would be added to the purse of prize money available (Fielden 1: 7). Since Teague's name fails to appear in the final race results, it seems fairly likely that Bill France disagreed with Teague's idea, which caused Teague—a race car driver himself—to boycott the race in act of protest.

NASCAR banned several drivers from racing in its Charlotte debut. Four Modified drivers were not allowed to post entries because of NASCAR's determination they were guilty of "actions detrimental to auto racing" (Fielden 1: 7). Three other drivers, Buddy Shuman, Ed Samples, and Speedy Thompson, were dismissed from competition because of an alleged incident at a NASCAR Modified event earlier in the year where thumb tacks were thrown onto a track's surface prior to a race. Another driver was accused of similar charges, but given a one-year probation and allowed to race (Fielden 1: 7).

NASCAR's attitude toward drivers who violate rules or misbehave has changed over the years, especially as the sport became more publicly recognized and sponsor-oriented. The operating procedure of NASCAR today seems to involve some consideration of just who is guilty of violating a rule. If it is a driver and/or car owner who is well-sponsored, popular with race fans, and consistently competitive, NASCAR tends to turn the other cheek and level a fine, or perhaps a probationary period. Some of the teams are kept out of competition for brief amounts of time. In the cases of drivers like Curtis Turner and Tim Flock, their attempts to unionize race car drivers in the 1960s resulted in permanent suspension.

One controversial situation occurred in 1983 during the Miller High Life 500 at Charlotte Motor Speedway. Richard Petty, who won the race for his 198th career victory, was penalized after the event for running with illegal tires and an oversized engine ("Petty Fined" C7). Petty, easily the most beloved driver in NASCAR's history, was fined $35,000 and lost 104 Winston Cup championship points earned that day. The fine, then the largest ever leveled against a driver by NASCAR, was an easy way to cushion the violation incurred by Petty's team—even though Richard Petty admitted that he knew nothing about the wrong tires and motor.

According to racing historian Greg Fielden:

The NASCAR rule book is specific regarding proper tires and engine specifications, but it has a wide latitude in assessing penalties. "Penalties for violation of NASCAR rules are determined by the gravity of the violation and its effect on safety and good reputation of stock car automobile racing. Such penalties may include disqualification, suspension, fines, and/or loss of points . . ." read [*sic*] the 1983 NASCAR rule book. (4: 399)

Petty, based upon NASCAR's interpretation of his team's violation, was fined and stripped of points, although his win was allowed to stand. This decision angered many Winston Cup drivers and teams. Darrell Waltrip, who finished second to Petty at Charlotte, was quoted as saying, "This is all in total contradiction of two of the most flagrant rules violations. There was supposed to have been some standard set procedures about these things. . . . Maybe it had something to do with who was first and second, or vice versa" (Fielden 4: 399).

Such assumed favoritism, as perceived by observers of the "Pettygate" affair, is believed to be common within NASCAR. This kind of situation appeared once again during the 1993 Winston Cup season, when the No. 25 Kodiak Chevrolet Lumina of Ken Schrader was caught with an engine violation at Daytona's July event. Schrader's race car was fitted with an illegal carburetor for his qualifying attempt at the Pepsi 400. A series of holes allowed air to bypass the restrictor plates used on stock cars running in Winston Cup races at Daytona and Talladega. According to Deb Williams, writing about the violation in *Winston Cup Scene:*

Small holes had been drilled through each throttlebore wall and into each stud bolt wall. This created a passageway through which air flowed. The air was then channeled downward and directly into the intake manifold, where other holes had been drilled. The intent was to get more air into the intake manifold by bypassing the carburetor restrictor plate. ("National Stock Car" 29)

Schrader and his team owner, Joe Hendrick, initially received a four-race suspension as a penalty for the rules violation. This was reduced to a $5000 fine for both parties after an appeal was made—by Schrader—to the National Stock Car Commission, a 21-member governing committee, who lifted the suspension ("National Stock Car" 28). Winston Cup participants were critical, and vocal, about the commission's decision.

Some members questioned the independent decision-making abilities of the National Stock Car Commission, implying that NASCAR itself had leveled some pressure upon the appeal process. The National Stock Car Commission is similar to the Grand National Advisory Board, which was created by NASCAR following an attempt by drivers to unionize in 1961. Racing legend and Winston Cup car owner Junior Johnson commented:

I think they [the commission] did what they were told [by NASCAR]. If the rule says what everybody says it does, I don't know, I haven't read it, then it's just another typical [NASCAR President] Bill France deal. Do something, put it out and then do it the way he wants to, not the way the rules say. I wouldn't be surprised at nothing he would do. I never read the rule book because they never go by it. (qtd. in Williams, "National Stock Car" 28)

Johnson's sentiments were echoed by many throughout the sport of Winston Cup stock car racing, especially with regard to NASCAR's original 1947 commitment to making racing fair and just for all competitors.

One anonymous respondent in the sport called the commission's decision "the most significant thing that has happened in Winston Cup racing in 10 years." Lifting the Schrader/Hendrick suspension, according to one person, "changed the whole reason we [Winston Cup race teams] are here." The National Stock Car Commission made it so that teams "could no longer justify all of [their] honest hard work and the sacrifices" ("National Stock Car" 28). Once again, Winston Cup stock car racing was faced with a possible credibility problem because of NASCAR's doctrine of absolute control and power within the area of rules interpretation.

Such absolute power can lead to consistent inconsistency. If NASCAR has no one to answer to but itself, backpedaling over rules violations and their subsequent enforcement is left entirely to the whims of those near the head of the organization. Prior to the 1993 Schrader/Hendrick incident, however, there had been three separate situations— over three consecutive seasons—where NASCAR had stuck to its guns and made its penalties stick.

A questionable carburetor was under fire during a race at Richmond, Virginia, in 1990. Mark Martin piloted a Jack Roush-prepared Ford Thunderbird to victory, only to be fined $42,000 and stripped of 42 Winston Cup championship points by NASCAR ("National Stock Car"

29). The penalty was upheld by the sanctioning body, and it ultimately cost Roush and his race team substantially more. Mark Martin wound up losing the 1990 Winston Cup title to Dale Earnhardt by 20 points, and the Ford Motor Company lost the 1990 manufacturer's championship to Chevrolet.

In 1991, NASCAR penalized Junior Johnson and his Budweiser Ford racing team after an oversized engine was found during an inspection after The Winston—an all-star race—at Charlotte Motor Speedway in May. Considering that The Winston is a non-points paying event, the penalty leveled against Johnson; his crew chief, Tim Brewer; and his driver, Tommy Ellis, was quite harsh. A 12-week suspension was recommended by NASCAR, but an appeal persuaded the National Stock Car Commission to reduce it to four. As a result, Johnson and Brewer missed four important points paying races during one of the busiest stretches of the schedule. The Budweiser Ford was turned over to Johnson's wife, Flossie, who served as its "owner," and the Thunderbird carried the number 97 instead of its usual number eleven (Phillips, "Flossie Johnson" 10). NASCAR declared that Johnson was not even allowed to attend the races in person. The sanctioning body feared the media would pay more attention to him and his plight than to the races themselves (Egan 120).

The third incident also occurred at Charlotte Motor Speedway, only this one happened during the 1992 Winston Cup season. Martin Birrane, owner of Bobby Hillin, Jr.'s Team Ireland ride, was fined by NASCAR for running "an illegal engine part" ("National Stock Car" 30). Because of this violation—and its subsequent fine—Birrane's team was unable to remain in competition, and his shop closed its doors for good later that same week. The questionable judgment in this case stems from the fact that Birrane purchased the engine from an "outside vendor" ("National Stock Car" 30). Had Birrane's own team built the controversial engine, the penalty would have been no question. Guilt would have been obvious. Because the engine had been bought from an outside source— apparently one capable of building Winston Cup motors—(and in the business thereof)—Biranne's career-ending penalty seemed a bit severe. His team was forced to close because it trusted a firm contracted to build its engines, and NASCAR took its penalty out on the car owner rather than the company at fault.

This scenario was similar to 1993's Ken Schrader/Joe Hendrick situation. In the Schrader/Hendrick case, the illegal carburetor was on an engine built by B&R Engines, located in Winston-Salem, North Carolina. Rick Hendrick, who runs three Winston Cup teams through his Hendrick Motorsports facilities near Charlotte Motor Speedway, "acquired an interest in the firm a few years" earlier ("National Stock Car" 29). Unlike Martin Birrane in 1992, who had no apparent connections to the engine builder in question, it seemed as if there was a conflict of interest concerning Rick Hendrick and B&R Engines. In any case, all speculation aside, the end result was that Ken Schrader and Joe Hendrick were given slaps on their wrists. Martin Birrane is nowhere to be found around the NASCAR Winston Cup Series today.

This scenario could strike any team, and many were preparing their defenses for future accusations by the sanctioning body. Some car owners would use the Schrader/Hendrick alibi as their way out against NASCAR. According to a story about the commission's decision in *Winston Cup Scene:*

[Junior] Johnson said the engine men he'd talked with since the ruling said they were going to contact an outside source for their engines . . . "so when they get caught they've got an excuse to get by the rules." Johnson said he would have been a lot more surprised if the commission had upheld the suspension [of Schrader and Hendrick] than he was with the eventual ruling. "[William] France [Jr.] has been able to kinda put the clamps on everybody and make them like what he does," Johnson said. ("National Stock Car" 30)

If NASCAR is a "benevolent dictatorship," then we might see a reason for its questionable patterns of judgment. First of all, the sanctioning body must maintain a standard of fairness for the teams who participate in the sport. Stock car racing is, however, a sport that possesses the qualities of a spectacle. The Winston Cup Series "is first and foremost a show, and constant adjustments are made to keep the show working. . . . Rules can be bent or closely observed, depending on the demands of showmanship" (Egan 119). Fairness, in this sense, is determined according to the demands of the sanctioning body. Such random interference is a part of NASCAR's autocratic nature.

Secondly, NASCAR must beware of damaging its reputation with corporate America. The late Neil Bonnett often said that race cars run on money. NASCAR is aware of this fact, and this sometimes causes the organization to walk a fine line between motorsports competition and its Madison Avenue relations. The governing body—as a result—finds itself between the proverbial rock and a hard place. It must make every attempt to keep Winston Cup racing fair, honest, and equal, while making an attempt to keep its corporate sponsors satisfied and anxious to be involved with the sport. Because of NASCAR's largeness, and its ability to freely manipulate the protocol of both business and sport, many of the corporations close to Winston Cup racing often receive special attention.

Unfortunately, this results in big teams with powerful sponsors getting preferential treatment over smaller teams with less well-financed racing programs. Drivers who draw sponsorship dollars seem to get favorable treatment when rules are broken.

Given such authoritative control, NASCAR has been able to govern stock car racing as it sees appropriate. Sometimes its government overlooks the needs of those ultimately responsible for putting spectators in the seats—the drivers and teams who run for the national championship. This has resulted, on two occasions, in attempts to organize the participants who make up stock car racing's workforce. As we will see in the next chapter, both attempts at unionization met with the wrath of "Big Bill" France's absolute control over NASCAR.

3

A Fight to the Finish:
NASCAR Versus Organized Labor

Perhaps, a better way to analyze France's control of the NASCAR Winston Cup Series is to look at NASCAR itself as a trust, for an understanding of what the sanctioning body is and how it became so powerful. The basic operational philosophy behind NASCAR, may show why the sport of stock car racing continues to grow each year.

According to economist John Moody:

the term "Trust" is applicable to any act, agreement or combination believed to possess the intention, power or tendency to monopolize business, interfere with trade, fix prices, etc. It will be noted that this embraces those enterprises which are popularly believed to have this intent, power or tendency, and not merely to those which have, by demonstration, been shown to be possessed of such power. (xiv)

Moody continues to explain trusts through the following description:

Thus, franchise corporations and groups are Trusts . . . possessors of exclusive powers or privileges of any sort, as well as mere producers on a large scale, must be looked upon as Trusts . . . the thorough-going Trust must be characterized by largeness. (xiv)

Given Moody's definition, we can identify NASCAR as a body that possesses the qualities necessary to be considered a trust. It possesses special privileges and powers; it has the ability to interfere with trade (namely the business of building and operating race cars); and it is, without any doubt, a governing body characterized by largeness.

From the earliest days of NASCAR, there are examples of how the sanctioning body has operated like a trust. William France routinely kept drivers under his authoritative rule. He banned drivers from the first NASCAR Strictly Stock race in Charlotte because of their questionable behavior at a Modified event a few weeks earlier, and drivers who participated in non-NASCAR races in 1950 were punished for their indiscretions (Fielden 1: 20). Two drivers who ran in "outlaw" events—Red Byron and Lee Petty—were stripped of points as a penalty by NASCAR. Loyalty was essential in these early days, and drivers who strayed were dealt with quickly and in a sometimes harsh manner.

One of the first drivers to receive the wrath of NASCAR as a means of punishment was Curtis Turner. He had been racing in the Strictly Stock division since its initial "official" event in June of 1949, when he drove a 1946 Buick Roadmaster to a ninth place finish (McCredie 124). Curtis Turner quickly assumed a role within the folklore of stock car racing, recognized for his aggressive driving style on the track and his aggressive partying style off of it. Turner had made a small fortune in the timbering business, selling lumber and operating three sawmills by the time he was 18 (Chapin, "Curtis" 51). Cutting timber was nothing compared to the battle Turner would have with "Big Bill" France in 1961.

Curtis Turner wanted to build a superspeedway near Charlotte, North Carolina, and he joined O. Bruton Smith in a partnership to begin planning the facility. The problems for Turner and his Charlotte race track began pretty much from the very start of construction. According to racing journalist Herman Hickman, the project was hindered by "bad weather" and "rocky terrain that complicated construction to the point of exceeding the budget by thousands" (33). Turner stated that workers "hit about half a million yards of solid granite . . . whole thing cost a half million dollars more than it should have" (Chapin, "Curtis" 52). Despite these setbacks, the track was completed, and Turner was named president of Charlotte Motor Speedway.

In 1960, the facility was used for the running of the World 600. The surface of the track broke up under racing stress, costing Turner and Smith additional money for repairs (Hickman 33). In a short time—after a less-than-stellar turnout for a fall event—many of the facility's stockholders were up in arms and looking for some retribution from Turner and his partner, who were now out of money and completely desperate.

Curtis Turner's desperation boiled over into his driving. He needed every dollar he could win. After losing the 1961 Rebel 300 to his Holman-Moody teammate Fred Lorenzen, Turner plowed into the winner in an act of frustration (Hickman 33). Losing the winning share of the race purse meant Turner had lost any bargaining power he had for future loans. Without borrowed money, the speedway was in grave danger of being closed. In a last ditch effort to rescue his race track, Curtis Turner turned to one outlet that could help him. He solicited loan money from the Teamsters, promising to try and organize NASCAR's Grand National drivers into a formal union in return (Chapin, "Curtis" 57).

Turner had a big job ahead of him. He would be attempting to unionize NASCAR drivers in direct conflict with the power held by "Big Bill" France. NASCAR was France's organization, and no one—not even the Teamsters—would be able to break his control over the sanctioning body. The stage was set for a battle between two automobile racing giants. France had made stock car racing a big business. Curtis Turner had no choice but to attempt a big gamble.

Curtis Turner utilized William R. Rabin, the accountant hired to establish the books for the Charlotte Motor Speedway. Rabin's connections led to Teamster leader Jimmy Hoffa, and he operated as a "liaison" between Turner and the union, working out the details of the loan (Fielden 2: 94). Turner's initial attempt to organize the drivers fell through after some advance work among his fellow drivers came up empty. In June of 1961, Turner was let go as president of the Charlotte Motor Speedway—despite not being present at the board of directors' meeting that decided his fate within the speedway's organization (Fielden 2: 94).

France could now make an example of Curtis Turner—through the guise of NASCAR—and demonstrate how the sanctioning body would continue to deal with participants who were willing to go against the status quo. In this kind of power structure—the "benevolent dictatorship" of the France family—NASCAR and "Big Bill" were one and the same. If the sanctioning body dealt with Turner harshly, then it would be fully understood where France stood in relation to the organized labor movement of the Teamsters. The Teamsters' failure to gain a stronghold with the drivers would result in NASCAR's "successful application of political and economic repression," common behavior for a capitalist institution threatened by its labor force (Sage, *Sport and American Society* 164). NASCAR's autonomous nature made union repression possible, while other governing bodies in professional sports accepted the inclusion of organized participants.

Once he had been removed as president of the Charlotte Motor Speedway, Curtis Turner decided to approach the Teamsters Union in an attempt to regain his position at the facility. The union was ready to spend whatever it had to in order to get the NASCAR Grand National drivers. It was part of the Teamsters' plan to organize athletes from all aspects of professional sport, including Turner's colleagues (Chapin, "Curtis" 57). This time Turner would use a direct approach and organize the drivers himself.

A meeting was held in Chicago between union officials and a variety of representatives from automobile racing divisions, among them Turner, Glenn "Fireball" Roberts, and Tim Flock, all drivers from

NASCAR. The Teamsters introduced their plans for the Federation of Professional Athletes, an organization that would provide drivers with collective bargaining strength against the oppression of their respective sanctioning bodies. According to the historical documentation compiled by Greg Fielden:

The purpose, they [the drivers and union officials] said, was to form a union of all professional drivers cutting across NASCAR, USAC [the United States Automobile Club], IMCA [the International Motor Contest Association] and other boundaries. Targeted benefits for members were, "(1) better purses, (2) pension plans, (3) more adequate insurance coverage, (4) a scholarship fund for children of deceased members, and (5) upgraded facilities for drivers at the speedways—including shower areas and lounge facilities." (2: 94)

Curtis Turner promised Teamster leaders that he would assume responsibility for organizing NASCAR's drivers. The Teamsters, in return, loaned Turner money in order to rescue Charlotte Motor Speedway from near-bankruptcy.

William France had different ideas. His reaction to Turner's public statement was fast and furious. "Big Bill" made his opinion known in a hurry, announcing that "no known Teamster member can compete in a NASCAR race . . . and I'll use a pistol to enforce it" (qtd. in Fielden 2: 95). This statement has since entered the folklore of NASCAR Winston Cup racing. Many memoirs of "Big Bill" relate this particular event, even if it is difficult to verify. What can be verified, however, is "Big Bill's" ultimate disapproval concerning Turner and his union involvement.

France registered his disapproval with the union activity and told the drivers that "before I have this union stuffed down my throat I will plow up my track at Daytona Beach" (Chapin, "Curtis" 57). He would fight any union's presence within NASCAR, a position that persuaded "Fireball" Roberts to resign immediately. A final decision was made and presented to the NASCAR participants—Curtis Turner and Tim Flock would be suspended by the governing body for "conduct detrimental to auto racing." These two top-notch drivers were to be suspended for life, based upon William France's ironic comment that automobile racing was "one of the few sports which has never had a scandal" (qtd. in Fielden 2: 95).

Examining France's comment from the perspective of today is a study of NASCAR's perception of itself during the early days. The sanctioning body's definition of a "scandal" was quite different from the drivers' definition. Whereas NASCAR believed everything was going smoothly, the drivers sought out better facilities and a more financially secure future. Since NASCAR—or France—wielded absolute power, the organization got its way while the dissenting drivers got a lifetime ban. This "flexing" of muscles proved NASCAR's intolerance of disloyalty, while—at the same time—showing participants how far the organization would go to remove "negative" elements.

The organized labor debate raged on between Curtis Turner and William France. Both sides of the issue railed against the other, each highlighting the evils of its opponent. One central figure in the whole scenario was NASCAR's Vice-President, Ed Otto. He maintained an air of maturity throughout the entire episode, and he made public statements that reflected a difference of opinion from NASCAR President France. Otto actually supported the notion of unionization, based upon his past personal dealings with "recognized and respected" labor organizations. He was quoted by racing historian Greg Fielden as saying:

I understand and respect our unions and have enjoyed a good relationship with them, and I surely appreciate the fact that their steps toward improving the status, income and living standards of the people of our country have been one of the major factors in enabling so many Americans to afford attendance at and enjoy the thrills and excitement of the great sport to which I have devoted the major part of my lifetime efforts and from which I have been able to earn a decent livelihood for myself and my family. I am sure I am a friend of labor, not an enemy. (2: 98)

Ed Otto followed this statement with his personal opinions on the involvement of unions within the sport of stock car racing. Ironically, a large portion of his comments leaned—not surprisingly—toward the NASCAR anti-labor platform. He expressed concern over the

many instances which conclusively indicate that the relationships of the people involved in automobile racing do not constitute a proper basis for unionization. It can only hurt the sport and it cannot help any union that attempts involvement in the sport on behalf of the contestants in the sport. (qtd. in Fielden 2: 98)

Such a commentary by NASCAR's second-in-command safely follows the company line. Above all, such comments reflect NASCAR's unwillingness to breach the sanctity of its exclusive privilege to limit the effectiveness of other groups who wanted a part of the stock car business.

The outcome of the Turner/Teamsters episode was two-sided. First, unionized drivers Curtis Turner and Tim Flock were banned from all

NASCAR competition. Both of their lifetime bans were lifted by the sanctioning body in 1965, but only Turner attempted a comeback. Tim Flock, who was already talking about retirement, bowed out with the Federation of Professional Athletes union episode in 1961 and ended his driving career (Chapin, "Curtis" 57).

This was not the first time that Tim Flock had encountered an uncomfortable situation with NASCAR. At one point—in 1955—Flock was voted the most popular driver by his Grand National peers. In protest of Flock's award, William France refused to recognize the prize in NASCAR's records because he felt Tim did not deserve to claim it (Fielden, *Flock* 144). Perhaps "Big Bill" was upset with the way Tim Flock had dominated the 1955 Grand National season. Flock won 18 races, the NASCAR championship, and the most popular driver award— all this after France attempted to tighten the point system to insure closer competition by rewarding consistency over winning races outright (Fielden, *Flock* 137). For Tim Flock, 1965 was four years too late for a return to NASCAR racing.

Sensing disharmony among fans and participants, and feeling pressure from speedway promoters, William France turned to the man whom he felt had the best chance of pulling NASCAR out of the hole it had fallen into. Curtis Turner was a throwback to the early days of NASCAR racing, when the sport was exciting and rough. He was the quintessential moonshiner-turned-racer, and he was still eager to mix it up on speedways across the country. Promoters felt that fans would be more likely to come to races if they knew a legend like Turner would be in the field. Luckily for France, he was willing to return to racing.

The second development that resulted from the Federation of Professional Athletes episode was the creation of NASCAR's Grand National Advisory Board. This group would administer numerous aspects of Grand National competition, including rules, payoffs of prize money, and promotion of the sport. The organization was similar to the National Stock Car Commission that oversees Winston Cup racing today.

The board was established to guarantee equal input from all sides of Grand National competition; it was to include two drivers, two car owners, two promoters, and two NASCAR administrators. Ned Jarrett and Rex White were the two drivers initially named to serve on the board, but they did so only after they renounced their short-lived memberships in the ill-fated Federation of Professional Athletes. Once they espoused the NASCAR "anti-union" perspective, they were named to their new posts. Under the Grand National Advisory Board's legislation, teams were presented with a better, more equally distributed prize money system and increased death and dismemberment benefits (Fielden

2: 100). In the end, the Grand National Advisory Board managed to accomplish what the Federation of Professional Athletes had planned from its very start—a better environment for NASCAR's top division of cars and drivers.

The union issue remained quiet for a few years, especially as NASCAR tried to correct its downturn in popularity and competition during the mid-1960s. Curtis Turner was satisfied to be back in a Grand National stock car, his "lifetime" suspension behind him. A shaken NASCAR now faced problems with automobile manufacturers, namely Chrysler.

Chrysler introduced its 426-cubic-inch "Hemi" engine in 1964. The hemispherical combustion chamber utilized by Chryco's cylinder heads helped the new motor design to generate over 405 horsepower (Craft, *Anatomy* 45). At the 1964 Daytona 500, Hemi-powered cars managed to win everything in sight: both qualifying races, both front-row starting positions, and the race itself, with Richard Petty taking the lead on lap 52 and staying there for the next 148 laps to earn his first superspeedway victory (Fielden 2: 248).

The problem with the 426 Hemi was that it was not a regularly available engine. It was a pure racing motor, not to be found in any 1964 production model. The fact that NASCAR allowed the motor to be used in competition angered many drivers and car owners, but such is the privilege of having absolute control with no chance of overrule or argument. NASCAR allowed the Hemi engine because it would liven up the Grand National division, increase competition among the Ford and Chrysler products, and provide the fans with a better show. As historian John Craft has stated, "Faced with the possibility of an all-Ford show following GM's withdrawal, it is obvious that NASCAR officials had decided to let Hemi cars run 'for the good of racing'" (Craft, *Anatomy* 46).

Ford countered the Chrysler Hemi with a "modified version of the 427 FE engine that featured radically raised intake runners" (Craft, *Anatomy* 46). This new powerplant—called the "High Riser"—was the big-block response that propelled NASCAR's Grand National division into an era of dangerously high horsepower. Numerous drivers were critical about the motor war, especially since tire companies were unable to produce a compound that provided safe wear at such high speeds. Men like Junior Johnson and Fred Lorenzen—drivers whose abilities to run the fastest cars made them national heroes—hoped to see speeds brought down.

NASCAR took it upon itself to change the rules of competition. "Big Bill" France and the administration of NASCAR decided to bring down speeds at the sake of the high-performance, non-production engines. Rule changes for the 1965 Grand National season were announced in October of 1964. As of January 1, 1965, Chrysler's Hemi motor—and Ford's High Riser motor—would be outlawed from NASCAR competition.

The rule changes were met with varying amounts of enthusiasm. Ford agreed with NASCAR's decision completely. Leo C. Beebe, the Ford Division Special Vehicles Manager, said that "the automobiles in stock car events should be as representative as possible of regular production models . . . NASCAR has provided manufacturers with greater opportunities to apply lessons learned on the tracks to improve passenger cars" (Fielden 3: 8). Chrysler, on the other hand, had a much different reaction to NASCAR's rule changes.

Ronney Householder, Chrysler's director of competition, made his disapproval loud and clear. Shortly after NASCAR's rule change announcement, Householder declared:

The new . . . rules put us out of business down South. It's pretty certain that we'll have to direct our stock car racing support to USAC, which is sticking with its 1964 rules . . . it looks impossible for us to continue in NASCAR. To the guys who are running our cars, it means a loss in factory support and a depreciation in their equipment, because the 1964 cars and engines won't be eligible. (qtd. in Muhleman, Jan. 1965, 54-55)

Chrysler had withdrawn, that quickly and that assuredly, from all NASCAR competition.

Chrysler's announcement failed to change Bill France's mind. France felt that if General Motors could produce a substantial race car to run in 1965, then NASCAR would not have to cater to Chrysler's whims. General Motors could catch up in NASCAR racing because the rule changes "would automatically make available GM engines more competitive" ("Spotlight on Detroit" Feb. 1965, 6). The only problem with this strategy was that GM was coming off of a major strike, and labor relations were much more important than the creation of a solid racing-based production model. At least for now, General Motors would be out of NASCAR competition.

With Chrysler and GM out of NASCAR Grand National racing, the Ford Motor Company enjoyed absolute success. In the 1965 Daytona 500, Fords captured the top 12 places—quite a difference from a year earlier, when Chrysler's Hemi-powered machines dominated Speedweeks. Overall, Fords took 17 of the first 20 finishing positions at Daytona (Blunk, "Lorenzen" 36). By May, NASCAR's hopes of a

GM return were dashed. Chevrolets were entered at Darlington, a debut that had been delayed since a hoped-for start at the Atlanta 500 in March. Bill France never let on that the Chevrolets were struggling, telling a radio reporter that he was "real pleased to see these Chevrolets doing so well," despite the fact that one car would finish tenth, and the other one would not finish at all because of a broken crankshaft (Fielden 3: 12).

Union rumblings were heard again during the 1969 season, when the NASCAR Grand National teams prepared to run the sanctioning body's newest superspeedway in Alabama. As always, "Big Bill" France was firmly at the center of the controversy.

In August of 1969, NASCAR's Grand National teams gathered for the Yankee 600, which was to be held at the Michigan International Speedway near Brooklyn. On the Thursday evening before the race, 11 NASCAR drivers held a meeting in nearby Ann Arbor to discuss the prospect of starting a union like the one proposed by Curtis Turner back in 1961. The central figure in the meeting was Richard Petty, one of the most popular and recognized names in automobile racing. Petty and his fellow drivers apparently had been thinking about creating a union for quite some time; they kept their discussions quiet in order to avoid publicity and the wrath of Bill France. Richard Petty once said, "Eleven of us—all drivers—formed it to begin with . . . it was an idea many people had been working with for a long time. We got together one night up in Michigan and agreed" (qtd. in Fielden 3: 209).

What came out of that Ann Arbor meeting in August of 1969 was an organization called the Professional Drivers Association (PDA). The primary purpose of the PDA was to improve the sport of automobile racing. NASCAR Grand National drivers sought better conditions for themselves and their teams, including paved areas where mechanics could work, washrooms, and a pension plan. These goals were similar to Curtis Turner's original plans for the Federation of Professional Athletes (FPA) except that the PDA was not tied to organized labor. Richard Petty theorized, "If we can clean up the sport from the inside out, it will draw more people and the promoters will then make more money and can undertake the costs necessary to maintain a pension plan" ("Top NASCAR Names" 3).

This organizational movement was news to Bill France, who announced in no uncertain terms that things at NASCAR would remain unchanged. He stated, "We're not planning to change NASCAR. . . . We'll post our prize money and they're [the PDA] welcome to run if they want to. If not, that's their business" ("Top NASCAR Names" 3). The PDA, despite its high profile roster of members, was already facing a struggle against the autocracy of "Big Bill" France.

France, revered as the "czar" of stock car racing, explained to the media how Grand National competition had improved under the watchful eye of NASCAR. According to him, conditions had already been improved. "Big Bill" told the press:

NASCAR has been pretty great to this bunch. I drove in a day when there was zero prize money posted and the track operators were rinky dink guys who were not responsible people . . . these fellows have gotten to be big heroes and they have apparently forgotten how they got there. (qtd. in "Top NASCAR Names" 3)

France had seen exploitation by promoters and track owners during the 1930s, as stock car racing began evolving into a popular sport out of an environment of confusion. Rules and specifications were unclear and unfair, yet the thrill of production-based automobiles on a stretch of dirt attracted crowds. Stock car racing, as France saw it, was the proverbial diamond in the rough; the promise of professional sport was there, it just needed to be made more fair and regulated. The regulation, however, would be controlled by the sanctioning body according to its own vision of the sport's future.

NASCAR was in an unusual position by 1969. The sport stood poised on the brink of national popularity, ready to vault toward the followings once limited to professional baseball, football, or basketball. Despite this, Grand National drivers were unorganized as a negotiating body. The Grand National Advisory Board had been instituted in 1961—in response to attempted unionization by the Teamsters—but only two drivers were included as representatives. There was no organization to protect the drivers' best interests.

Other professional sports had bargaining units, but stock car racing was not an ordinary sport. Each team functioned as its own separate organization, with its own division of labor and power in place. Unlike a football team, which might have 50 players on one franchise's roster, a Grand National race team would have just one "player." Even with factory involvement, where several teams and drivers shared the same types of cars and equipment, each team functioned independently. Given that NASCAR was an autocracy, it was apparent that stock car drivers could not "be compared with golfers, football players, or other athletes that already have bargaining units" ("Top NASCAR Names" 3). With one man in charge, and no rule that could not be overturned, the PDA faced a challenge.

What made the Professional Drivers Association so strong was its roster of members—one that included some of the biggest names in the sport. Unlike Turner's attempt at unionizing drivers, this new effort utilized the immediate involvement of NASCAR's best and most famous competitors. Richard Petty was named president of the PDA. Cale Yarborough and Elmo Langley were made vice presidents. The PDA's board of directors read like a who's who of NASCAR Grand National racing: Bobby Allison, Donnie Allison, Buddy Baker, Pete Hamilton, Charlie Glotzbach, David Pearson, LeeRoy Yarbrough, and James Hylton. Compared to Turner's Federation of Professional Athletes, the PDA carried major racing weight. Petty and Baker were second-generation drivers; Pearson was quickly becoming one of the sport's top stars. What the PDA had that the FPA did not was depth—more than just one or two big names at the administrative top.

The Professional Drivers Association went public prior to the Southern 500 at Darlington Raceway. Richard Petty responded to France's initial statements with one of his own, announcing that the Professional Drivers Association would "devote its effort to the betterment of the sport by seeking to work in harmony with NASCAR, the promoters and others involved in auto racing" ("Top NASCAR Names" 25). Petty spoke of harmony and cooperation, while Bill France hinted at disloyalty and greed. Confrontation seemed certain, and the battlelines were drawn over a piece of NASCAR's property near Talladega, Alabama.

Bill France sought to expand his racing empire by building a facility that would accommodate the ever-increasing speeds of the NASCAR Grand National competitors. His plan was to create a large superspeedway near Talladega, Alabama, that would be the biggest and the fastest in America. Its debut was to be September 14, 1969, with the running of the Talladega 500 at the newly completed Alabama International Motor Speedway (Laye, "Talladega's" 34). As the track became a reality, however, it was criticized by several NASCAR drivers who drove its high banks and questioned its safety.

Several drivers who tested at the Alabama International Motor Speedway felt that the track's surface was too rough. There was also some concern about how the track would be on tires, given its harsh pavement and anticipated high speeds. As a demonstration of his facility's safety and race-readiness, Bill France himself took the wheel of a Ford stock car, driven by Mario Andretti in several USAC events, and turned laps nearing 175 miles per hour (Fielden 3: 211). The 59-year-old France accomplished two things with his "practice run" around the high-banked oval. He generated publicity for his speedway, while—at the same time—showing that the complaints of the Grand National drivers were unfounded.

Bill France then attempted to undermine the entire union. He submitted an entry for the inaugural Talladega 500, then asked PDA board member Bobby Allison if he could join the union since he was going to run in the event (Fielden 3: 212). This would allow France to see the PDA's inner workings—and gave him a chance to attack the union from within.

It became more and more apparent that the Talladega 500 would turn into a confrontation between "Big Bill" France and the PDA. Things got underway with practice sessions, where drivers of faster cars had some routine, new-track tire troubles. Bobby Allison had made unofficial laps at over 197 miles per hour ("Bobby is Fast" 3). The PDA was concerned because no tire had ever been built to withstand such speeds, and it appeared the Talladega race would generate 500 miles of flat-out driving. By the time teams got their cars ready for qualifying, tires were falling apart under the stress of high speed—some after only three laps—and cars were bottoming out "as many as a dozen times each lap" ("Alabama Speedway" 13).

France recognized the potential for problems, especially when only nine cars attempted to qualify for the first 15 starting positions. Tires "blistered" during qualifying, which prompted Goodyear and Firestone to assure competitors that better tires were on their way. Unfortunately, neither company had a significantly safer tire for the new speedway.

Teams experimented with different kinds and brands, thanks to France's lifting the NASCAR rule that forces cars to start on the same tires used in qualifying. Finally, a decision was made that would attempt to determine once and for all what tire was best for the facility. A test session was established, with one car trying the tires from Firestone while another ran all of the tires sent by Goodyear. It was a dangerous test that challenged not only the tires from both companies, but also the nerves of the two drivers—Donnie Allison and Charlie Glotzbach—who sat behind the steering wheels. In the end, the session proved one thing. Neither manufacturer possessed a tire compound that could safely withstand the stresses of racing at the Alabama International Motor Speedway.

Once again, the power structure of NASCAR—and the absolute control of Bill France—is reflected by a single incident. After the informal tire test, Firestone examined its product and decided not to run the event. According to W.R. McCrary, general manager of racing for Firestone, the company's tires would not "'live on this track and we won't consider running a tire that will hurt the drivers'" ("PDA Drivers Must Post Bonds" 3). Goodyear was ready to announce the same thing— except that "Big Bill" France "convinced Goodyear's Public Relations Manager Dick Ralstin to hang around a little longer. After a private conference with France, Ralstin said Goodyear would bring in another tire by race time Sunday" (Fielden 3: 213).

What was said in the "private conference" will probably never be known, but the one-on-one dynamic of the meeting reflected France's ability to persuade people—and even companies—to play ball with the man in charge. This is possible when the leader of a trust possesses absolute control. With "Big Bill" France in the catbird seat, Goodyear found itself in a possible hot seat. Above all, the NASCAR Grand National drivers found themselves headed for their drivers' seats. That was until the PDA stepped in and made a decision of its own.

PDA President Richard Petty got the decision-making process moving. On Friday evening, Petty called a meeting of the PDA and a "preliminary decision" was made that the drivers would meet with Bill France on Saturday morning. The meeting allowed the PDA to voice its concerns before France, and the union quickly requested that NASCAR postpone Sunday's race. Bill France refused the PDA's suggestion, and proclaimed the track safe "at racing speed," which he estimated at 175 miles per hour ("PDA Drivers Must Post Bonds" 26). Since practice speeds were in excess of 190 miles per hour, the PDA knew that France's calculations were too low to be considered realistic.

Richard Petty responded to France's estimate, backed up by his fellow drivers: "Who is to say what the racing speed would be on this or any other track? To win, it might require us to race at 190 or 195 miles an hour . . . the track is not safe at the speed we would be required to run" (qtd. in "Alabama Speedway" 13).

Purposely racing at less than wide open could create more trouble, especially if some drivers decided to run flat-out while others held back and ran slower. Such traffic inconsistencies might lead to accidents between drivers trying to second-guess their cars at high speed, the condition of their new tires, and the handling characteristics of the superspeedway.

Bill France remained firm, declaring, "We will have a 500-mile race here tomorrow, and the prize money that has been posted will be paid . . . Whether you run for it will be up to you to decide" (qtd. in "Alabama Speedway" 13). He then directed a comment toward Richard Petty, who had accused France of building his new speedway too quickly. France said, "Richard, if you don't like the track, load up your car and get out" (qtd. in "PDA Drivers Must Post Bonds" 26).

Petty, angered by France's insinuation, called for another PDA meeting after their requests to NASCAR were ignored. France had refused to cancel Sunday's event, so the PDA refused to drive. By late Saturday morning, over 12 teams had loaded their cars and had prepared to leave the speedway. Richard Petty made the PDA's decision public by announcing it to the media. PDA Vice President Cale Yarborough stood with Petty as the driver boycott was declared. According to *National Speed Sport News*:, "Petty said the drivers had discussed the possibility of running their cars 'slow'—in the 170-180 mph range. But he said, 'We came to race. We came to run wide open. We feel this track isn't ready and the PDA has decided we will not race'" ("PDA Drivers Must Post Bonds" 26).

Cale Yarborough added, "'A piece of iron can't stand that kind of pounding for 500 miles. . . . We're breaking things that have never broken before'" ("PDA Drivers Must Post Bonds" 26).

Despite the PDA's withdrawal from Sunday's race, NASCAR still went ahead with its Talladega schedule. A 400-mile Grand Touring event, one of the supporting divisions that sometimes ran in conjunction with Grand National races, was scheduled for Saturday afternoon. Ken Rush averaged 151.27 miles per hour and won the accident-free event, and no team had problems with shredded tires for the entire 151 laps ("Rush Takes First" G2). As of late Saturday afternoon, no Grand National drivers had yet left the speedway. The die was cast shortly thereafter, according to racing historian Greg Fielden:

As darkness spread . . . a booming voice was heard over the public address system. . . . It belonged to Bill France. "All those who are not going to race, leave the garage area so those who are going to race can work on their cars." . . . Within a few moments, a truck motor cranked up. It was the Petty Enterprises truck. The headlights came on and the famous #43 was pulled from the garage area. Others followed. A total of 32 cars were hauled out. (Fielden 3: 213)

The PDA drivers immediately came under fire for their actions at Talladega. One PDA member accused his fellow drivers of making a decision for him, since the majority of PDA members voted to leave the facility. NASCAR veteran Buck Baker, whose son Buddy was on the PDA's board, said:

Things must have gotten a little plush for a lot of these guys, or they must want it a little better than it is . . . When I sign an entry blank, I'll race . . . But today it's different, and they have made it [money and fame] fast . . . the drivers . . . won't realize this until they walk down the street one day and no one knows who they are. (qtd. in Economaki, "Editor's Notebook" 4)

As France had planned, the Talladega 500 took place on Sunday, September 14, 1969. NASCAR Grand Touring teams were used to fill out the starting field, which took the green flag in front of 65,000 spectators. Initial figures called for over 100,000 spectators, but NASCAR officials determined that the PDA boycott affected ticket sales at the gate ("Dodge's Brickhouse" 26). Each fan in attendance received a printed statement written by Bill France. It explained the situation at hand, told fans how the field had been composed, and offered fans a "two-for-one" deal allowing them to see a second race for free. The statement, in part, proclaimed:

I am very much surprised that some of our drivers and car owners would wait until the last day prior to a major event and withdraw their automobiles from a race. . . . When the drivers qualified for the event, everyone expected they would race. It would be unfair to the spectators who traveled to Talladega to see a race to postpone it. It would also be unfair to the drivers and car owners who wish to compete . . . Persons who attend the race, and those holding reserved seat tickets for the Talladega 500 and who do not attend, will be allowed to exchange them for tickets for a race at Daytona Speedway or for a future event at Alabama International Motor Speedway. ("Talladega: The Principals" 37)

Such a decision—allowing the fans to see a second event for free—is fitting for a "benevolent dictatorship" like NASCAR. France, as the "benevolent dictator," enabled NASCAR to inflict rules with an iron hand, while showing compassion for its dedicated fans, giving them an added benefit as an act of kindness. This act made up for the fact that Sunday's field was missing some of the biggest names in the sport. Such is the behavior of NASCAR as a trust. The organization has the exclusive power to interfere with trade based on its largeness. Its act of beneficence, the thousands of free tickets given to fans for another race, lets the sanctioning body appear to be benevolent, even though the free tickets are part of an ulterior motive. Giving to the fans now is a means of winning their support later if the drivers should ever attempt another boycott or confrontation with NASCAR.

The inaugural Talladega 500 was won by Richard Brickhouse, a PDA member who broke his ties to the union over the public address system on raceday morning. Brickhouse, driving a Dodge Daytona Charger vacated by PDA member Charlie Glotzbach, averaged 153.78 miles per hour in an accident-free race that exhibited no apparent tire problems ("Brickhouse Seizes Chance" 17). The young driver was met in victory lane by William France, who told the first-time winner—and the 65,000 spectators, "This race reminded me of what the great Cannonball Baker [the first national commissioner for NASCAR] used to say, 'Quitters never win and winners never quit.' The guys who raced today were the real winners" (qtd. in Fielden 3: 215).

The "guys" who did not compete—the members of the PDA—spent time addressing their reasons for leaving on the eve of the race. On September 18, 1969, the PDA gave its formal and official response, which declared, "Our members are race drivers first and accept the risks involved, but when these life and death risks become both unreasonable and unnecessary then corrective action is essential" (Fielden 3: 215-16).

France, attempting to regain control over the cars and drivers of NASCAR, issued a counter statement in which he made it clear the sanctioning body had a major responsibility to address, and that was to the fans. The reaction of race fans to the Talladega/PDA incident, according to France, was "favorable toward NASCAR because we ran the race and I think they [the fans] saw a good show" (quoted in "Talladega: The Principals" 104).

France also added a "good faith to the public pledge" to entry forms issued by NASCAR for future Grand National events. The pledge, just two paragraphs long, was designed to avoid another "mass withdrawal of drivers on the eve of a racing event" ("NASCAR Asks" 3). NASCAR had labeled the PDA a band of troublemakers who could not be trusted, and the good faith pledge was a simple way to embarrass those who boycotted Talladega.

The pledge, like the one used in the Automobile Dealer Franchise Act of 1956, was intended to mediate the power balance and bargaining leverage between opposing groups. Automobile dealers during the mid-1950s accused car manufacturers of "enfranchising too many dealers" and of using "high-pressure methods to force sales." Dealers felt the manufacturers produced too many cars, then "expected" them "to keep selling regardless of profit" ("While Auto Industry Booms" 26-27). As a result, in order to sell surplus cars, some dealers were forced to reduce prices and profit margins to 0.6 percent ("Help for Dealers" 81). In this particular situation, "good faith" was meant to protect auto dealers from "conditions . . . brought about by . . . Ford and Chevrolet, with their chain-store and factory controlled agencies" (qtd. in "While Auto Industry Booms" 27). NASCAR believed that the PDA's actions at Talladega were an attempt at intimidation. France demonstrated that even without the sport's top drivers, the show would still go on.

Part of the good faith pledge declared that "both the driver and the car owner recognize their obligations to the public and race promoter . . . we agree to compete in the event if humanly possible unless the event is postponed, canceled or the car fails to qualify" (qtd. in "NASCAR Asks" 3). This statement was leveled in direct retaliation against the PDA, who demanded that the Talladega event be postponed until safety concerns could be addressed. Now NASCAR's cancellation policy was in writing, and posted publicly for every Grand National driver to see. "Big Bill" had won again; no NASCAR race would be postponed or canceled merely by the politicization of drivers or car owners. As one NASCAR official put it, "this [pledge] just ties them [drivers and car owners] down a little stronger on their obligations once they enter a race" (qtd. in "NASCAR Asks" 3).

The good faith pledge was designed more for racing fans than it was for racing teams. NASCAR wanted to assure its spectators of star-studded fields, something that was promised to the fans at Talladega but not delivered. If anything, the pledge symbolized an impasse between the PDA and Bill France. France expressed concern over the fact that PDA members may have "prodded" some drivers into boycotting the Talladega race. "I think," France declared, "a driver is obligated to race after he qualifies" ("Talladega: The Principals" 104).

Other administrators in automobile racing did not agree with France's treatment of the PDA and the entire Talladega incident. NASCAR's most outspoken opponent was Larry LoPatin, president of American Racing, an organization that controlled five speedways. LoPatin argued that France was tyrannical in his handling of the Talladega event, and his solution to the problem was questionable with regard to the future of automobile racing. LoPatin was quoted by Chris Economaki as saying:

You're seeing the end of an era. This [handling of the Talladega situation] will bring a lot of changes. A lot of people [race promoters] are going to reassess their operation. You can't run anything without order . . . you've got GT [Grand Touring] cars running with GNs [Grand Nationals] and a lot of rules have been suspended. You just can't operate that way. ("Editor's Notebook" 4)

LoPatin's diatribe against "Big Bill" France centered on the fact that NASCAR allowed another division—the Grand Touring cars—to run with the larger, more powerful Grand National cars. To make the competition more equal, NASCAR overlooked rules that governed the Grand Touring cars. The rule changes made a better show for the fans, despite threatening the safety of the less experienced Grand Touring drivers. LoPatin disagreed with France's logic.

LoPatin went on with his complaint against France, commenting that

when one considers that there were 23 GT cars and 13 bigger Grand Nat'l [*sic*] cars and drivers ready to go and over $300,000 in the till, the decision to suspend some rules to get the show in might be looked upon by the stockholders as a master stroke rather than a lapse in management policy. (Economaki, "Editor's Notebook" 4)

Larry LoPatin's opinions in the national racing press failed to endear him to Bill France. He saw "Big Bill" as a man with too many conflicts of interest in everything from enforcement of rules to management of speedways. Such involvement would lead to unfair governing practices within the sport, part of the trust-like behavior exhibited by a national power such as NASCAR.

LoPatin suggested that cooperation could ease the pressure between NASCAR and the PDA. He told *National Speed Sport News:* "Auto racing is an industry with common problems . . . and we have to solve those problems together. . . . If France continues his fight with the drivers and . . . suspends them . . . what can the rest of the promoters do?" ("NASCAR Asks" 23).

William France had some obvious conflicts of interest. Along with being NASCAR's president, he was also president of the Daytona and Talladega speedways. These facilities are now incorporated as the International Speedway Corporation, a public company that earned $60 million in revenues in 1993 and includes tracks at Darlington, South Carolina, and Tucson, Arizona. ISC also owns 50 percent of Watkins Glen International Speedway in New York (Byrnes 52).

It is interesting to compare how France reacted to both situations where unionization threatened NASCAR's control over its drivers. When Curtis Turner attempted to bring the Teamsters into Grand National racing, France responded by pressuring drivers into resigning under the threat of "lifetime" suspensions from NASCAR's premiere division. Turner and fellow driver Tim Flock disregarded France's threats, and both found themselves out in the cold. Bill France lifted Curtis Turner's "lifetime" suspension when stock car racing experienced a period of stagnation during the mid-1960s. Fans lost interest in the sport, and rule changes caused companies like Chrysler to back out of NASCAR involvement. Turner gave the sport of stock car racing a much-needed boost of excitement, based on the folklore and history behind his career.

Bill France had to react differently during the unionization scare of 1969. This time, the union movement involved several big name drivers—including Richard Petty. France had to use a diplomatic judgment in this situation, for fear of alienating the thousands of Richard Petty fans all across America. The lifetime suspension would be a virtual kiss of death for NASCAR in this case. Suspending such names as Baker, Allison, and Petty would mark the end of Bill France's dream.

Whereas Curtis Turner was suspended, Richard Petty was given the chance to compete in future events because of amendments made to NASCAR's rules. Bill France tried to guarantee that a boycott like the one at Talladega would never happen again. Rather than getting rid of the union leader completely, as was the case with Turner, France instead tried to work around the PDA and its famous president. Banning Petty would have been professional suicide for NASCAR. Turner's skill and daring style was eventually needed to help bolster the sagging sanctioning body in 1965. Petty's talent and fan appeal was needed immediately. A four-year suspension would have brought NASCAR precariously close to financial failure.

The Professional Drivers Association remained a thorn in Bill France's side during the 1970 season. Petty and his fellow union members disagreed with the "Good Faith to the Public" pledge. Its new version, found on 1970 NASCAR entry forms, had been changed to give the sanctioning body additional control over each race car. Grand National cars, according to the 1970 pledge revision, "must remain and be raced unless withdrawal is approved by the NASCAR competition director" (Economaki and Laye 3).

The 1970 good faith pledge stated, in part, that

the undersigned car owner . . . further agrees with NASCAR . . . (1) to start the described car in the 1970 Riverside [CA] "500" . . . provided the described car qualifies or the appropriate NASCAR officials assign it a starting position, and (2) to utilize, if necessary, a substitute driver for the described car if the driver executing this entry blank is for any reason unable or unwilling to drive this car. (Economaki and Laye 3)

Richard Petty and several other PDA members refused to sign forms bearing the revised pledge. They returned their blanks with the pledge scratched out. Petty commented that France wanted "to keep control of 110 percent and it can't be done." The sport of stock car racing, according to Petty had "outgrown a one-man operation" (qtd. in Economaki and Laye 13).

Unfortunately for the PDA, the automobile manufacturers were siding with NASCAR. Chrysler advised Richard Petty to sign the entry forms regardless of what they said; it was the only way NASCAR would let him compete. Petty did so, and "Big Bill" got a step up on the PDA. Car owners checked into the legality of NASCAR's demands and found everything to be binding, a revelation that upset many drivers even more because it meant car owners would be forced to appoint a substitute driver if the PDA demanded another boycott.

NASCAR, functioning as a trust, felt no obligation to negotiate with the PDA. Drivers operated independently of NASCAR. They were not considered "employees" of the sanctioning body, thus leading Bill

France to ignore their existence. This was the same argument made concerning France's disdain for the Teamsters Union. NASCAR felt obligated to acknowledge nothing but itself.

Bill France declared that he was thinking only about the fans. "The clause was added," he said to the media, "for the protection of the public. We will not change it." Part of this stemmed from the Talladega boycott, which made raceday ticket sales drop because fans did not want to see a race without the biggest names in NASCAR. France, once again, assured stock car fans that they would be guaranteed to see the show they were promised, regardless of how the drivers felt. "NASCAR will do everything in its power to protect the public," William France announced, "without the public we have no sport" (qtd. in Economaki and Laye 13).

In the end, it was NASCAR that outlasted both the Federation of Professional Athletes and the Professional Drivers Association. By the time the R.J. Reynolds Tobacco Company came along to help NASCAR with some financial assistance in 1971, the PDA was pretty much relegated to automobile racing history. Bobby Allison, when questioned about the PDA in 1969, argued that "Every other major sport has its players organization" (Fielden 3: 211). Bobby Allison seemingly forgot one very important fact. Not every major sport exists under a "benevolent dictatorship." NASCAR sees all, knows all, and controls all. When someone tries to wrestle part of that control away, the sanctioning body changes its plans. Proposed unions become threats to private enterprise, successful teams become threats to close competition, and unfair advantages become threats to NASCAR's mythic history of equality for all of its competitors.

Current NASCAR President, William France, Jr., has said that "None of our rules are written in stone" (qtd. in Vehorn, *Farewell* 119). Such is the legacy of "Big Bill" and all of NASCAR's history. From early attempts at unionization to the influx of major corporate sponsors and millions of dollars through marketing and promotion, NASCAR is one of professional sport's most successful money machines. Most of NASCAR's success has come from its overwhelming ability to wield authority through its advantage of being a massive enterprise with almost unlimited power. Like a trust, NASCAR possesses exclusive privileges that enable it to affect the economic, political, and competitive workings within the business of American sport.

4

A High-Banked Learning Curve:
Acculturation and Stock Car Racing

Racing is just plain harder in the Winston Cup Series than anywhere else, but that makes the rewards a whole lot more special as well.

—Johnny Benson, Jr., 1996 NASCAR Winston Cup
Rookie of the Year (*NASCAR Online* 6 Nov. 1996)

When young children are exposed to certain activities like "stick and ball" sports, they obtain a level of cultural programming—or acculturation—where the values, beliefs, and certain accepted behaviors of their society are internalized. As a result of this internalization, young people are "taught" about the major sports within our culture, such as football, baseball, basketball, and ice hockey. Along with these "major" sports come such events as golf, tennis, bowling, and soccer. What makes each of these an accepted part of American sporting culture is their ability to be played with relative ease—referring to the availability of proper equipment, facilities, and an understanding of the game itself. Such accessibility allows a sport to become part of mainstream culture.

Inaccessibility hinders our cultural education. This is the case with NASCAR Winston Cup stock car racing. Despite the fact that most people have access to an automobile, and can operate the vehicle according to state and local laws, few have actually experienced the sport of stock car racing except in its most mythic presentation. The difference comes from a lack of access to this distinct subculture. Many Americans can shoot a basketball through a hoop or hit a baseball from an early age, but few Americans—even during adulthood—can handle a 3,400-pound stock car putting out over 700 horsepower and capable of reaching speeds over 190 miles per hour. Driving a car on the streets is one thing, and it is something most of us over the age of 16 can do. Adding the competitive aspect of stock car racing, with its high speeds and close competition, is simply a part of American sports that few of us are acculturated into. A young boy or girl can grow up with basketball or baseball, but few children grow up with access to the unique socialization required for life within the Winston Cup subculture.

The socialization of children is affected by their exposure to certain cultural behaviors and stimuli. American children can experience traditional sports, like baseball or football, because they are often part of the youngsters' basic cultural environment, unlike "specialized" sports like automobile racing. This is the case with highly specialized careers such as circus performing, where "children usually learn the act from their parents." Young people who pursue specialized occupations, like race car driving or acrobatics, often "grow up in the environment and receive training and instruction" from family members or others working in that particular specialized field (Linde 17).

Most traditional sports are introduced to young people in America at a very early age. Children's toys mimic the sporting equipment used by adults. Some companies market small basketball goals, for example, complete with adjustable poles and breakaway rims, making it possible for a toddler to "shoot baskets" like older children or adolescents. Oversized baseballs and bats are also marketed for small children, providing them with the opportunity to develop and sharpen the appropriate skills necessary for when they begin tee-ball. A parent can buy miniature football uniforms for his or her child in the colors of professional teams, complete with shoulder pads and helmets with face masks. The accessibility of such "traditional" athletic equipment allows children to discover America's sports at an early age, when such cultural stimuli make their greatest, most lasting impression.

This same idea holds true during later childhood, when young athletes take part in a variety of community-supported, operated, and managed sports teams. By this time, the children have already been introduced to the basic equipment and rules of their specific event through their use of sporting "toys" like those mentioned in the passage above. The organized sports made available to these young athletes may include Little League baseball, "Pop" Warner football, church or school basketball leagues, junior ice hockey, or AYSO (American Youth Soccer Organization) soccer leagues. Such sporting activities are common within American communities because they help children develop such character-building traits as accepting defeat, good sportsmanship, and the virtues of teamwork. From the viewpoint of acculturation, however, we see another "lesson" being aimed at the young athlete. Such "traditional" sports acculturate the young American athlete into an understanding that "mainstream" sports are an accepted part of our national experience. In other words, these "stick and ball" games are what constitute American sports.

By the time a young man reaches his freshman year in college, it is highly conceivable that he has played a single sport for over 12 years. A boy who begins playing tee-ball at the age of five can then "grow up" into Little League baseball, which can lead to some kind of teenaged league—like American Legion baseball—and end up with the young man playing for his junior and senior high school baseball teams. This scenario involves organized baseball play, which goes over and above any informal baseball the young man could play throughout his life. Granted, the player has to avoid serious injury and demonstrate some interest and ability, but such a pattern is not uncommon. Acculturation, in this sense, occurs quite easily. The player has almost constant contact with his sport, and the dominant culture provides him with sufficient external stimuli in the form of such things as televised professional baseball games, newspapers and magazines about baseball, baseball cards and memorabilia, and the historic and cultural mythology that defines baseball as America's "pastime."

Such constant attention and lifelong acculturation can also help a young athlete turn professional, a position of high social status in modern-day America, by the age of 22 or 23. If the athlete happens to play college football or basketball, sports that produce large amounts of university revenue, he might be offered a professional opportunity before he even graduates from college. Such was the case with Chris Webber, the University of Michigan basketball star who signed a 15-year, $74.4 million contract with the Golden State Warriors after two seasons of college play. Webber left the University of Michigan for big money and professional competition. His decision is all well and good, but what does this tell us about America and its attention to mainstream sports?

Mainstream sports often allow for participation with little or no adverse expense or effort. Pickup games of baseball can be accomplished with little more than a simple ball and bat. Urban children organize stickball games with a rubber all-purpose ball and an old broom stick. Basketball can be played with a variation of a hoop and net, with something as unorthodox as a milk crate taking the place of an "official" goal.

What separates a sport like stock car racing from these traditional childhood events is its dependence upon unique types of equipment. A gravity-powered soap-box racer is a homemade beginning, but it is a stretch from the gasoline-fueled, internal combustion engines required for even the most entry level foray into automobile competition. For many children aspiring to make it into Winston Cup stock car racing, the best way to start is with a go-cart. Go-cart racing allows children to achieve direct experience with the basics of driving, competition strategy, engine repair, and chassis setup. One quickly learns, however, that children involved with go-cart racing have often been introduced to the sport by their parents. In some situations, there is a direct overlap between automobile racing and go-cart competition for children.

Go-cart racing fits into the acculturation process because it provides children with the experience needed to handle a low-level type of automobile once they reach the age of 15 or 16. A child who has several years of carting experience will be more at ease with a stock car, at least in terms of driving strategy, chassis setup, and the nature of racing competition (passing, finding the fastest line around a track, and so forth). Whereas today's Winston Cup drivers often spent their youth ramming around empty fields in old cars, or hot-rodding around the backroads of their hometown, the Winston Cup stars of tomorrow will have extensive go-cart racing experience. Winston Cup drivers like Ricky Rudd and Lake Speed already come from carting backgrounds.

Part of the traditional acculturation process involves having access to automobiles from an early age—not necessarily driving them as a child (although it would not be that unusual in a rural community where the roads were for the most part open) but at least being around cars and all of the things that are associated with them, such as engines, parts, tools, and other aspects of automobile operation. This is where the young person begins his or her acculturation—exploring under the hood of an automobile and learning the parts and the procedures. This is also where the acculturation of children can sometimes go astray. Most people in today's society do not attempt their own automobile repairs or maintenance, especially with the advent of high-technology engines with computer chips and electronic fuel injection. Here we see a vital part of the acculturation process disappear. In order to develop the skills needed to become a good driver, you must first become a good mechanic. That is the route taken by most people in stock car racing, as biographies and feature articles written about them indicate.

Unlike the football player who wins a college scholarship, the stock car driver attends the school of real life. There is no easy way to learn the business of stock car racing. Acculturation into the sport is based on the individual's work ethic and how much the young person wants to get behind the wheel. Such is the case with former Winston Cup driver, and current Winston Cup car owner, Bobby Allison, who spent most of his career building, maintaining, and repairing his own race cars. Throughout his career, Bobby Allison always had a "safety net" of sorts; he was always able to diagnose problems in his stock car, especially while on the track in either qualifying or racing conditions. This skill came from the days and nights he spent under the hood of his own race car, doing anything that had to be done by himself.

Bobby Allison's interest in stock car racing developed during his childhood years in Florida. His maternal grandfather, Arthur Patton—a relative of General George Patton—was a great follower of sports, and one sport that caught his attention was stock car racing. Patton took Bobby with him to a local dirt track to watch Modifieds one summer evening, and the young boy was hooked. This experience changed Bobby Allison, and "there was no doubt as to which direction his life would take" (White, *Circle* 18).

By 1955, Allison was a senior in high school. Hialeah Speedway was running an amateur division as part of its season, so the young Allison took a 1938 Chevrolet coupe and decided to begin his ascent toward a racing career. In his first outing with the coupe, Allison managed to finish seventh out of 40 cars. Two weeks later, he scored his first win, beating sixty cars in a twenty-five lap race.

Allison's success came with little help—if any—from anyone else. Entering the sport of stock car racing required little more than an old car and a box for parts that were removed for safety. Bobby Allison had been maintaining and repairing a variety of late model vehicles for his own transportation, a typical situation for a young man growing up in a family without much money. Such self-reliance made Allison a good mechanic—before he had even climbed behind the wheel of a stock car.

Stock car racing had not been Bobby Allison's first sporting experience. While in high school, Allison tried playing football. His slight build made him quick, but it also made him a target for larger defensive players. At his coach's suggestion, Allison made a move toward stock car racing, a decision that would change his life. This decision in Bobby Allison's life gives us an opportunity to consider an interesting difference between "mainstream" sports and stock car racing. A more traditional sport like football or baseball often requires some natural athletic ability in order for the player to enjoy the experience. A good soccer player, for example, must have strong running skills and sharp foot/eye coordination.

A sport like automobile racing, on the other hand, requires a different level of ability. Stock car drivers are very athletic—as a four-hour race on a mid-August afternoon will attest. Racing creates an entirely different set of demands upon its participants than found in other more typical sporting events. Driving a 3,400-pound Winston Cup stock car requires hand/eye coordination, an ability for sustained concentration, and a talent for sensing exactly what a race car is doing on the track. Racing requires well-developed arms, legs, shoulders, wrists, hands, and necks. Consequently, an increasing number of drivers and pit crew members are taking part in regular exercise and weight-training programs. Athletic ability is, however, just a piece of the racing puzzle.

Winston Cup stock car drivers must also understand the inner workings of a high-performance automobile, which is a complicated and highly detailed piece of machinery. Knowing precisely what to expect from a race car comes from years of driving and mechanical experience, the lessons often learned through shadetree trial and error. A good Winston Cup driver—or any racing driver, for that matter—is one who can "diagnose" a sick motor, a poor suspension setup, or the changing conditions of a racetrack. Unlike baseball, where the ability to throw a 100-mile per hour fastball is a natural talent, one a player must be born with, automobile racing is more of a science. In an interview shortly after his retirement, four-time Indianapolis 500 winner Al Unser said that "racing . . . can be taught . . . [an] experience can be translated and we can . . . use it for ourselves" (Woolford, "Inside Track").

In a sense, taking this idea into consideration, we see how Bobby Allison was able to "teach" himself how to drive a stock car based upon his ability to maintain and understand the automobile itself. Allison's self-education as a race car driver continued during the late 1950s, while he worked for the Mercury Outboard Motor Company (White, *Circle* 22). He drove stock cars at Hialeah Speedway on weekends, constantly sharpening his skills behind the wheel. It was during those earliest days when Allison, like most other successful drivers, discovered just how difficult operating a stock car could be. Like many of the sport's "first generation" drivers, he had to prove his worth as a stock car driver on regional short tracks. Allison himself ran for years on the bullrings of Alabama and Florida, all in the hopes of keeping his family and his racing operation afloat financially.

The year 1961 marked Bobby Allison's first foray into NASCAR Winston Cup racing, at that time called Grand National racing. A statement by NASCAR in 1950 reported that the "Grand National" name indicated "superior qualities," an attempt to distance the sport from its rough-and-tumble moonshining origins (Fielden 1:18).

Bobby Allison's Grand National debut at Daytona International Speedway marked a familial changing of the guard in NASCAR racing. In one of the two qualifying races held to determine the starting grid for the Daytona 500, the 100-mile race that Allison ran in as a rookie, veteran driver Lee Petty was injured in an accident that threw his Plymouth over a retaining guardrail and into the parking lot. The injuries suffered by Petty, who had won the inaugural Daytona 500 in 1959, were severe; they included massive internal damage, multiple fractures of his left chest, a punctured lung, and a broken collar bone (White, *Circle* 31).

Hospitalized for four months, Lee Petty rested while his sons, Richard and Maurice, took over the family's racing business. Richard Petty describes their tasks in his 1986 autobiography:

picture two boys, twenty-three and twenty-one years old, running a business, when all they ever did before was bolt things together and drive. It is amazing to me, when I look back at it, that we got to all the races. It was tough at times, there's no doubt about it. There was so much to be done. (*King Richard* 180)

From 1961 on, Richard and Maurice Petty assumed a competitive role as the operators of Petty Enterprises. Lee's major injuries that year made him retire as a driver, allowing young Richard to assume the family's mantle as its primary driver.

Even Richard Petty, when reflecting on his experiences in the 1961 NASCAR season, found a difference between first and second generation drivers. Petty has written that

getting started was tougher for me than it had been for Daddy [Lee]. When he started, everybody was new at it, but by the time I was running the show I was competing against many of the all-time greats—guys with years of experience like Junior Johnson and Joe Weatherly and Fireball Roberts. . . . Some were one hundred percent drivers, some were fifty percent. All were zero percent car-builders. I was one hundred percent everything. (*King Richard* 180-81)

Petty's transition into the Grand National series was considerably less tenuous than Bobby Allison's, especially given Petty's family background. His career as a NASCAR driver began with him working as a mechanic on his father's stock car. The acculturation of Richard Petty into NASCAR racing was propelled by his childhood environment, one where automobiles and speed were commonplace, a part of everyday life.

Richard Petty's childhood was spent in and around the small town of Level Cross, North Carolina, where he was born on July 2, 1937. As a boy, Petty looked to his family—and their close-knit community—for lessons in living and growing. It was here that his acculturation into rural southern life and, ultimately, stock car racing, began. The process shaped Richard and his brother Maurice on two distinct levels. First, the acculturation process established expectations set by their overall community. This is reflected by Richard's comments concerning his education, values, and a basic system of culturally created—and accepted—behavior. Petty writes:

We all lived a pretty sheltered life around Level Cross, particularly when I was growing up during World War II. It was made up of work and picnics, and work and church socials, and work and visits with other members of the family. Did I mention work? Well, I can't stress work too much, because it's the first thing parents taught their kids . . . kids in our area did whatever they were told to do . . . I sure am glad I learned at an early age that work won't hurt you. They have been important lessons in life, and ones I've tried to teach my kids. (*King Richard* 17)

Richard Petty's emphasis on work, family, and community—not uncommon within American character development—outlines the beginning of his own socialization. This process would be passed on from Richard to his children, including his son, Kyle, as he learned about life in a racing family and prepared for his career as a third generation stock car driver.

The second element of the acculturation process experienced by Richard and Maurice Petty involved the introduction into their family's automobile-related environment. Richard traces his family's fascination with cars back three generations, writing that it all started with his great-grandfather Judson Petty, who—at the age of 98—raced "around the countryside in his stripped-down Model T Ford" (17). Thus began the Petty legacy that led to ten combined NASCAR driving championships and eight Daytona 500 wins.

The southern charm and grace that Richard Petty has displayed to the fans, the media, and the people living near Level Cross has been attributed to Richard's grandfather, Judson Petty. Richard's description of Judson refers to him as "a quiet, God-fearing Quaker gentleman" (18). This familial combination of conservativism and an addiction to raw speed resulted in the first of the professional racing Pettys— Richard's father and one of the NASCAR Grand National pioneers, Lee.

It is Lee Petty who had the most influence upon the education and acculturation of young Richard. Lee's interests in automobile racing and speed were inherited—or at least realized—during the years of his adolescence. Richard writes that his father "traded his bicycle for a Model T. . . . The first thing he did was strip down the Model T and race it. . . . You'll have to admit that he was living up to his heritage" (18). Lee fueled his sons' interest in stock car racing, and they evolved into two of the sport's greatest figures; Richard became NASCAR's winningest driver with 200 victories, many of them with brother Maurice along pit road as his crew chief.

In the earliest days of stock car racing, before NASCAR even existed, local drivers were limited as to where they could work on their cars. Most of today's race teams have elaborate facilities that measure better than 22,000 square feet. Such was not the case for Lee Petty when his racing interests developed; he had to operate as a shadetree mechanic.

This experience affected the young Richard, who learned about automobiles through direct observation and participation. He explains,

"There was always a car in the front yard or the side yard, or wherever there was a shade tree to work under. And it was always apart, in one stage or the other, being modified to make it run faster" (18). Unlike many of the South's first stock car drivers, who started as bootleggers seeking bragging rights against their fellow moonshine runners, Lee Petty raced simply for the fun of it. In fact, Petty had a career operating a small trucking firm in Randleman, North Carolina (Yates, *Drivers* 79). His racing was limited to taking a car—either new or old—and trying to wring as much speed from it as possible. Lee's earliest races, writes Richard Petty, made him the "king of back-road racing around the Piedmont" (42).

Richard Petty was taking part in an orally directed process of acculturation. Lee's "social circle," which gathered around the stove down at the general store, introduced Richard to the importance of the automobile within their regional community. Richard has admitted that "the conversation was always about cars. . . . It [sitting around the stove] was part of the storytelling routine. . . . There was a lot of ritual" (19). Petty, perhaps inadvertently, recognizes this type of communal behavior to be the oral narrative tradition rooted in our country's folklore, an aspect of acculturation that functions as a vehicle for the next generation to achieve an understanding of its history, civilization, ideals, and values. Young Richard thought he was merely listening to these stories as entertainment; he was actually experiencing a cultural rite of passage that declared his "acceptance" into the community of mechanics and racers that made up his father's peer group.

The popular argument that arises when someone discusses the Petty family, and Richard's "rags-to-riches" ascent into the sport of NASCAR stock car racing, is that there was an easier process of assimilation for him than there would be for most other aspiring race car drivers. In his 1992 book about Richard Petty's career, Frank Vehorn writes about the stigma that often followed Richard through the garages and pits on the NASCAR circuit:

"Richard used to become irritated if anyone even hinted that he just stepped into a winning operation and made the most of it. 'No one ever [*sic*] gave the Pettys nothing,' he reminded. 'We worked for everything we got.' " (*Farewell* 41)

It seems that some of these hints came from competitors like Bobby Allison, especially when Bobby and Richard became fierce rivals in the late 1960s. According to Frank Vehorn, Bobby Allison "started . . . at the very bottom . . . on NASCAR's minor league circuits, where he became . . . a national champion before getting a self-made opportunity to compete in racing's spotlight" (*Farewell* 41).

Speaking of his detractors, Richard Petty has admitted that "they're right, Daddy *did* give me a race car to start with . . . he let me drive the second car for Petty Engineering—a car I had built. So, you see, I wasn't handed anything on a silver platter—pewter maybe, but not silver" (132). Lee made a deal with Richard, that the young man would not start driving a race car until he turned twenty-one (113). Once Richard turned 21, he faced a choice that was based, in part, on his family's involvement in NASCAR racing. He could attempt to race on the convertible circuit, established by NASCAR in 1956, or—if driving did not suit his interests or abilities—he could return to being a mechanic and crewman for his father.

A similar situation occurred when the sons of Bobby Allison and Richard Petty decided to attempt careers as stock car drivers. The acculturation processes experienced by their fathers were then reflected in how both young men were advised to go about starting their respective climbs toward NASCAR's highest level. For Kyle Petty, it was a matter of beginning at the top, much like Richard did at the urging of his father, Lee. For Davey Allison, it was a matter of starting out at the lowest possible level—running local short tracks in a hand-built car—like his father did. Davey was expected to work his way up the NASCAR ranks through his own skill and motivation.

The acculturation process for Davey Allison was another where automobiles and high performance were part of everyday life. This situation is a given within the equation of how stock car drivers are—in most cases—developed. In Davey Allison's case, he worked as an employee for Bobby Allison Racing. He was given shop space, an old Chevrolet chassis, and a used engine. Like his father, he would be expected to gain experience through trial and error on the short tracks of Alabama. Only after his duties as an employee were completed could he work on building his own race car (Bolton and Bolton 15).

John Ozley, a former employee of Bobby Allison Racing, has stated that the team was too busy preparing race cars for Bobby:

We were building short track and sportsman (now Grand National) cars for Bobby, so there wasn't time to build a car for Davey. . . . Donnie [Bobby's brother] had the shell of an old Nova he had raced a few years before, and he gave it to Davey. Bobby had the engine out of an old show car that had sat on an engine stand for more than a year. It had a lot of miles on it. He gave that engine to Davey to use. Bobby always contended that you learned to race with a car that didn't have a lot of power. You learned to race the car you had. (qtd. in Bolton and Bolton 15)

Davey's acculturation process was one that required following a learning curve that would ultimately provide him with the skills and experience necessary to earn his promotion into the big time. This second generation driver would have to demonstrate his desire and motivation through his own actions, not on the generosity of his successful father.

We can compare the experiences of second generation stock car driver Davey Allison to the experiences of third generation stock car driver Kyle Petty. As Davey Allison followed his father into NASCAR racing, Kyle Petty followed his father as well.

Kyle Petty was granted an opportunity similar to that given his father. When Kyle admitted in 1978 that he wanted to drive a stock car, Richard decided that the best way for him to learn was by starting out at the very top. Since Kyle wanted to someday run at a track like Daytona, Richard believed that it was best for him to try it first hand at the beginning. Petty observes:

There is an ARCA—Automobile Racing Club of America—race the week before the Daytona 500, so that seemed like a good place for Kyle to get started. I figured he might as well start at Daytona, since his grandfather had won the first race they ever had there, and I had won my first superspeedway race there. That track meant a lot to the Pettys. (238)

This was not a typical way to try driving a race car for the first time, but it was typical for the men racing in the Petty family. The family business had become family tradition.

Kyle Petty has endured these pressures throughout his entire life. His decision to become a stock car driver was not really a big surprise within the subculture of the Winston Cup Series. As sportswriter Bones Bourcier reported in the August 1993 issue of *Stock Car Racing* magazine, the NASCAR Winston Cup Series "had some unusually high expectations of him" (42).

According to Bourcier, "It wasn't enough that the son stepped into his father's profession. The world wanted him to fill his father's shoes, too" (42). Kyle Petty never felt that kind of pressure—at least personally—from his family, despite the pressure leveled on him by the motorsports' media and fans. Kyle has admitted:

He [father Richard Petty] was just another guy, and racing happened to be his job. My parents told me, "You don't have to be a race driver. You've got three sisters, and they're not going to race. They're going to be teachers, or lawyers, or whatever they want to be. Whatever you want to do, we'll help you. (qtd. in Bourcier 42)

What Kyle Petty wanted to do was to become a stock car driver.

Stock car drivers with children find themselves facing a hard choice: do they assist their son or daughter with entry into the sport, or do they stand back and let their child attempt the sport on his or her own? Supplying equipment, facilities, and advice is often the easy part. Supplying talent, skill, and desire is fully up to the child.

This idea struck home during the summer of 1980 when I was attending a Winston Cup event at Pocono Raceway. Kyle Petty and his wife, Pattie, were the new parents of a baby son, Adam Kyler. During pre-race ceremonies that Sunday afternoon, the Pettys were presented a baby buggy painted to resemble Kyle's stock car. This was when he was driving for Petty Enterprises, so the buggy was in the Petty blue-and-red color scheme and markings of the team's STP sponsorship. Carrying the number 42, it looked just like Kyle's car, and it sat on pit road with the starting field for the day's race, which was lined up for the command to fire engines.

Such a gift followed the pattern of acculturation perfectly. Just as Kyle had never known anything but stock car racing during his entire life, neither would his son. Before interests and talent were even identified, the fourth generation of Petty racers was already supplied with a "ride." Naturally such a gift was out of sheer fun, but the basis for assimilation was already in place. This baby had been born into one of America's most famous racing families, making it certain that his eventual acculturation would involve stock car racing. Everyone along pit road had a good time that afternoon, celebrating the arrival of this new little Petty, but one could not help but think about the images and assumptions that were projected by the little buggy with the fancy paint scheme and the STP sponsorship.

Children often recognize their parent's career, even though they may not understand the level to which the parent is involved. Kyle Petty has said that he, for a long time, assumed that everyone's father drove a stock car. On his television program *Winners,* the late Neil Bonnett spoke in 1992 about Kyle's childhood impressions of his father, reporting that "he was ten or eleven years old before he learned that not everybody's father was a famous race car driver like Richard Petty. He [Kyle] didn't think there was anything special about the man they called the King."

One thing special about the King is that he recognizes what kinds of pressures go along with being the offspring of men whose careers have elevated them to a level of stardom in their chosen fields. The reaction to Kyle Petty's embarking on a racing career—and the expectations connected to his family name—was the same as when Davey Allison moved into the Winston Cup ranks. A major part of this issue is that second and third generation race car drivers must be compared to drivers with similar amounts of experience or seat time, not to their famous fathers or grandfathers who learned the sport through years of labor, trial, and error. As Richard Petty writes about Kyle: "If you want to compare him, compare him with other drivers who have the same amount of experience; don't compare him with me. Don't compare Davey Allison with Bobby. It's not fair" (*King Richard* 242).

In Winston Cup racing, familial relations often evolve into business and/or team operations, as was the case for Kyle Petty following his 1979 ARCA victory at Daytona. It was shortly after this win that Kyle became the second driver at Petty Enterprises, running a second STP stock car with his father. This step seemed natural, especially considering Richard's assimilation under the guidance of his father, Lee, during the late 1950s. Kyle was able to—once again—benefit from the facilities and experience of his father's racing team. The younger Petty had race cars at his disposal, a term the inexperienced driver took all too literally.

According to the late Neil Bonnett, tearing up race cars is a "traditional [racing] family rite of passage." It happened often during Kyle's early Winston Cup career, and it made racing an expensive occupation for the Petty family. By the early 1980s, when Richard and Kyle were both running out of the family's shops, Winston Cup racing was becoming more expensive each season. Corporate sponsorship made racing teams more evenly matched, and a new medium—cable television—carried Winston Cup racing to homes all across America and the world. The sport grew, and so did the importance of fielding a successful Winston Cup effort.

Increased competition meant increased costs; it also meant a sharp increase in the pressures leveled against Winston Cup teams. Winning became even more of a commodity because now more than team and/or familial pride was at stake—now a sponsor had to be taken into consideration. A satisfied sponsor often showed its pride by increasing its team's racing budget, a move that correlated to the team being able to afford better equipment, more speed, and—most of all—more victories.

In the case of Petty Enterprises, increased competition costs meant implementing some sort of organizational change. Preparing, maintaining, and racing two Winston Cup cars became too costly for the team. By the start of the 1984 season, Petty Enterprises had been trimmed to a one-car operation—with Kyle Petty as driver. A decision had been made. Richard Petty would move to another team. He wrote:

Kyle had to be tired of living in the shadow of "King Richard," and Chief [Richard's brother, Maurice, who served as the team's engine builder] surely was fed up with trying to build engines for two Pettys, making each one as strong as the other-and not favoring either one. (*King Richard* 243)

Richard started driving in 1984 for California businessman Mike Curb, with the blessing and cooperation of STP and Pontiac. Kyle, on the other hand, inherited the daily operations of Petty Enterprises, the most successful stock car shop in America. The pressures of multi-generational ties to the sport once again became apparent. Suddenly, Kyle Petty was an intimate part of the family business, free from his father's presence and completely on his own and responsible for the team. As Richard puts it, "Nobody knew better than I what it was like to live in the darkness cast by a giant" (243). Richard had found himself in this same position back in 1961, after Lee had his accident at Daytona. Now Kyle was in the driver's seat—figuratively and literally.

Kyle Petty found the task to be daunting, especially since he was running the entire operation. He admitted: "I just couldn't do it . . . I couldn't run the business and run the race car, and make the hotel reservations, and get the people to the race track, and get this and get that . . . At that time, I wasn't but twenty-three, and I just couldn't do it."

By the end of April 1985, Petty Enterprises had closed its doors. Kyle had been offered a ride by the Wood Brothers, one of automobile racing's most famous teams, and Maurice Petty continued to prepare Ford Thunderbirds for drivers like Morgan Shepherd and Dick Brooks, even though his health and his spirits seemed to be failing. According to Kyle Petty: "It was hard to leave Petty Enterprises, where a Petty had always driven—no matter what—for the last thirty or thirty-five years. And, all of a sudden, they've left it to you, and then you're the last one to walk out and close the door."

Despite his hard feelings when he left Petty Enterprises that year, Kyle Petty found himself enjoying a second acculturation as part of the Wood Brothers racing team. Kyle has admitted that the experience of driving for another team was highly educational. He said, "I learned more from Leonard Wood in the four years I worked there than I've learned in racing the whole time I've raced . . . just about cars, and what makes them tick." This education enhanced the process of acculturation into the sport of stock car racing that Kyle had already undergone with his family and his environment.

The move away from the safety of Petty Enterprises was, most likely, a good one for Kyle Petty. According to Peter Golenbock: "Kyle was having a lot of fun in his life, but from 1979 through 1985 he failed to win a single Winston Cup race. He was criticized for not being hungry enough because he had grown up with a silver and Petty-blue spoon in his mouth" (388). By being responsible for another team's race car, as opposed to being the sole operator of Petty Enterprises, the young Petty had to follow the instructions of someone else. In this case, it was the Wood Brothers. This team, based in Stuart, Virginia, had single-handedly revolutionized pit strategy. Pit stops conducted by the Wood Brothers were faster and far more polished than any seen on the NASCAR circuit before. Their cars, thanks to quick pit work, had won the Daytona 500 several times with a variety of talented drivers like Cale Yarborough, Tiny Lund, A.J. Foyt, and David Pearson at the wheel. The success of these drivers while with the Wood Brothers carried them to stock car stardom, and Kyle Petty found himself poised for the same opportunity.

It was a familial issue that ultimately cost Kyle his driving job with the Wood Brothers in 1988. The team had different ideas about where it was headed, and a driver change seemed to be part of the formula. As Kyle said, "In a family-type organization, the easiest thing to change is the non-family member." He found himself without a ride at the beginning of 1989, although by March he was already driving the Sabco Racing Pontiac. He made 19 starts that season as the driver for Sabco Racing, and finished 30th in the final Winston Cup point standings that year (Fielden 4: 626).

Things have changed again following those dark days in Level Cross during the spring of 1985. Richard, who retired as a driver after the 1992 season, is once again at Petty Enterprises. Today he owns the No. 43 STP Pontiac Grand Prixs driven by Bobby Hamilton, the fifth driver in five seasons to climb behind the wheel for the King. Kyle hinted during the early 1990s, when he was driving Pontiacs for multi-millionaire businessman Felix Sabates, that he might return to the family stable where so many winning stock cars have been built and maintained, where so many first place trophies rest on shelves in the small museum located across from the garages. When interviewed by the late Neil Bonnett in 1992, Kyle admitted:

When Felix decides that he doesn't want me anymore, and he kicks me out, and it's time for me to shuffle on down the road, then I'll probably end up back at Petty Enterprises. That'd be fine for me. Blood's thicker than water, and it's a whole lot thicker than money, and at some point and time, I'll end up back working with Richard Petty again.

Dale Inman, Richard's cousin and a longtime employee at Petty Enterprises, has said, "He'll probably come back . . . I'm sure someday he'll be the owner of Petty Enterprises." Nothing would suit the Petty family, diehard Petty fans, or the Petty-intensive media more than to have Kyle behind the wheel of a Petty Enterprises stock car.

The fantasy became reality in late October of 1996 when Kyle Petty announced he was starting his own Winston Cup race team in conjunction with Petty Enterprises. Kyle was leaving Sabco Racing at the end of the 1996 season, which was a perfect time for his return to the family fold. "I guess I'm proof, " Petty declared to the media, "that you can go home again" (qtd. in "Kyle Petty, Mattel"). Kyle's new team, named PE2, would be a separate operation away from his father's shop in Level Cross. While Richard's cars would continue to carry STP sponsorship, Kyle's new Pontiacs would be financed by Mattel, Incorporated's "Hot Wheels" line of toys. Foremost on everyone's mind, however, was the fact that Kyle would be back working with his family's team once again.

The importance of family and tradition became an important part of Kyle Petty's decision to return home. "My grandfather [Lee] started this whole deal, and I want to keep the tradition alive . . . I have two sons, Adam and Austin, who both seem pretty serious about racing, so who knows, maybe they will take it to the fourth generation" (qtd. in "Kyle Petty, Mattel").

Richard Petty echoed his son's sentiments, saying, "There's a lot of history at Petty Enterprises. We're proud of what we've done, and proud that Kyle is coming home." The younger Petty also spoke of history and the fact that "raising a family makes you appreciate your own background" (qtd. in "Kyle Petty, Mattel"). Reuniting father and son fulfilled the hopes of many close to NASCAR Winston Cup racing. It solidified almost 50 years of stock car racing success, and provided a positive look toward the future of the sport.

Any positive future for the Allison family took a tragic turn during the early 1990s, as both Davey and his brother, Clifford, died in separate accidents at different racetracks. Their father had already retired from driving following a near-fatal wreck at Pocono in 1988. Davey, by that time, had made the move from ARCA competition to the Winston Cup Series. He won the rookie-of-the-year title in 1987, capturing two wins (Talladega and Dover) that season. Bobby had become a Winston Cup car owner and was happily watching his two boys assume their place in the sport of stock car racing.

Clifford, Bobby's youngest son, was working his way through the ranks of ARCA and Busch Grand National racing in hopes of making it to the Winston Cup Series. By 1992, he was running both divisions and showing great promise as yet another member of the famed "Alabama Gang." Clifford's run at the big time came to a tragic end, however, when he was killed in a crash during practice for a Grand National event at Michigan International Speedway. Davey had had a serious accident at Pocono just a few days earlier, but the painful injuries he suffered in Pennsylvania could not compare with the pain he felt of losing his brother.

The Allison family came back from Clifford's death to continue campaigning on the Winston Cup circuit. Davey, by the summer of 1993, was in hot pursuit of the division title. Driving for veteran car owner Robert Yates, Allison had won at Richmond earlier in the season, and had managed to notch a third-place finish in the inaugural race at New Hampshire International Speedway. As fate would have it, the first Winston Cup race at New Hampshire would turn out to be Davey Allison's last.

The next afternoon, Davey and family friend Red Farmer flew to Talladega Superspeedway to watch a Grand National test session driven by David Bonnett, son of fellow "Alabama Gang" member Neil Bonnett. Allison had recently purchased a helicopter in hopes of easing the pressure of travel required by life on the NASCAR circuit. Davey was attempting to land the helicopter when it smashed into the ground. Red Farmer escaped with minor injuries, but Davey Allison was not as lucky. By the next morning, Bobby and Judy Allison's oldest son was gone. Two second-generation drivers had been taken by injuries and accidents, yet Bobby Allison continued to try and shape the future of NASCAR by running a race team.

Another second generation driver has assumed his place within the changing of the guard, despite the fact he has been racing for almost 20 years. This driver, Sterling Marlin, is the son of Clifton "Coo Coo" Marlin, a journeyman driver who never won a race on the Winston Cup (then the Grand National) tour. For 17 years, Sterling Marlin followed his father's distinction as being a non-winner. While other second-generation drivers won races and fought for positions in the points championships, Marlin just kept getting beaten. He scored nine second-place finishes during his career, only to watch the winner drive off toward victory lane and adoring crowds.

That all changed when Sterling Marlin won his first Winston Cup race—the Daytona 500 on February 20, 1994. It happened on national television in front of a record-breaking crowd of 165,000 spectators—not counting the television viewing audience. In just a few laps around the Daytona International Speedway, Marlin drove from near obscurity to national headlines. By the time he pulled his car into Victory Lane, he was already a celebrity based on the telling of his story by network commentators.

Marlin's story is one of classic acculturation, the boy who learns about race cars by working on his father's. Young Sterling worked on his father's pit crew, changing tires and traveling the circuit as part of a low-budget operation. No big corporate names were on the side of Coo Coo's car—although the really huge sponsorship push did not occur until after Coo Coo had retired from racing and Sterling had made the switch from crewman to driver. Sterling's car was sponsored by Kodak, and in one victory he made almost as much as his father did during his entire career (Tuschak, "Marlin Family Win").

During the CBS broadcast, a story was told about Sterling as a boy ten years of age. He worked in his father's "shop," a tin-roofed building with nothing more than a gas heater for warmth and comfort, maintaining his father's race car in Columbia, Tennessee. As the commentators told the brief story, Marlin was racing toward his first career victory, living proof that one can learn through adversity and hard work. From helper to crewman to driver to the Daytona 500 champion—the path to success in stock car racing lies along family tradition, environment, and acculturation. Growing up in a racing family provides the proper setting for entry into such a demanding sporting activity. The cars, the tools, and the equipment have to be there. If they are, then a child's education will come from experience and—if the desire is there—a need for greater challenges and stiffer competition. Experience is the foundation upon which success—or at least opportunity—is built.

Sterling Marlin was greeted by numerous mechanics and crewmen as he rolled down pit road toward Victory Lane after the race. He spoke of the experience later in a press conference, saying, "I've been in Winston Cup racing since I was 14 or 15 and I was one of those guys for a long time, changing tires and working on my daddy's car. . . . It was pretty emotional and I appreciate what those guys did" ("Better Late Than Never" 15).

The praise came from peers who not only wanted to see Marlin finally make it to the winner's circle, but from men who—in many cases—have had the same kind of upbringing. A quick look at a roster of Winston Cup teams shows numerous familial connections. Brothers, nieces and nephews, cousins, sisters, and relatives through marriage comprise large portions of NASCAR teams. Notice the drivers who are brothers: Darrell and Michael Waltrip; Geoff, Brett, and Todd Bodine; Chuck and Jim Bown; Rusty, Kenny, and Mike Wallace; Benny and Phil Parsons; Terry and Bobby Labonte; Jeff and Ward Burton; and the late Davey and Clifford Allison. Father and son pairs are also prevelent among NASCAR drivers: Ralph and Dale Earnhardt; Ned, Glenn, and Dale Jarrett; Ed and Jimmy Spencer; and Lee, Richard, and Kyle Petty.

But what about drivers who are not of southern descent? Most of the previous examples involve drivers who were born and raised in the South. What about participants who come from above the Mason-Dixon line? Does their process of acculturation differ? A number of factors have affected the socialization of northern drivers in the sport of Winston Cup racing, including the mass media, family background, and recognition from influential figures in stock car racing itself.

One of the first northern drivers to find success as a NASCAR Grand National competitor was Fred Lorenzen, who was raised in the town of Elmhurst, Illinois, not far from Chicago. Lorenzen became familiar with NASCAR racing while camping out with friends in his parents' backyard. In a 1992 interview, Fred Lorenzen said that he and his friends "would always listen to this race on the radio called the Southern 500 . . . I used to say that someday I would drive in the Southern 500" (qtd. in White, "Lorenzen" 50).

This sounds, at first, like the wishful thinking of a young boy who dreams of becoming a race car driver. In Lorenzen's case, it went on to become more fact than fiction. As a teenager, Fred Lorenzen participated in street races on local roads in his 1952 Oldsmobile (White, "Lorenzen" 49). His ascent to the ranks of professional stock car racing was slower than that of drivers like Richard Petty. Lorenzen believed this was because he grew up in the North, where automobiles were less of an influence on daily life. "Down South," Lorenzen has said, "drivers were brought up at 10 or 11 years old to learn how to drive a car . . . they were all brought up on the backroads . . . There's no comparison" (qtd. in White, "Lorenzen" 50).

Lorenzen eventually made it into stock car racing's big leagues, but not before gaining experience on short tracks around Chicago. Southern racers saw Lorenzen's talent. He won two USAC stock car championships, then climbed behind the wheel of a Ford owned and maintained by John Holman and Ralph Moody in Charlotte. Before he retired on April 25, 1967, Fred Lorenzen had won 26 races and over $400,000 (Thomy 136).

The pressures of Grand National racing forced Lorenzen out at the age of thirty-one, a time when most drivers have yet to reach the peak of their careers. Suffering from ulcers, he stepped from his "blue-and-white No. 28 Ford" and got into real estate back in Elmhurst. At Lorenzen's retirement, Jacque Passino, Ford's chief of performance, declared that "No man since Barney Oldfield has contributed more to the performance image of Ford" (qtd. in Thomy 140). Lorenzen made his contribution from the suburbs of Chicago, one of stock car racing's success stories from the North.

Another Northern stock car success was the late Alan Kulwicki from Milwaukee, Wisconsin. Kulwicki's acculturation into Winston Cup racing was more typical; his father, Gerry, was an acclaimed engine builder in the Midwest. Alan played "traditional" sports in school—both football and basketball—but he raced go-carts at the age of 13. Kulwicki had "to decide whether to go to training camp for football or to race go-carts" (qtd. in Golenbock 349). He decided to race, and he set out to become a professional driver.

One unique element of Alan Kulwicki's acculturation process was that he managed to earn a bachelor's degree from the University of Wisconsin while gaining experience on the short tracks near his home. Gerry Kulwicki wanted his son to forsake a racing career and become "an engineer or a doctor—anything but a race car driver" (qtd. in Golenbock 349). At the time of Alan's death in 1993, he was the reigning NASCAR Winston Cup champion and owner of his own racing team.

Alan Kulwicki was praised for his individualistic spirit; it was the motivation that carried him from Wisconsin to Charlotte in search of stock car racing success. Kulwicki's success came from more than that, however. It was also the confidence he learned as a second-generation engine builder and college-educated mechanical engineer that made him a Winston Cup champion. Like many drivers before him, Kulwicki gained a strong background in automobiles and the sport of racing through his family, which was closely tied to midwestern motorsports. The process of acculturation, therefore, operates effectively away from stock car racing's Southern roots.

Winston Cup driver Derrike Cope, a native of Washington, was another second-generation automobile racer. Cope's father "was a top fuel drag racer, a professional from Southern California . . . we moved to the Pacific Northwest, he retired from drag racing and opened an engine-rebuilding facility" (Golenbock 395).

Derrike Cope was initially interested in a baseball career. Stock car racing took a backseat to his days as a catcher. He played on the team at Whitman College in Walla Walla, Washington, and was scouted by the Chicago Cubs (Golenbock 395). Cope's dream of a possible baseball career came to a sudden end after he caught a cleat in some grass and blew out his right knee (Granger 98).

Cope began helping his brother who was working with a Late Model Sportsman car. Once Derrike actually tried driving, his career plans took an unexpected turn. "I got behind the wheel," Cope once said, "and that's when I felt like that was what I was meant to do" (Golenbock 396).

Cope's father was receptive to his son's career plans, giving him advice that would help the young driver make it to the Winston Cup ranks. Derrike said, "I told my Dad I wanted to race, that I was willing to put in the hours required. He said I needed to travel with some racers and learn about it [the sport] before I got involved" (qtd. in Granger 98). Derrike's father told him to find "the best people possible," and to learn how to "be an excellent spokesman outside the race car" (Golenbock 396). Cope took classes, worked with various media, and gained experience that made him "comfortable" doing public relations work.

The experience of Derrike Cope is a new area in the process of acculturation. Unlike the stock car driver of the past who learned mechanical and/or driving skills at the hands of a parent or relative, today's Winston Cup drivers are being acculturated to meet the demands of corporate responsibilities. Success as a race car driver means working as a company spokesman, being articulate at a sales meeting as well as fast on the racetrack. Many drivers have managed to secure their racing careers on the merits of being a popular figure with consumers. A driver like Michael Waltrip is incredibly popular as a spokesman for Citgo gasoline, despite going winless in Winston Cup competition. The "high-speed salesman" is an important aspect of NASCAR's Winston Cup Series—based upon the sport's need for big dollar corporate sponsorship. Learning public relations skills is a necessity for up-and-coming stock car drivers. Derrike Cope learned these skills early in his career, and now he is a successful driver with solid sponsorship.

Acculturation affects everyone within a society. It is the way in which cultural values, beliefs, and traits are passed from one generation to another, from one person to another. Processes of acculturation occur in different ways; most of them happen in common, rather indistinguishable ways: through education, through religious upbringing, through community, and through ethnicity. A major aspect of our acculturation, however, comes from the lessons taught to us by those around us, by those closest to us. In most cases, such lessons are taught by family members—especially those who live in close contact with us as children, such as parents or siblings. This is how we learn to interpret the culture around and within us.

Fig. 1. Brett Bodine poses for a photograph with a young fan during a personal appearance in 1996. (Photo by Mark Howell)

Fig. 2. Ward Burton signs autographs for fans before qualifying at Pocono in 1996. (Photo by Mark Howell)

Fig. 3. Bill Elliott, an eleven-time winner of the NASCAR Winston Cup Series' Most Popular Driver Award, with the author's parents, Glenn and Virginia Howell, during a 1996 personal appearance at a McDonald's in Pennsylvania. (Photo courtesy of Glenn and Virginia Howell)

72

Fig. 4. Junior Johnson, the "Last American Hero," scored 50 NASCAR wins before becoming a car owner. A moonshiner-turned-racer, Johnson is a significant figure in the folklore of the sport. He retired from racing after the 1995 season. (Photo by Mark Howell)

73

Fig. 5. Joe Nemechek focuses on his upcoming qualifying attempt. With more teams and sponsors trying to get into Winston Cup racing, qualifying has become a pressure-packed event. (Photo by Mark Howell)

Fig. 6. Lake Speed with his daughter at Pocono. Speed began his career in go-carts and was the 1978 World Karting Association Champion. By 1980, he was driving a stock car on the Winston Cup circuit. He won a race at Darlington in 1988. (Photo by Mark Howell)

Fig. 7. 1995 Winston Cup Champion Jeff Gordon at Pocono in June of 1996. Gordon won ten events in 1996 en route to a second-place finish in the championship standings. (Photo by Mark Howell)

Fig. 8. Mark Martin holds off a charge by Jeff Gordon at Pocono. The small appendage over the No. 6 Valvoline Ford's windshield is a television camera. This camera angle provides viewers with a driver's-eye perspective of Winston Cup action. (Photo by Mark Howell)

Fig. 9. Winston Cup cars are hauled in rolling garages that come complete with lounges, ample storage space, and enough room for two stock cars. This hauler carries Pontiacs built and maintained by Petty Enterprises. (Photo by Mark Howell)

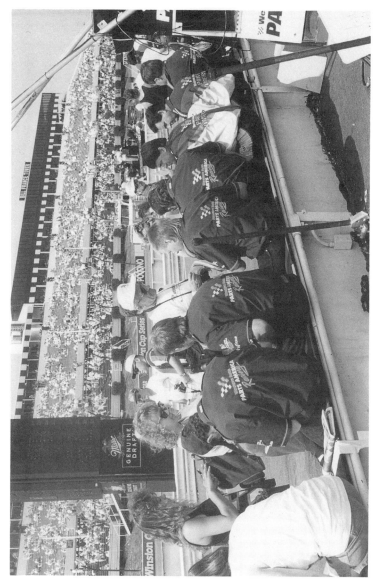

Fig. 10. Darrell Waltrip's Western Auto Parts America pit crew signs autographs for fans prior to the UAW-GM Teamwork 500 at Pocono in June of 1996. Increased television coverage has given pit crews celebrity status. (Photo by Mark Howell)

5

Changing Identities in American Culture: Sponsorship and Drivers' Roles in NASCAR's Winston Cup Series

Automobile racing in the United States is in its infancy. It can be made a tremendously high class sport, or it can fall into the hands of professionalism. Both are all right in their way and should be encouraged, but a close study of events will prove that automobiling will have a very similar career to football. No professional football team was ever made permanently successful . . . Let us guard this great, big, far-reaching sport in its infancy, so that it may develop into a being, which shall be a constant source of delight, satisfaction and pride to us all.

—Burr McIntosh, 1904

Stock car racing, as explained in *Social Aspects of Sport* by Eldon Snyder and Elmer Spreitzer, is a prole sport—it attracts followers from the proletariat or working class level of society. Prole sports, which include such events as motocross racing and professional wrestling, place an emphasis on speed and power rather than physical grace or skill. These sports are attractive to working-class people, according to Snyder and Spreitzer, because the events derive from artifacts common to the proletariat lifestyle, such as automobiles and motorcycles, and fans can identify socially with the participants (179).

NASCAR Winston Cup stock car racing, as seen through its history, meets this criterion. In its current state of existence, however, this division of stock car racing has attracted a following quite removed from that of its earlier days. As a result, the responsibilities and images of today's stock car drivers have changed in relation to the sport's growth and nationwide recognition. Major international corporate sponsorship has elevated Winston Cup racing far above its earlier position as merely a prole sport. Television coverage of Winston Cup events has created additional demands for drivers and other participants, as well as a different, non-prole audience.

In this chapter, we will examine the changing identities of stock car drivers and the sport of NASCAR Winston Cup racing itself. A Winston

81

Cup driver wears many hats; a full day's schedule might include testing a new car, doing an interview, signing autographs at a designated site, approving souvenirs that will carry the driver's name or image, and having a dinner meeting with a business manager or corporate sponsor. Free time for family is a valued commodity. Today's driver is always in demand; the driver is a spokesperson, a salesperson, an ambassador, an employee (or employer if the driver personally owns a team), and a media personality. The days of a race car driver simply racing are over.

Since the very beginning of the automobile's history, companies have recognized the role that racing plays in the selling and marketing of products. The first companies to utilize racing as a means of promoting their products were the automobile companies themselves. Henry Ford thought people would consider his new car to be worthwhile if it had a proven competition record. The idea had worked for the Duryea brothers; their cars raced throughout the United States and England during 1895 and 1896, earning them a reputation as the finest automobiles in America. The Duryeas' racing successes gave them major media coverage; their victories were celebrated by newspapers throughout the country (Georgano 16).

Ford saw the attention automobile racing was receiving, and he believed that a strong, competitive race car would give him an edge against other manufacturers trying to prove their worth. His 1896 "quadricycle" failed to receive media attention because Ford failed to announce its public demonstration. His second car had received newspaper coverage, but he believed winning an important race would generate the publicity his newest automotive creation deserved (Finch 63-64).

Henry Ford prepared a racer for a ten-mile sweepstakes race in Grosse Pointe, Michigan, on October 10, 1901. Another automobile builder, Alexander Winton, was favored in the event on the merits of his previous speed trials. Mechanical trouble with Winton's car that day gave Ford an easy victory and the national publicity he sought (Collier and Horowitz 40-41). Ford's win at Grosse Pointe was a key moment in the history of automobile racing because it marked a turning point in the hierarchy of racing teams. Prior to the win, Ford—like Alexander Winton—was compelled to drive his own racing car in competition.

Ford recognized the possibilities for racing, especially in terms of dollars and publicity to be won, and became associated with a former bicycle racing champion named Tom Cooper. The men built two racing cars—one called the Arrow (although some sources refer to it as the Red Devil) and another called the 999 after a famous New York Central train—but neither partner was courageous enough to climb behind the wheel in competition (Georgano 33). There was one person, however, who—according to Cooper—was a fearless competitor and eager to give the cars a try. The driver was a bicycle racer from Wauseon, Ohio, named Barney Oldfield.

Oldfield's hiring as Ford's driver marked a change in racing as the world knew it. As race cars became more powerful, car builders decided—perhaps in a moment of great wisdom—to forsake the heroics of competition and leave the danger to professional drivers. This allowed Henry Ford to "retire" from racing while still keeping his cars in competition (and in front of the media). His use of Oldfield as a professional driver, and Oldfield's success behind the wheel in a variety of competitive events, helped elevate Ford and his cars to the forefront of the automotive industry. It also helped to create one of America's most recognized sports personalities. Barney Oldfield, with a cigar clenched firmly in his teeth, was soon known throughout America. He became a household name from his success in automobile racing.

Barney Oldfield was America's first popular professional automobile racer. From his first races for Henry Ford in the 999, Oldfield became a nationally known public figure—a celebrity from the world of 20th-century American sports. His initial success came from racing bicycles; he had never been behind the wheel of an automobile prior to his association with Ford. October 23, 1902, was the first time Oldfield had driven the 999 alone in competition, and his debut came against Winton's Bullet, which—at that time—was the fastest automobile ever known (Oldfield 24). Oldfield, facing experienced and race-proven competition, won the event and instant recognition as a professional driver. As Homer George recorded in a biographical sketch of Oldfield, "his success won him immediate fame for it was due more to his daring and ability as a driver than to the superior excellence of the car" (Oldfield 25).

By December of 1902, Barney Oldfield was breaking records set by Winton's Bullet, unseating it as the fastest automobile in America. In May of 1903, Oldfield and the 999 established a new world's record for the mile, covering the distance "in one minute and one and three-fifths seconds" (Oldfield 25). A month later, Oldfield became the first person to cover one mile in less than one minute. Oldfield and the 999 were earning national fame by shattering speed records and winning races throughout the country. His success was planting him firmly within American culture.[1]

For the first time, a race car driver was a national folk hero. Barney Oldfield conquered this new technology and—in a sense—tamed it. His driving skills made automobiles look fluid, limitless, and, perhaps most important, thrilling. Oldfield was the one figure in America who could control the power of the automobile and channel it into useful and exciting form. No one had captured the American imagination like Barney Oldfield because no one had ever demonstrated such skill and bravery on this relatively untried invention.

After leaving Ford's 999 behind for other, more advanced racing cars, Oldfield began touring the country to conduct driving exhibitions. He proceeded to establish even more speed records and further his reputation as America's finest driver. His switch to other makes of cars proved that it was the man—not the machine—that could create spectacular speed. He demonstrated that all automobiles, at least those built with care and the best technological advancements, were capable of high performance. It was a matter of talent—which Barney Oldfield possessed—to make a car run at its best.

Talent meant more than wealth, and Oldfield proved this by going to Florida to run against some of the world's richest and most successful sportsmen. These amateurs, like William K. Vanderbilt and Henry L. Bowden, were able to spend inordinate amounts of money on racing cars from all over the world. It is this period in both automobile racing history and Barney Oldfield's career when the certainty of information becomes unclear. Various histories of this era in automobile competition provide conflicting statistics concerning the dates of speed trials, the men who made them, and Oldfield's role in the setting of these record marks. A 1961 book about Barney Oldfield reports that he did not establish record runs at Ormond Beach until 1910, when he set marks while driving the German-built Blitzen Benz (Nolan 100).

Homer George, on the other hand, wrote that Oldfield had "established a new competitive one-mile straight-away mark of forty-three seconds" at Daytona Beach during trials held either late in 1903 or early in 1904 (Oldfield 28). Such a discrepancy should not be surprising, especially given the amount of time that has passed since 1919, when George composed his biographical sketch for Oldfield's book, *Barney Oldfield's Book for the Motorist*. Such differences, however, cloud our view of the role that Oldfield played in terms of conquering the speed records that so many millionaire "racers" hoped their money could buy. If Barney Oldfield did indeed set new records in either 1903 or 1904 in Florida, it proves his ability as a driver outweighed the wealth that could purchase such superior equipment. We will see that by the time Winston Cup stock car racing becomes a national phenomenon, the idea of "how fast can you afford to go" will be a rule rather than an exception.

Given the racing successes stated above, Barney Oldfield found himself to be a popular figure with the American public. He was a sports hero and a media celebrity. His public persona was so strong that in

1905, Oldfield was hired as an actor. He played opposite Elsie Janis in a Broadway musical entitled *The Vanderbilt Cup,* based on the races of that same name. According to Homer George, Oldfield "had the satisfaction of seeing his name shine in enormous electric lights on the 'Great White Way.'" The show generated standing room only audiences, and Oldfield even toured with the production when it went on the road for "ten successful weeks" during 1906 (Oldfield 31).

Oldfield's acting career would not be limited to the musical theater. The inherent appeal of automobile racing—a new sport not witnessed by many Americans during the early years of the 20th century—would provide the perfect setting for motion pictures. Barney Oldfield, as America's first true (and best known) automobile racer, was the perfect hook for studios planning to produce racing stories. Even if audiences were not familiar with the specifics of automobile racing, the fame and celebrity status of Barney Oldfield would give them a reference point, an individual they would recognize as a significant player within the sport (or business—even at this early date in its history).

Barney Oldfield would make several motion pictures during his acting career. His first movies were produced by Mack Sennett at Keystone Studios in 1913. In one film, *Barney Oldfield's Race for a Life,* the driver saves the damsel in distress from a certain death, the heroine being tied to railroad tracks by the villains. Such a role promotes Oldfield's image as a brave and heroic race car driver, fearless in the face of danger since that is the way in which he makes his living on the race track.[2]

Another movie featuring Oldfield is actually a testament to the growing popularity of race car drivers in general as figures of celebrity within American sport. This 1913 picture, entitled *The Speed Kings,* centers around a father and daughter who favor different drivers in an upcoming race. The father wants to see Stutz driver Earl Cooper win. Cooper, according to the dialogue, is "a speed demon." The daughter, played by Mabel Normand, wants Teddy Tetzlaft to win because he is her true love. Tetzlaft is presented to the audience as "the speed king," which establishes a typical good-guy versus bad-guy scenario. As expected, the winning driver will also win the hand of Normand, giving a new definition to the term "trophy girl." Barney Oldfield has a cameo as himself, adding his celebrity status to the importance of the racing event depicted. Cooper wins the race, but—as usual—true love prevails and Normand gives her love to Tetzlaft and his Fiat American racer. Oldfield, on the other hand, looks into the camera from behind the wheel of his car on the starting line and validates the race's authenticity.

Oldfield would make several more films; his last—*Blonde Comet*—was released in 1941 by the Producers Releasing Corporation (Babich and Zucker 345). Once again, Oldfield plays himself, this time in a story about parts manufacturers and their attempts to find success in automobile racing. Such "autobiographical" roles would become common for stock car drivers as their sport—and their public personae—grew in recognition and developed a place within American popular mythology.

Barney Oldfield was, in actuality, a stock car driver. The machines he drove were "stock" in physical appearance, despite a variety of innovative powerplants tucked under their hoods. This is not all together different than the stock cars seen on today's NASCAR Winston Cup circuit. The racing machines built by men like Henry Ford, and driven by men like Barney Oldfield, were essentially stock cars. Racing would help make the forthcoming, mass produced automobiles better and more practical. Until then, what these pioneers of automobile racing built and drove were "stock" in configuration and construction.

As automobile manufacturers made better and faster cars, risks for the racing drivers increased. To compensate for these added dangers, race teams modified their cars to make them stronger and safer. These modifications cost money, as did the price increases of newer year models which teams had to buy in order to meet NASCAR's changing regulations.

Safety modifications turned the stock car of the late 1940s into the "stock" car now seen running America's high-banked superspeedways. Such modifications meant purchasing aftermarket, or specially designed replacement parts such as drivers' seats, roll bars, and puncture-proof fuel cells. These purchases cost money over and above the basic costs of preparing an automobile for racing purposes. To defray as many of these additional costs as possible, race teams sought the financial assistance of area businesses. The businesses would serve as sponsors and help pay expenses for a team in return for promotional consideration displayed on the automobile's exterior sheet metal, usually somewhere along a fender or across the hood or trunk lid.

Sponsorship dramatically changed the face of traditional stock car racing. Early in the sport's history, sponsorship was limited to businesses that dealt with automotive products (with many of the better teams running "factory" cars supplied by the automobile manufacturers themselves—as done by Henry Ford in 1902 for his "factory" driver, Barney Oldfield). By the 1980s, added media coverage attracted sponsors from more domestic companies serving all social classes and regions.

Television coverage—especially the broadcasts provided by specialty cable networks like ESPN and TBS—carried NASCAR racing to viewers all across the United States, introducing them not only to the fast-paced excitement and close competition fans in the South had come to recognize, but also the wide-ranging cast of characters that the sport involved. Stock car racing found a national audience watching these cable stations. Cable sports coverage allowed for more specific audiences, unlike those viewers limited to watching free network television. Instead of pandering to all viewers, the cable networks could customize their schedules to meet unique viewing demands. Such specialized broadcasts generated interest among corporations seeking new and more focused outlets for their products. This newfound national audience also attended races in person; attendance figures report over three million people witnessed the 29 regular-season events on the 1990 NASCAR Winston Cup schedule (Thigpen 55). The millions of fans interested in NASCAR racing represented millions of potential customers for those businesses willing to sponsor some aspect of stock car competition.

Corporations, according to Ian Robertson in his *Sociology,* compete through the use of advertising instead of through product quality or price (469). David M. Potter, in his *People of Plenty,* remarked that advertising is the most characteristic American institution. He calls advertising "the institution of abundance," one of our country's "instruments of social control" (176). Advertisements, in fact, do much more than promote a company's products. Most advertisements have latent functions, such as the ability to create markets where there were none before. This arouses customer desire for goods previously nonexistent to a region or social class (Robertson 469).

Corporate sponsors initially saw stock car racing as a means of gaining customers among the working class. Fans in the rural South could identify with a product much as they could a stock car driver. This same driver identification is now being seen with fans from all social classes nationwide. Such knowledge lured corporations toward stock car racing, using a "we'll scratch your back if you'll scratch ours" approach. NASCAR Winston Cup teams require massive amounts of capital to maintain highly competitive racing programs. Corporations, conversely, need national exposure to generate more customers, whose business will create increased profits.

Winning a customer's trust by becoming affiliated with a race team means higher profits because the customer associates his or her favorite driver with his corporate sponsor, often motivating the fan to buy that sponsor's products. This involvement between the fan and the sponsor develops a feeling of participation for the fan-consumer. By purchasing a sponsor's products, the fan believes that he or she is actually helping to finance that company's racing operation. The identification of fans with Winston Cup stock car drivers has been commodified by corporate sponsors in search of these new sales markets. Fans are, in a sense, exploited because of their association with a particular racing team. This association creates a three-way relationship: fans identify with drivers, who identify themselves with the company that sponsors them, which—in turn—creates a relationship that lures fans into buying the sponsor's products. If the driver's appeal with the fans is strong enough, the product's sales amounts will increase dramatically.

For example, when Procter and Gamble decided to sponsor Darrell Waltrip's Tide Machine in 1989 and 1990, the company hoped his popularity with fans would provide the product with increased numbers of users. Waltrip, who was voted NASCAR's most popular driver in 1990, was featured on a special package of the soap powder. According to Harry Reasoner of CBS News, Procter and Gamble "introduced a . . . 42 ounce box of Tide that prominently featured Mr. Waltrip's car coming out of the Tide sun [a graphic on the package]. Consumer demand caused the company to print 7.5 million boxes, rather than the 1.5 million initially planned (Reasoner, "King Richard").

Today's stock car drivers go through their careers emblazoned with a sponsor's colors, logos, and name. They wear shirts, jackets, and hats—each with tasteful placement of their sponsor's name—during personal appearances or press conferences. A formal meeting means wearing a tie with the sponsor's logo and perhaps a matching lapel pin. At the speedway, a driver goes about his work wearing a fireproof suit with his sponsor prominently splashed across his chest. Helmets and gloves sport logos and slogans, and a collection of baseball caps is waiting to be worn in Victory Lane with the sponsors' corporate images displayed for all the television and still photographers to see. Drivers and their race cars are rolling billboards and, because of this, a driver assumes a specific responsibility for his corporate backers. Racers represent major corporations in a high-speed, four-hour long "commercial."

Winston Cup stock car racing, unlike most other professional sports, allows its participants to enjoy long and competitive careers. Some drivers compete for 20 years or more. Richard Petty, who drove a Pontiac Grand Prix sponsored by STP, was a regular on the Winston Cup tour for 35 years. Better than twenty of them were run in financial association with STP (Reasoner 1989). Upon his retirement from driving in 1992, Petty remained with STP, which now sponsors the Pontiacs he builds for driver Bobby Hamilton. Because of this, the name of Richard Petty and the symbols and products of the STP company are almost synonymous.

The same goes for Harry Gant, former driver of the Skoal Bandit Chevrolet, who notched 18 victories during his 21-year Winston Cup career. He drove the green and white Skoal Bandit stock car for a stretch of thirteen years, his best season being 1991 when he won five events, including four consecutive races late in the year. Fans will forever associate "Handsome Harry" with the number 33 and U.S. Tobacco's Skoal brand.

The length of a driver's career and his association with a particular sponsor creates a subliminal relationship of sorts. Seeing a car sponsored by a particular company for several years, whether it be seen in races or in promotions, can establish a recognition of a driver with his specific sponsor, whether the audience follows racing or not.

Today's stock car driver realizes that his commitment to a sponsor means more than merely winning races. From the 1950s through the 1970s, a driver could afford to concentrate on driving—and often living—hard and fast. Meeting the press in years past came after winning a race. Today's stock car driver is surrounded by media people who record his every move both on and off the racetrack.

During the 1950s and 1960s, a driver like Curtis Turner, a former Virginia bootlegger, could be proud of his reputation for fast living. Turner's behavior—both on and off of the track—reflected a life dedicated to fun. His reputation for socializing with celebrities and beautiful women attracted to the romantic life of professional automobile racing was the stuff of legend. Many of the stories still told about the wild side of stock car racing involve some aspect of Turner's life. He was considered by many to be the most talented driver of his era, a natural behind the wheel, educated by running moonshine through the mountains of Virginia (Girdler 58). Turner was not afraid to make waves throughout the sport; in 1961 he was banned from all NASCAR competition because of his involvement with the Federation of Professional Athletes, an organization associated with the Teamsters Union (Fielden 2: 14). He was suspended until 1965 when, at the age of 41, he returned to competition and won the American 500 at the North Carolina Motor Speedway in Rockingham (Fielden 3: 15). Turner's penchant for hard living finally caught up with him in October of 1970, when he and a companion were killed in an airplane crash near Du Bois, Pennsylvania. His Aero Commander 500 went down—reportedly because Turner had been drinking at the controls—enroute to Roanoke, Virginia (Fielden 3: 312).

Curtis Turner was one of stock car racing's characters, the basis of numerous stories pertaining to the adventures of life on the circuit. The NASCAR drivers of today, on the other hand, live under a media microscope. When a driver does misbehave, it often strikes the sport painfully and deep. Two such cases, occurring within the last ten years, involved drivers Tim Richmond and Rob Moroso.

Tim Richmond was one of NASCAR's young rebels. He, like so many drivers in the early days, gained a reputation around the sport for his exploits with ladies who were attracted to the romanticized lifestyle of stock car racing. Richmond's tactics were the foundations of folklore. This "swashbuckling rider of the stock car circuit" was known to stay out late chasing women and drinking, only to be found asleep in the garage area before starting races. He dressed like the stylish characters on the television series *Miami Vice,* and longed for a chance to begin an acting career of his own (Gross 75).

As a driver, he scored seven victories in 1986, only to drop out of competition in 1987 due to illness. Richmond recovered enough to run a few events that year and earn wins in his first two races back behind the wheel. By 1988, NASCAR officials were worried about his health and asked Richmond to submit to a drug test, which he failed.

Two days later, Richmond passed a second test. NASCAR's findings discovered high levels of over-the-counter medications used to fight colds. The sanctioning body agreed to let Richmond drive only if he released his medical records for inspection. He refused, and never drove a stock car again. On August 13, 1989, Tim Richmond died in a West Palm Beach, Florida, hospital due to complications from AIDS at the age of 34 (Gross 81).

Despite his reckless approach to life, Tim Richmond was still a part of the modern stock car racing business. It was as if he had combined the lifestyle of the past with the responsibilities of the present. Rick Hendrick, Richmond's former car owner, said of the late driver:

Tim had a reputation of being a hell-raiser, a party guy, a Curtis Turner-type individual. But when I got Tim in '86, he went to Daytona in a suit, he cut his hair, he went to the Procter and Gamble meetings [their car was sponsored by Folger's Coffee] and he couldn't have been a better representative of our company. (Berggren, "Rick Hendrick" 68)

Business is a top priority on today's stock car scene, unlike the precorporate days when the fastest way around a speedway was foremost on every team's agenda. Again we see the driver placed into new roles of responsibility that were rarely considered during the sport's early and developmental days.

Another, more recent incident involved Rob Moroso, who lost his life in a traffic accident in the fall of 1990, just hours after competing at North Wilkesboro, North Carolina. Moroso, a standout in other divisions and predicted by racing experts to be the sport's next big star, was found with a blood alcohol level of .22, twice the legal limit recognized by police. Ironically, Moroso had just turned 22 years old a week earlier. Like Curtis Turner so many years before, Rob Moroso learned the hard way that drinking and driving are often a fatal combination (Berggren, "Rob" 13).

Rob Moroso's skill with a stock car earned him NASCAR's Rookie of the Year Award for 1990, even though there were still four races scheduled after his death (Berggren, "Rob" 13). This award, typically, is presented with great fanfare and attention. In 1990, the posthumous award was announced with little excitement at all, much to the anger of the Moroso family. We can only conclude that NASCAR's corporate connections were embarrassed by Moroso's fatal accident, fearing a comparison drawn between Moroso and Curtis Turner, since both men died under similar circumstances (Berggren, "Rob" 58). Such behavior is far from accepted by Madison Avenue.

The stock car driver of today, unlike those of the past, has little time to concern himself with getting out of the accepted line. As a spokesman for a major corporation, which is providing between $4 million and $7 million a year in sponsorship (and sometimes more than twice that to promote the race team), drivers find themselves in almost year-round demand. According to Dale Jarrett, a second-generation driver who mans the Quality Care Ford Credit Thunderbird, "the sponsors would keep you busy to the point of having absolutely no time if you would let 'em, but you just have to say, 'Look, I have a life just like you do'" (qtd. in Kleber 80).

Serving as a spokesperson places the driver in direct contact with fans, all of whom represent potential customers for the sponsor's products. Unlike stock car drivers of the past, today's NASCAR drivers are often under legal contract to make appearances and meet the public. Dale Jarrett—winner of the 1993 and 1996 Daytona 500 and the 1996 Brickyard 400—has commented: "That's part of my job. I enjoy very much meeting people and talking to the fans. I think what sets our sport apart is the fans' accessibility to the drivers—to get those autographs and be up close and talk with them" (qtd. by Kleber 81). Fans are able to identify with drivers because of the access granted to them before and after races, unlike most professional sports which keep fans behind closed doors.

Being in front of the public is considered when corporations decide which drivers they want to sponsor. One promising young driver on the Winston Cup circuit during the early 1990s was a Californian named Chad Little, who drove a Ford Thunderbird sponsored by Tyson Foods, a company that packages and sells chicken to supermarkets. NASCAR observers considered Little to be "disarmingly handsome" and that his "good looks, which don't show up nearly as well on film as in person," would "surely help his driving career" ("Two Hundred MPH" 101). Notice that the observers emphasized Little's "in person" appearance. This may have helped Tyson attract customers by the fact that women shopping for groceries could meet Chad during one of his many supermarket promotional visits. Unfortunately, Tyson terminated Little's sponsorship package because of the new team's poor performances in Winston Cup events. Little has since gone on to earn driving jobs, or "rides," with other sponsors; his most recent deal is a Winston Cup ride sponsored by John Deere equipment. When Little is not racing, he often works as a television commentator.

Another telegenic Winston Cup driver is Jeff Gordon, who broke into the national spotlight during his rookie season in 1993. Gordon, the 1995 Winston Cup champion, is the perfect package of talent, courage, charm, and good looks—a driver as comfortable in front of television cameras as behind the wheel of his Dupont Chevrolet. He is the blend of old and new: a driver of consumate skill who is a consistent winner and an articulate spokesman who appeals to a broad consumer audience. A large portion of this audience is comprised of young women—who have become NASCAR fans because of Gordon's notoriety. He possesses a natural flair in front of the camera, regardless of the venue; not only does he do "professional" interviews for racing broadcasts, but he can match wits with David Letterman, be energetic the next day on *Good Morning America,* and make entertaining commercials for his sponsors.[3]

All in all, the involvement of major corporate sponsorship in NASCAR Winston Cup racing has placed added pressures upon the men and women who compete each week. The stock car drivers of today, unlike their counterparts of the past, are faced with the rigors of nationwide public recognition. Television coverage has carried the sport to viewers all across the country, making drivers—and even pit crew chiefs—overnight celebrities.

Such is the case with Ray Evernham, crew chief for Jeff Gordon's No. 24 Dupont Chevrolet. Gordon's Winston Cup championship was the result, in part, of Evernham's hard work and team management skills. The two have become synonymous with automobile racing success, symbols of the changing guard in NASCAR. Evernham has become a common sight on Winston Cup broadcasts; he even does feature pieces about technological developments within the sport for The Nashville Network. The formation of a Mechanic of the Race Award sponsored by the Miller Brewing Company has put many crew chiefs in the media spotlight, the prize often being presented during the latter stages of a race. A surprised crew chief, usually in the throes of a close battle for the win, finds himself on live television being handed a plaque for his toil that day. It is this kind of recognition that puts mechanics in the public eye—something the corporate environment of today's Winston Cup Series encourages.[4]

Crew chiefs are not the grimy mechanics of yesteryear. They do not usually travel with their drivers to take part in public appearances, but Ray Evernham is just as revered as Jeff Gordon. The two were asked to give a lecture to first-year engineering students at Princeton University in the fall of 1996. It was a packed event, attracting more than just engineering students. Evernham and Gordon talked about the Winston Cup Series, the role engineers play within the sport, and fielded questions from a knowledgable and enthusiatic Ivy League audience, most of whom were familiar with the rules and regulations of NASCAR racing from television ("A Day in the Ivy League"). Evernham is the first Winston Cup crew chief to be a featured speaker at Princeton, and probably any other major university. The type of people who identify with NASCAR drivers and mechanics has changed significantly over the years, elevating their status, acceptance, and skill.

Steve Hmiel, former crew chief on Mark Martin's Valvoline Oil Ford Thunderbird, reflected changes in the sport of stock car racing in this way:

As racing gained some well earned respectability, some new folks started coming out to watch us [NASCAR teams] run. They were women, children, and corporate people who may have spent last Sunday on the golf course. They understand that racing is not a pack of drunken rednecks that spin their tires and rain chicken bones down on each other from the upper seats. It took a long time, but racing is a respected business in the country club, the board room, and even Mother's kitchen. (Hmiel 10)

The respectability of today's stock car racing has indeed attracted new spectators into the grandstands. Women now make up almost 50 percent of stock car race attendance (Thigpen 55). This statistic is highly important to corporations looking for tax deductions through new avenues of advertising and promotion. Harry Reasoner, in a feature done for CBS News in December of 1989, reported that he

was told that if you started interviewing women leaving stores and one of the questions you asked was, "If Heinz [maker of food products] sponsored a car, would you buy Heinz [products]." And 18 out of 20 of them said, yes. Barbara Behrman of Heinz Marketing responded, "That's pretty close," and said later, "it was 87 percent." (qtd. by Reasoner, "King Richard")

As a result of findings like these, NASCAR teams are now being sponsored by products and firms like Eastman Kodak, Procter and Gamble, the McDonald's Corporation, Coca-Cola, General Foods, and Kellogg's. Sponsors within the past ten years have included Slender You Health Spas and Underalls Pantyhose, far from typical company names expected to be seen on the fenders of stock cars. Teams are still sponsored by the traditional "male" products like breweries and automobile parts suppliers, but the trend has shown noticeable changes due to the discovery of female fan interest. Women have begun to play a more integral part in the business of NASCAR Winston Cup racing.

Unfortunately, the number of women drivers in NASCAR has failed to increase with much regularity. One of the first Strictly Stock drivers was Sara Christian, who ran well against her male counterparts. Women like Patty Moise and Shawna Robinson have driven stock cars against men since the late 1980s, and Indianapolis 500 veteran Janet Guthrie tried Winston Cup racing for a while during the mid-1970's. Most recently, it was announced that Geoff Bodine Racing would put a woman behind the wheel in the NASCAR Craftsman Truck Series. Tammy Jo Kirk, a regular on the NASCAR Slim Jim All Pro Series roster, joined Bodine and brought along her All Pro sponsor, Lovable intimate apparel ("Sponsor News"). Such an arrangement—a female driver with a female-oriented sponsor—should be received well, especially given the growing numbers of women following NASCAR. The number of women working behind the scenes in NASCAR has been growing as well, women such as Deb Williams, editor of *NASCAR Winston Cup Scene;* Beth Tuschak, who covers NASCAR racing for *USA Today;* Patty Wheeler, an executive with World Sports Enterprises; and Lesa Kennedy, executive vice president of International Speedway Corporation, the enterprise that runs all of the speedways NASCAR owns.

Women's identities in NASCAR racing have changed in front of the scenes as well. In the days of trophy queens, women could be found parading before crowds in swimsuits and sashes, alongside the name of a sponsor or race supplier. Such women are still seen at local speedways across America, but NASCAR's Winston Cup Series has managed to change with the times. Advances in women's rights paved the way for more responsibilities and greater respect; the beauty queens gave way to corporate spokeswomen like Miss Winston and the Unocal Race-stoppers. These women are company representatives who meet the public, work with the media, and function as liasons between the racers, the sponsors, and the fans. Swimsuits have given way to tasteful uniforms as these women add a corporate touch without the sexploitation.

Family-oriented sponsors have even committed money to purse funds that are available to all competitors, no matter who their primary sponsors are. Companies such as Heinz, Gillette, Sears, Roebuck and Company; Armour Canned Meats, Dinner Bell, Van Camps, and Goody's headache powders, provide money "pools" that reward drivers and teams who excel in specific race performances but fail to win the event. For example, a driver who suffers from bad luck in a race may win $750 offered by the "Goody's Headache Award." Even in this way, corporations have recognized the appeal of Winston Cup stock car racing and the benefits of a close association with the sport.

The involvement of Winston, a tobacco product of the R.J. Reynolds Company, has meant major changes for the sport of stock car racing. Sponsoring stock car racing is considered vital to the cigarette company's marketing exposure because cigarette advertisements are banned from television. The Winston brand has sponsored stock car racing's premier division since 1971, when it joined with NASCAR to create a points championship award as incentive for the race teams. In 1985 the company developed the Winston Million, which guarantees one million dollars to the driver who wins three of the four major superspeedway events in one season. Bill Elliott won that bonus during its inaugural year. Since that time, R.J. Reynolds has boosted its championship cash prizes by adding a bonus award of one million dollars that is presented to the driver winning the year-end points title. In 1996, the Winston brand of R.J. Reynolds provided $6 million in awards to NASCAR Winston Cup drivers, with over $4 million tabbed for the NWCS point fund. In 26 years of involvement with NASCAR Winston Cup racing, the R.J. Reynolds Tobacco Company has given over $55 million to the series.

Such financial prizes carry with them an incredible amount of pressure, much in the same way that major sponsorships do. These also affect how the drivers carry themselves both on and off the racetrack. Today's drivers, like Barney Oldfield, are media figures because they possess a special talent found in few other people. They walk a tightrope between their sport and their responsibilities to those who provide them with a ride. All the while, they live and work in the public eye as celebrities, heroes, and role models.

Despite these new roles, many stock car drivers find themselves associated with the image of NASCAR propagated by popular culture and the cultural myths of the South. The sport's rural past is a part of NASCAR's stereotyped present, which emphasizes the rough-and-tumble nature of full-bodied automobile racing. Drivers are professional athletes who must work full-time in order to assure themselves of having a chance for victory. Once a driver makes it to the Winston Cup Series, he or she is no longer a part of the proletariat.

We have seen that NASCAR Winston Cup racing has exceeded the parameters established by a definition of prole sports. Corporate sponsorship has carried the sport beyond the simple identification between fan and driver; it has carried the sport far beyond its origins. Its economic power over the teams involved as regular competitors has changed the way in which racers approach the sport. The difference with NASCAR's Winston Cup Series is that it requires a multimillion dollar sponsorship package to cover its high costs. Winston Cup racing has far exceeded its past, when "wheelmen" challenged each other over dirt ovals at a southern fairgrounds for the bragging rights of the county. Today's stock car drivers face the responsibilities of being corporate representatives long before they ever climb behind the wheel of a car at Daytona.

Perhaps the best summation of the relationship between stock car racing and American business was given by the late Harry Reasoner, who said that "if the aim of a professional sport, as is so often said, is to operate as a successful business, the most successful business in American sports is stock car racing" (Reasoner, "King Richard"). The relationship has indeed been successful. Corporations have found an increased consumer audience, while stock car racing has established a level of national acceptance. The development of new markets where none had been before, due to the close identification of fans with their favorite NASCAR Winston Cup drivers, has become very profitable for corporate America.

It is hard to imagine that the actions of Henry Ford in 1902 would have an impact on the world of stock car racing in 1997. A simple decision made out of fear—hiring a professional driver to race his high-powered automobile in competition—changed not only the sport of automobile racing, but the demands on racing drivers as well. In order to promote a corporate image, a company's name and trademark, the driver must assume the roles of a spokesman, a salesman, an ambassador, and an employee. The cost of racing has made sponsorship essential, required for success in the Winston Cup Series. Drivers, through their corporate connections, have become public figures—media personalities that make commercials, speak to large audiences on behalf of the sponsors who pay their bills, and appear in motion pictures. (In chapter 6, stock car drivers and film will be discussed in more detail.)

Considering these changes, perhaps it is time to examine proletariat sports in America. There are contradictions in the traditional definition that fail to address the complexities found within NASCAR's Winston Cup Series, especially concerning how people of the "proletariat" make their way into competition. Since it is unforeseeable that Winston Cup racing will regress to fit the traditional definition of a prole sport, maybe it is time to remove the label of "proletariat sport" from the NASCAR Winston Cup Series.

Perhaps it is time, as well, to redefine the NASCAR Winston Cup Series with regard to the deeply rooted southern stereotypes that have long been associated with the sport. NASCAR has, over the last 50 years, grown into a sport of international interest. It is a subculture that reaffirms American qualities and traits while glorifying the most influential technology to ever reach our shores—the gasoline-powered automobile. As the Winston Cup Series approaches the 21st century, its participants and fans should remember the actions and words of Richard Petty. In 1975, at the height of his driving career, Petty was "modest, folksy, and beyond corrupting glitter and materialism explaining to a *New York Times* reporter: 'A man don't want to get above his raisin's, you know'" (Kirby 109-10).

Fig. 11. Jeff Gordon's "Rainbow Warriors" push his Dupont Chevrolet onto pit road at the June race at Pocono. Cars and crew are now just as recognized as the drivers themselves. Fans gather near a barrier to take photographs as the car rolls by. (Photo by Mark Howell)

Fig. 12. Fans crowd around the garage exit as Geoff Bodine's No. 7 QVC Ford is pushed toward the starting grid. NASCAR's "open door" policy has attracted many fans to the sport, yet it can make preparations difficult as crews must negotiate hundreds of spectators while getting ready for the day's competition. (Photo by Mark Howell)

Fig. 13. The No. 29 Cartoon Network pit crew prepares for action. The sign at left serves as a target for the driver. Headphones worn by the pit crew allow them to communicate via radio. Communication between driver and pit crew is key, especially when changes to the car are being made. (Photo by Mark Howell)

Fig. 14. The Winston Trackhouse, sponsored by R.J. Reynolds provides fans with an upclose look at the world of NASCAR Winston Cup racing. Part museum, part amusement park, and all advertisement, the Winston Trackhouse entertained a steady stream of visitors all during the race weekend at Pocono International Raceway in 1996. (Photo by Mark Howell)

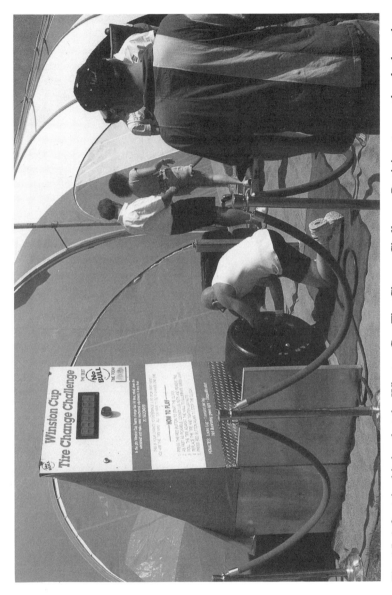

Fig. 15. A fan tries his hand at the Winston Cup Tire Change Challenge. Participants race the clock as they attempt to change an actual stock car wheel and tire. (Photo by Mark Howell)

Fig. 16. Race fans await their turn in the Winston Simulator, a "ride" that allows them to experience the thrill of high-speed action. Before their trip is over, these fans will have raced in the Smokin' Joe's hydroplane and the Smokin' Joe's Winston Cup stock car. (Photo by Mark Howell)

Fig. 17. Simpson World in the Lakeside Industrial Park in Mooresville, North Carolina, is a NASCAR Winston Cup souvenir showplace. Not only can the usual items (T-shirts, caps, jackets) be bought here, but it is also a showroom for the latest in Simpson safety products like firesuits, helmets, and driving shoes. (Photo by Mark Howell)

Fig. 18. Glenn Jarrett interviews Dick Trickle for Speedvision during qualifying for the 1996 UAW-GM Teamwork 500 at Pocono International Raceway. Qualifying is often aired live on such networks as ESPN2 or Speedvision in conjunction with a larger national broadcast of the race itself on a network like ESPN or TNN. In this case, qualifying was shown on Speedvision and the actual race was shown on TNN. (Photo by Mark Howell)

Fig. 19. One way to learn about stock car racing is to work for a team from an early age. This is how drivers like Sterling Marlin and Kyle Petty gained experience. Joey Knuckles, pictured here with driver Tighe Scott in July of 1977, worked for Walter Ballard then and is today part of Robert Yates Racing. (Photo courtesy of Tighe Scott)

Fig. 20. The famous Barney Oldfield, "The Wizard of the Track." (Photo belonging to the author)

107

6

Made in America:
Ritual, Folklore, and Cultural Mythology
of the NASCAR Winston Cup Series

Stock car drivers, like the horsemen of the American West, occupy a special place within American culture. Just as frontier scouts and cowboys have become a romanticized part of our national history, Winston Cup drivers have become symbols of the character traits that Americans admire. The meaning of the NASCAR Winston Cup Series, and its role in the world of professional sports, must be analyzed, interpreted, and treated as an important component of life in the United States.

Culture, according to Clifford Geertz, "denotes an historically transmitted pattern of meanings embodied in symbols, a system of inherited conceptions expressed in symbolic forms by means of which men communicate, perpetuate, and develop their knowledge about and attitudes toward life" (89). These symbolic forms "serve multiple purposes," depending on the cultural meaning that needs to be transmitted (113). Each symbol has a specific "function" based on "a people's ethos . . . and their world view—the picture they have of the way things in sheer actuality are" (89).

Geertz uses Balinese cockfighting as an example of the way symbols, and their culturally constructed meanings, function. The sport is highly symbolic and ritualistic, and its actions serve as a means of interpreting Balinese beliefs and experiences. Geertz explains:

What sets the cockfight apart from the ordinary course of life, lifts it from the realm of everyday practical affairs, and surrounds it with an aura of enlarged importance is not, as functionalist sociology would have it, that it reinforces status discriminations . . . but that it provides a metasocial commentary upon the whole matter of assorting human beings into fixed hierarchical ranks and then organizing the major part of collective existence around that assortment. Its function . . . is interpretive: it is a Balinese reading of Balinese experience, a story they tell themselves about themselves. (448)

These cockfights synthesize a variety of motions and behaviors in a way that reflects Balinese society. The cockfight combines what Geertz calls "themes"—"animal savagery, male narcissism, opponent gambling, status rivalry [and] mass excitement," and it binds them "into a set of rules." These rules create a "symbolic structure in which . . . the reality of their inner affiliation can be intelligibly felt." By examining such cultural rituals, a person should be able to "see a dimension of his own subjectivity" (449-50).

NASCAR Winston Cup racing is such a cultural ritual. It addresses the nature of American society—a society occupied with automobiles, technology, consumption of material goods, and competition. Those who participate in the sport are folk heroes and media celebrities; they are professional athletes and daredevils. The Winston Cup stock car driver is considered fearless, intuitive, physically adroit, and emotionally cool. Like the scouts who tempted death along the Great Plains, NASCAR drivers tempt death on high-banked ovals at speeds of better than 200 miles per hour. There is little difference between dodging bullets along a trail in Wyoming and dodging concrete walls along a straightaway at Daytona; both have the power to stop a man quickly and permanently.

What makes the stock car driver so unique within American culture is his ability to use and manipulate technology. This is not unlike the frontiersman who gained acclaim for his abilities to shoot, hunt, track game, and ride. Whereas the majority of Americans climb into their cars for their daily commute to work, the Winston Cup driver climbs into his car to try and defy principles of physics and engineering. The stock car driver tries to test every aspect of the 3,400-pound machine under him: its engine, its handling characteristics, and its durability. While the daily commuter worries about spilling coffee on his dress clothes, the NASCAR driver worries about keeping his car on its wheels. As Rick Mast, driver of the No. 75 Remington Arms Ford, put it:

you're more worried about . . . what you can do to make the car better. The very instant you get in trouble, when that baby goes wrong, then you feel like you're going 200 mph, or more like 2000 mph. Those cars are made to go in one direction and when they aren't going in that direction, you get scary wind noises, the wall flying by, tires squealing, you know it's not going to be good. But you don't think about that, you just react when it happens. ("Rick Mast Chat Session")

Because their talents transcend average human ability, NASCAR Winston Cup drivers are considered heroes. They do something that most of us can only think about. We drive every day, but our arena is the highway, the city street, the crowded parking lot near our office. Stock car drivers, like the frontier heroes of old, challenge their environment and test themselves against the unknown. The rest of us simply stand by to observe and admire. These brave men become the subject of our conversations as we dream of their talents and tell stories about their accomplishments. Admirers of such men elevate these individuals to folk hero status. They become symbols for our society and our lives; they set the standards that we wish we could follow.

Folk heroes often come from the ranks of professional athletes. Even touring entertainers like Buffalo Bill and Annie Oakley followed this pattern—their talents in the horse ring earned them many admirers who followed their exploits and paid to see them perform in person. As sports turned professional and became more recognized as popular entertainment, athletes became a central part of our culture. Athletes soon became the focus of our popular folklore as Americans began to swap stories about the lives, talents, and accomplishments of these newfound celebrities.

One professional athlete to take his place within American popular folklore was Barney Oldfield. Oldfield—the first professional race car driver in America—was a man of rural heritage and working-class upbringing, yet his name became synonymous with fearlessness (or recklessness, depending on how you define such things) and the sport of automobile racing. His father was a veteran of the Civil War, and his mother was the local blacksmith's daughter. Berna Eli "Barney" Oldfield was born, according to Homer C. George, "of sturdy but humble farming parentage, in a little loghouse three miles from Wauseon, Fulton County, Ohio" (Oldfield 18).

George's allusion to Oldfield's birth in "a little loghouse" projects a strong image of traditional American life. As history reminds us, a loghouse was home for many of our nation's heroes. Such modest beginnings are a breeding ground for excellence and a classroom for determination according to the American experience. Oldfield's family heritage and childhood upbringing follow this historical stereotype closely, as do the lives of such national folk heroes as Daniel Boone and Abraham Lincoln. Personalities like these, the great heroes who shaped America, are often perceived as the products of simple rural environments, which instill in them a work ethic central to the basic philosophy behind individual success.

For Barney Oldfield, like other American heroes, success came through hard work. His personal history seems to have been torn from the pages of a Horatio Alger story. Like Alger's characters—who achieve respectability and success through their dedication to honesty, sincerity, strong morality, and the sweat of their brow—Barney Oldfield "struggled upward" persistently to earn national honor and recognition. As Homer George wrote of Oldfield:

At the time of his birth, January 29th, 1878, his parents were struggling under the burden of a mortgage, on a quarter section of poor farmland which yielded meager returns for their toil. For eleven years, Oldfield remained on the home farm, living the slow, laborious life of the farm youngster of that period, rising at dawn to do the chores, little dreaming that fame and fortune were waiting for him in later years. (Oldfield 18)

Oldfield's dedication to helping his family fit the mold found in today's NASCAR Winston Cup mythology. Such loyalty to family and community are strong traits in the image of stock car racing, and Oldfield set the stage for the drivers who would follow him decades later.

What made Oldfield a folk hero was his common, even lower-class upbringing. A public school dropout, Barney Oldfield made his living by pursuing his dream of being a bicycle racer. It was a gamble but a gamble he was willing to take. This, in and of itself, made Oldfield a hero to some. Here was a man who followed his dream, even though his father believed racing bicycles was "a fool's game" (Nolan 29). Barney Oldfield threw caution to the wind, his feet upon the pedals and rode into sports history.

Barney Oldfield's accomplishments made him the subject of public discussion and amazement, in part because newspaper reporters followed his career closely. The media trumpeted his 1910 Daytona Beach record in great detail, thanks to the efforts of Oldfield's press agent, William Hickman "Will" Pickens. The Alabama-born Pickens had been working with Barney since 1904 as his "advance man," setting up racing dates and handling public relations for the Ohio hero (Nolan 71). It was Pickens who carefully crafted Oldfield's public image as a fearless competitor. At a race in Dallas, Texas, on a cold and windy December afternoon in 1909, Will Pickens showed the crowd his driver's tenacity by seeing to it "that Oldfield's hands were dramatically pried loose from their 'frozen' position on the steering wheel," even though the driver had waved to his fans as he crossed the finish line to win the event (Nolan 97).

Barney Oldfield, not unlike other athletic figures, became a folk hero to millions of Americans. He was an ordinary man who possessed extraordinary skills—skills that were accentuated by the fact that he could manhandle and manipulate this new thing called an automobile. Oldfield used automobiles to defy laws of physics and science; he traveled faster than anyone in history and lived to tell his story. While the majority of Americans still used horses and buggies, Barney Oldfield was using tomorrow's marvel of technology today.

Barney Oldfield was America's best known race car driver, thanks to the efforts of Will Pickens and the interpretation of Oldfield's life and accomplishments through the repetition of American popular culture and modern folklore. Many people create heroes by identifying with a person who reminds them of themselves, and they assign specific qualities to this person that separates him or her from the mediocrity of their own everyday life. Most everyone drives a car, but not everyone can be a Barney Oldfield, even though he was a "regular" person like the rest of us—he earned a living, was a husband, a son, and personable despite his fame, fortune, and celebrity status. As Dixon Wecter has explained, "the major idols of America have been men of good will. . . . No hero must announce that he is infallible. He must be greater than the average, but in ways agreeable to the average. . . . he must keep his personal modesty, his courtesy toward the people who gave him that power" (11).

Heroes, whether they are sports figures, politicians, or some other socially significant individual, exist in two separate spheres. As the age-old dilemma of history goes—what people did and what we *say* they did are often two different things. Such is the nature of folklore; an emphasis on people—the "folk"—makes it a circumspect way of gathering data about important topics. The advantage of human fallibility is that it opens doors to us regarding the *why* and *how* certain people are remembered as folk heroes, which is often more important than the issue of *who* is considered a hero in the first place.

Examples of this are not hard to find. Christopher Columbus was remembered as the man who "discovered" America, and praised as such, yet we now know the details of his travels. The "facts" about Columbus and his journey in 1492 are different than the "fiction" that has been committed to public memory. Atrocities toward the Arawaks who encountered Spanish explorers have been conveniently overlooked. Even Charles Lindbergh, the first to fly across the Atlantic Ocean alone, can be interpreted in two distinct ways: he was the "Lone Eagle" in 1927, but he was also recipient of the Order of the German Eagle in 1938. As Dixon Wecter puts it, "the Lindbergh legend had been stamped with a swastika" (441). At some point, these memories, these "facts" and their varying interpretations, or "fictions," have become part of our history. Ordinary people remind each other about these stories, these events, these famous people, and the tales get revised every time they are retold. The revisions come from our culture, from the things we consider important at any particular time in our lives, and these revisions color our history until it is time to tell the stories again.

Winston Cup stock car drivers, like other professional athletes, become folk heroes because they spend most of their careers—and personal lives—under a media microscope. The general public learns far more than it rightly deserves to know. Regular consumers of sports news learn where athletes live, how much money they make, details about private affairs, and explicit information regarding the not-so-private ones. Professional athletes become news items away from the field of competition, especially given their wealth and social status. They can also earn column inches and airtime for a lapse in personal judgment, as the New York Yankees's Dwight Gooden and the St. Louis Rams's Lawrence Phillips can demonstrate.[1] Such is the situation for a man or woman making millions of dollars each year from playing a game in front of paying audiences.

We buy seats to stadiums and arenas, we thrill to the exploits of an individual participant, we find ourselves fascinated with a player, and we search out more information about the player-turned-person. By learning intimate details about the athlete's life, we can then associate ourselves with him or her; we compensate for his or her athletic ability by learning about the athlete's faults and foibles. Michael Jordan thrills us with his ability to slam dunk a basketball, but he also pacifies us with the knowledge that he was once cut from his junior high school basketball team. Suddenly the legend seems more normal, more mediocre. Suddenly the professional athlete seems like us, a revelation introduced from within the society we live in.

Societies utilize folklore and storytelling to enhance the mystique of revered figures like professional athletes, often exaggerating or highlighting less well-known events to enhance their public images. Baseball fans and historians argue over the semantics of Babe Ruth's "called shot" in 1932, but regardless of its historical accuracy, the tale has become a metaphor for Ruth's personality and demeanor. Drinking and womanizing aside, the stories about Babe Ruth—or Barney Oldfield, for that matter—become more than retellings of historical facts. The stories we tell about sports heroes reaffirm who we are as fans and citizens, and who the hero is as an entertainer and a cultural symbol.

Many stories serve as a means of explaining an individual's greatness. Sheer talent is rarely enough; there is often some life experience that affects the creation of a sports hero. Such is the case with Junior Johnson, whose tenacity on the racetrack was formed, according to sports folklore, from years of doing battle against federal agents on the backroads of North Carolina. Racing lore also credits Johnson with originating the "bootlegger's turn," a move used during races when a car gets spun in an opposite direction.[2] Whether Junior Johnson created such a move or not is left up to debate. What makes this an important issue is that it has become a part of NASCAR folklore—a story told across generations of racing fans—and Johnson has become a legend in the process. Legions of stock car followers learn these stories, interpret them, and take from them the cultural contexts they consider to be most important at that particular time.

Stock car racing is a fertile field for the creation of such folk legends. It is a sport that thrived on word-of-mouth in the years before mainstream media accepted it as a major force in American athletics. Stories circulated from dirt tracks throughout the country by way of garages and schoolyards, over gas pumps and barstools. The exploits of local drivers who battled for glory at shrines like Darlington and Daytona became part of auto racing lore. As those drivers—men like Tim and Fonty Flock, Curtis Turner, Red Byron, Lee Petty, and Junior Johnson—worked their way from dirt to asphalt, their stories reflected some of the issues emerging from NASCAR's infancy. Moonshine haulers became athletes, recognized names throughout the country, and their stories—now a part of NASCAR folklore—addressed the culture from which they came.

This recognition even transcended lines of race, as in the case of the late Wendell Scott. Scott, a moonshine hauler from Virginia, became the first African-American to drive in the NASCAR Grand National division. During his career, Scott won one event—a 100-lap dirt track race in Jacksonville, Florida—on December 1, 1963 (Fielden 2: 243). He became nationally recognized after Richard Pryor played him in the 1977 motion picture *Greased Lightning,* which emphasized Scott's driving talent, bootlegging background, and the racism he encountered while working his way up to the big time.

Despite Wendell Scott's Grand National career, few minorities today are involved with the Winston Cup Series. Much has been made about NASCAR's "whiteness" and the fact that the sport has few minority fans. However, one African-American, John Gordian, is a volunteer member of Ricky Rudd's pit crew, working on the Tide Racing Team Ford Thunderbird. Currently there are no African-American drivers in the Winston Cup Series. Willy T. Ribbs, the first African-American to drive in the Indianapolis 500, was offered a ride for the World 600 at Charlotte Motor Speedway in 1978, but the ride was rescinded after Ribbs failed to show up for two practice sessions. The Ford ride reserved for Ribbs was then given to Dale Earnhardt for his fifth Winston Cup start (Fielden 4: 219, 232). Felix "The Nighthawk" Giles, the first African-American to win the Baja 1000 off-road race, has considered moving into NASCAR competition. In 1996, Giles considered qualifying for a Craftsman Truck Series event in Las Vegas, but failed to make the starting field ("Elliott Leads"). Because race trucks and stock cars are similar in structure, running at Las Vegas would have been a natural launching pad for Giles to move toward the Winston Cup Series.

NASCAR's fans are predominately white, a fact that Bill France, Jr., has acknowledged with wonder. "Why don't more [African-Americans] come?" France has said, "I can't give you a good answer for that." There's no game plans to keep minorities away. . . . We would like to see them as competitors and certainly as fans. We don't have a problem with a black driver or black team" (qtd. in Knotts 58). Opening new Winston Cup markets—especially in large urban areas within reach of new facilities, like the California Speedway near Los Angeles and Quad-Cities International Raceway Park near Chicago—might be the catalyst to attract minorities as fans and participants. Breaking NASCAR's ties to its traditional Southern identification might be enough to get a culturally and ethnically-diverse audience involved in the sport. A driver like Wendell Scott, moonshiner-turned-folk-hero, proved the liquor business was an economic necessity that crossed racial barriers.

The outlaw element of stock car racing derived from these early days of NASCAR. These "outlaws" were already the subjects of regional folklore: Curtis Turner, a teenaged liquor-hauler-turned-lumber-tycoon, and Junior Johnson, arrested by federal agents while standing guard at his daddy's still. These stories reflect a variety of cultural elements central to life in the American Southeast, primarily aspects involving self-reliance and personal economic survival.

Junior Johnson serves as the best example of these rough-and-tumble days. A native of Wilkes County, North Carolina, Johnson's days of running moonshine were the subject of an essay written by Tom Wolfe for *Esquire* magazine in 1965 titled "The Last American Hero is Junior Johnson." Wolfe describes Johnson as "a country boy . . . who learns to drive by running whiskey for his father . . . one of the biggest copper-still operators of all time. . . ." A career behind the wheel of a legitimate stock car made Johnson "a famous . . . driver, rich, grossing $100,000 in 1963, for example, respected, solid, idolized in his hometown and throughout the rural South" (72). Johnson, who served a ten-month jail sentence in Ohio because of his family's bootlegging business, eventually earned 50 NASCAR victories before retiring to become a stock car builder and team owner (Thigpen 55). Following the 1995 Winston Cup season, Junior Johnson sold his stock car enterprises and retired from racing all together. Despite this change, Johnson remains the southern folk hero Tom Wolfe "discovered" over 30 years ago.

Hollywood and American popular culture immortalized the legend of Junior Johnson by translating his story onto film. *The Last American*

Hero, a 1973 motion picture by Twentieth Century Fox, presented the saga of Johnson and his family's moonshine business in contemporary terms. "Junior Jackson" hauls the corn liquor made by his father and winds up discovering stock car racing, eventually becoming a winning driver on the national circuit. The boy from the mountains makes good, and leaves bootlegging behind to find his fortune in professional sport—not unlike Wolfe's version of the real-life hero from the Brushy Mountains.

The regional strength projected by NASCAR racing history—its ties to southern culture and folklore—creates a stereotypical depiction of drivers. This image exists even though many of the first successful stock car drivers were natives of the North and Midwest. Because of this depiction, a perspective of stock car racing has been produced that applies to these distinct regional stereotypes. The modern-day sport of Winston Cup stock car racing is tied to a rural, southern past, yet it exists as a part of corporate America. It is corporate America that utilizes stock car racing as a "vehicle" for marketing and promotion, using traditional, mythic images of drivers as a means of generating consumer activity and loyalty.

The rural, southern nature of Winston Cup stock car racing is responsible for America's initial conception of drivers and their place within the domination of professional sport. Some of the earliest stock car racers, according to folklore of the rural South, were men who hauled moonshine through the mountains of North Carolina during the 1930s and 1940s. They faced arrest and imprisonment if caught; this provided them with the inspiration to make their automobiles the fastest and strongest available.

Stock car racing in the 1940s was "a game of cops and corn." Moonshine runners had fast cars, as did the federal alcohol tax agents. Wheelmen either went straight and left the bootlegging business, got sent to prison, or ended up dead from a chase. All of them lived by a code of honor, a "'law of the West,'" meaning that those runners who were caught did their time according to the law (Petty, *King Richard* 47). Folklore of the South represents these men as noble renegades who were willing to pay the price for their illegal practices when—and if ever—caught.

Once again, popular culture capitalizes on this folklore through the use of film, where the stories of these "noble renegades" may be recreated and retold. The film *Thunder Road* (1958), which has been raised to cult status, and more recent productions, like *Moonshine Highway* (1996), continue to weave heroic tales of the American South. Hauling moonshine is seen as honorable work among the families who populate the backwoods and mountain clearings.

In *Moonshine Highway,* the future of bootlegging is summed up in one word: racing. In 1957, a mechanic named "Hooch" Wilson tells his moonshine-running friend, Jed Muldoon, that liquor haulers are using their talents on the race track. "They make money, those racers," Wilson says in the film, "get more all the time. Crowds . . . they love it. See all those good ol' boys drivin' sideways, door-to-door about 140 [miles per hour]. That's the future, boy . . . racin.'"

Early stock car races were held on the backroads of rural North Carolina between two men who decided to see which one had the fastest car in that particular area. Such "wheelmen" as these quickly gained a following as local racing heroes, whether they competed on or off of the track (Petty, *King Richard* 41). These early challenges expanded onto the dirt horse-racing tracks of southern fairgrounds, where several moonshine runners could race each other without fear of getting caught by authorities. What the moonshiners wanted was an opportunity to test their driving abilities at an equitable venue. Each ran independently when on the roads hauling corn liquor—the main objective there was to not get arrested. Bragging rights were hard to settle without head-to-head contests, and fields of cars were unable to run effectively at night on the backroads. It was not until 1949 that these amateur race car drivers had a chance to compete against each other—and other skilled competitors—under regulated and lawful conditions.

The first official NASCAR Strictly Stock event was held on June 19, 1949, on a 3/4-mile dirt track at the Charlotte Fairgrounds (Fusco 40). A driver had to run under NASCAR regulations, which stated that cars were to be "new model," or no more than three years old and of showroom quality. This meant the cars were to be entirely stock, except that headlights could be taped over and hub caps and mufflers removed (Petty, *King Richard* 65). For moonshiners, this was automatically a step backward since they drove cars modified to outrun the law. Moonshine cars were not "stock," even though they were used on open roads, and so deemed illegal according to NASCAR. In this new "Strictly Stock" division, victory would be based on the skills of each individual driver, not on the modifications of his car. This race marked the beginning of what is today known as the NASCAR Winston Cup Series.

Glenn Dunnaway, from Gastonia, North Carolina, won this first event, only to be disqualified after a post-race inspection discovered that the rear springs of his 1947 Ford had been altered by the addition of wedges (Fusco 40). These wedges were placed between each leaf of the springs to reduce shifting of the car's weight. Wedges made the car ride straighter which, in turn, made the car faster through the corners. This old bootlegger's trick, done to the winning car by Hubert Westmoreland who owned it and hauled moonshine in it, failed to meet NASCAR's regulations. As a result, the official winner was declared to be Jim Roper, from Great Bend, Kansas, who finished second to Dunnaway in a 1949 Lincoln (Fielden 1: 9).

Early moonshine-runners-turned-stock-car-racers were deemed by rural southern fans heroes because they symbolized a challenge to the oppressive federal agents who jeopardized their household income. Bootlegging, in the days before NASCAR provided wheelmen with a legalized venue, was part of a cottage industry that dates back to the Whiskey Rebellion of 1794. Then, as was the case during the 1930s and 1940s, the moonshiners found themselves harassed by federal agents who demanded the farmers and mountain men pay taxes on the alcohol they distilled.

There was only one difference between the Whiskey Rebellion of 1794 and the making of moonshine during the early years of the 20th century—the Whiskey Rebellion occurred in Western Pennsylvania near what is today the city of Pittsburgh. This historical fact addresses the cultural myth of moonshining—that it was a business limited to the southeastern states. Our common understanding of bootlegging is that it was a southeastern activity. That is the "fiction" of American history.

During the post-colonial period of American history, Western Pennsylvania was a rugged and primitive landscape populated by trappers, hunters, scouts, and Indian tribes. According to historian Thomas P. Slaughter:

The vast majority of poverty-stricken people in the western country were not town-dwellers . . . most frontiersmen sought to scratch a living from the environment in which they lived. . . . With the exception of Indian corn, their crops were those of medieval England—wheat, oats, barley, rye, buckwheat, flax, and hemp. Their ploughs showed no improvement over those of ancient Romans. . . . The new curved moldboards that Thomas Jefferson and others were experimenting with had not yet arrived in western Pennsylvania. Harrowing was done by dragging thornbushes across the fields. Farmers planted corn "Indian fashion," scattering seeds over unploughed land. (70-71)

Some crops, like wheat, managed to prosper occasionally, despite the lack of agricultural technology along the western frontier. Such "periodic excesses," mixed with "the scarcity of hard cash in the West," and an increase in the "non-agricultural population of the region" fostered reliance on a barter-based economy (Slaughter 71). A variety of items could be used for barter, including beef, flour, ashes, wheat, oats, and whiskey.

Making whiskey served two needs along the Western Pennsylvania frontier: it was a product in demand within the frontier community, and it could be used as a form of currency within the barter system (Slaughter 71). Of whiskey's two uses in Western Pennsylvania, we can argue that perhaps its greatest benefit to settlers was its power to dull the senses. As Slaughter has written:

The capacity of most stills was less than 100 gallons and provided little more than was necessary for home consumption. . . . Even with the benefits of rich soils and large quantities of local whiskey to numb settlers against the cold, the work, the fleas, and the prospects of annihilation by Indians, life in the western country was a delicate balance between dearth and excess. Settlers lived both physically and psychologically at the edge of subsistence. (71)

The frontier population lived free in the wilderness, despite the horrors and dangers that lurked within the woods around them. These people were "fiercely independent," and they "demanded total liberty . . . to trade in markets wherever they could be found, and to spend the meager profits of their labors as they saw fit" (Slaughter 72).

Ratification of the Constitution put a stop to the frontiersmen's independence as the federal government excised control over all its people, even those living far from the halls of government in Philadelphia. A national Constitution affected everyone in the United States, even those living on the edge of total wilderness who had had little contact with organized law. The primary point of contention was in regard to taxation, especially the taxation of whiskey. Whiskey on the frontier was mainly for personal use, commercial use was "only a secondary function of distillation" (Slaughter 73). Refusal to pay taxes on whiskey pitted frontiersmen against the federal government in a struggle between the control of the government and the freedom of the individual.

This was the spirit that drove the Whiskey Rebellion toward its violent fruition in 1794. The frontiersmen believed in personal freedom, even if it meant battling their own government. Distilling whiskey was an act of survival, not a luxury to be taxed. Over 12,900 federal troops from Pennsylvania, New Jersey, Maryland, and Virginia, and more than 7,000 frontiersmen from Western Pennsylvania, clashed in this struggle. President George Washington led troops West in an attempt to stop the frontiersmen (Slaughter 3). By the end of 1794, the insurgence had been put down. The federal government was victorious, despite the frontiersmen's disregard for authority (Slaughter 72).

The debate over excise taxes on whiskey stretched southward from Pennsylvania down through North Carolina and Georgia. People living in western North Carolina were subject to the same concerns over the power of the federal government as people in Western Pennsylvania. John Sevier, a Congressman from North Carolina during the era of the Whiskey Rebellion, saw what he considered prejudices against the tax (Slaughter 99). He felt that the people of North Carolina could probably ignore the law. The recognition and acceptance of these ideological and economic prejudices was the foundation for moonshining as it flourished during the first half of the 20th century.

Much of the frontier post-colonial ideology remained intact. As Alex Gabbard has written:

In the isolation of the mountains, some would say protection, laws and their enforcers tended to get lost on the (sic) way to the mountaineers. . . . These people had their own respect for the world they lived in. . . . Theirs was, by virtue of the demands placed upon mere survival, a simple life. A man was not measured by what he had, he was measured by who he was, and what outsiders might regard as a mean streak among some of them was, in fact, the last vestiges of the spirit of independence that had been the formative basis of this country. (7)

This was the "spirit" that possessed many families throughout the Southeast to distill their own whiskey. The need to live a life of independence, matched with the political and economic pressures of the 1920s and 1930s, caused many farmers to forsake their crops and lean toward a more lucrative, if illegal, industry.

Families made and distributed homemade corn liquor as a means of quenching the thirst for alcohol created by Prohibition, like excise taxes on whiskey, yet another piece of legislation from the federal government. "It was either make moonshine or starve," Junior Johnson once said, "Back in the '30s, it was that desperate" (Gabbard 33). Outlaws because of economic necessity, moonshine runners were numerous across North Carolina and throughout the entire South. As Tom Wolfe writes:

some nights there were so many good old boys taking off down the road in supercharged automobiles out of Wilkes County, and running loads to Charlotte, Salisbury, Greensboro, Winston-Salem, High Point, or wherever, it would be pretty hard to pick out one [particular moonshine runner]. ("Last American Hero" 72)

It is ironic that while the bootleggers ran modified cars as a means of transporting moonshine, their actual race cars were regulated to remain completely stock. Apparently a mechanical advantage was more important when trying to outrun the federal agents and a possible prison sentence. In the world of stock car racing, it was a matter of every driver racing for himself. Even Junior Johnson, once he retired from moonshining, had to trade in his "supercharged Oldsmobile engine" for a totally stock Oldsmobile Eighty-eight in 1955 to run the young NASCAR circuit (Fusco 46). Even a cultural icon like Junior Johnson—the "Last American Hero"—has to follow the rules.

These icons are the manifestations of cultural myths, the "stories taken from history" that Richard Slotkin refers to in his book *The Fatal Environment: The Myth of the Frontier in the Age of Industrialization, 1800-1890.* These stories, or narratives, have what Slotkin calls a symbolic function central to the society that has created and remembered them (19). Such symbols help us to define American society. They help us to define American society while providing us with a foundation for understanding who and what we, as a population, are.

Cultural myths, as defined by Richard Slotkin in *The Fatal Environment,* are "stories, drawn from history, that have acquired . . . a symbolizing function that is central to the cultural functioning of the society that produces them." They operate as part of our cultural "language," serving as an "encoded set of metaphors that may contain . . . all of the essential elements of our world view" (16). Such myths project images that reflect basic values within our society and reaffirm certain ideas or notions important to our ideology. These cultural myths, therefore, transform "secular history into a body of sacred and sanctifying legends" (19). Our cultural myths give us something meaningful from history to believe in—we are what our history says we are. The sport of stock car racing revolves around legendary men and machines, while projecting many cultural myths that are important to an understanding of what it means to be an American.

Cultural myths are a common part of television broadcasting since they touch on the symbols and ideals held by a viewing audience. Olympic gymnast Carrie Strug, who limped to victory under her own power after being injured at the 1996 Olympic games in Atlanta, created not just a picture of athleticism but one of determination and courage under adversity—cultural input that stimulated the minds and emotions of an acculturated audience.

Because Winston Cup races are broadcast live on national television, it is essential that cultural symbols and images are made a part of the television coverage. It provides a means by which the networks involved can have an impact on the largest number of viewers possible. Giving the audience culturally significant images is the best way that programmers can capture—and maintain—a large and loyal national audience. Some of these images include close-ups of flags (both American and Confederate) and women and children (symbolic of family in a male-dominated sport).

Hundreds of millions of television viewers watch Winston Cup races on TV each year. Such huge numbers demonstrate the effect that television coverage can have on a national scale. Just as popular television shows can affect the behavior of viewers, as in clothing styles, hair styles, or colloquial language, it is possible that cultural symbols can also be projected upon a national audience for their acceptance and acquisition.

Baseball is usually referred to as the quintessential mythic American sport, conjuring images of pastoral splendor played out under warm, sun-filled skies. The game has been adopted as our national pastime, based on criteria that reflect and interpret American culture. Baseball acquired its mythic significance by representing specific nationalistic qualities. According to sport historian Allen Guttmann:

The easy answer is that our national game is peculiarly American, fitted to American conditions and to the American character. As early as 1866, an observer of American pastimes wrote, "It is a game which is peculiarly suited to the American temperament and disposition. . . . From the moment the first striker takes his position, and poises his bat, it has an excitement and vim about it. . . . There is no delay or suspense about it, from beginning to end." (*Ritual* 95)

The reasoning behind baseball's acceptance as America's national pastime is that, like America itself, the sport is a product of the natural landscape. Baseball serves as a symbolic bridge between the American wilderness and the American city, the place where man conquers nature and brings control and civilization to the unsettled land. Baseball, as a game, was meant to be played outdoors. A piece of ground has to be marked off with base paths, a batter's box, a pitcher's mound—the landscape has to be physically altered through human intervention. The land is used by man for man's benefit—a natural resource suddenly impacted, changed by the culture living upon it. Such a view, however, has been deemed paradoxical. Annette Kolodny regards man's use of the natural landscape as "the essence of the pastoral paradox: man might . . . win mastery over the landscape, but only at the cost of emotional and psychological separation from it" (28). This idea of nature being bettered by cultural agency, despite its vast array of interpretations, remains a part of our national collective imagery.

Henry Nash Smith highlighted this point, writing that "The image of this vast and constantly growing agricultural society . . . became . . . a collective representation, a poetic idea . . . that defined the promise of

American life" (Smith 123). This "poetic idea" is the mythic quality of baseball; it represents America's connection to the landscape, while symbolizing the promise of individual and communal achievement.

However, even a sacred pastime like baseball has a two-sided history. There is the "fact" behind baseball: the quantitative element that involves wins and losses, batting averages, earned run averages, home runs, and runs batted in. Baseball, like other parts of our culture, also has a qualitative side: the great men and moments that embody the spirit and the ideology of the game. This is what can change with time and society—the "fiction" of the game that is interpreted according to what our culture feels is socially significant. Abner Doubleday's role in the creation of baseball has been pretty well refuted by sports historians, even though his name is a part of the game's cultural mythology—he is more "icon" than "individual."

This debate between historical "fact" and historical "fiction" is especially strong within the realm of the NASCAR Winston Cup Series. Heroes are defined by the things they have accomplished and by the images they possess. Interpreting history in these two ways has been a prime component in stock car racing, not unlike what Will Pickens did for Barney Oldfield's racing career at the beginning of the 20th century. This seems especially true given the fact that race car drivers, like Oldfield and the men who run stock cars today, are often identified by the public in two distinct ways. There is the driver as racer, and the driver as celebrity/spokesman. Barney Oldfield was the first to test these waters; today's Winston Cup drivers are swimming in them every day.

Certain stories about folk heroes are better if told in regionally relevant terms. For example, when Jeff Gordon won the inaugural Brickyard 400 at Indianapolis Motor Speedway in August of 1994, the news media emphasized his ties to the Midwest. Here was a 23-year-old from Indiana excelling in a sport born and bred in the American South. No matter that Gordon had been running stock cars since 1991, winning in Grand National and Winston Cup competition at tracks like Daytona and Charlotte; what mattered most was that a young man from America's Heartland had won a stock car race at the nation's most revered speedway. As Steve Waid put it in the *Winston Cup Scene* of August 11, 1994, "The favorite son of Pittsboro, Ind., the driver they call 'The Kid,' becomes part of auto racing lore by winning the first NASCAR Winston Cup race ever run at the venerated Indianapolis Motor Speedway." Ironically enough, the national media got so caught up in Gordon's win, many in the press neglected to say that Jeff Gordon was really a native of California, spending the early years of his life near Vallejo (Berggren, "Gordon" 26). His move to Indiana came because it was where a 13-year-old could purchase and drive a sprint car. From there, Jeff Gordon moved into NASCAR racing.

Identification with region is important in the creation of folk heroes. This, as we have seen, is how NASCAR's popular southern stereotype was formed in the first place. Labeling someone by the region from which they come generates connections with other social and cultural ties, and these too are often turned into stereotypes. Just like American culture stereotypes New York urbanites as loud and crass, Californians as laid back and superficial, and Texans as boastful and wealthy, American culture also stereotypes people from the Midwest. This is why Jeff Gordon's win at Indianapolis in 1994 was so socially significant, despite his origins out West.

The Midwest has been stereotyped in American popular culture as a quiet, rural environment where people dedicate themselves to their families and communities. This dedication often comes through personal sacrifice—sacrifice powered by the character trait of personal responsibility. Jeff Gordon received criticism following his Brickyard 400 win because of this issue. It was a situation that blended business and community with a healthy dose of responsibility. Through it all, Gordon's dedication to his "roots" were questioned by people who had watched him grow physically, emotionally, and professionally.

Jeff Gordon had agreed to make a personal appearance at Tri-County Speedway, a quarter-mile dirt track in Haubstadt, Indiana. It was one of the tracks where Gordon earned experience during his climb to stardom, the place where his legend began. The deal was for Gordon to appear at the local speedway on the day following the inaugural Brickyard 400. Had Jeff Gordon been an also-ran in the Brickyard, he would have made the appearance easily, but Gordon was anything but a back marker. His win made him an overnight sensation, and his appearance schedule suddenly got busier and more involved.

Jeff Gordon, in Victory Lane at Indianapolis, suddenly found himself obliged to attend a special post-race celebration at Walt Disney World, a duty that forced him to miss the Tri-County appearance (Bourcier, "Gordon" 44). Gordon was a champion between his home and a hard spot—he had an obligation to the Haubstadt racetrack, but he also had an obligation to NASCAR, the organization behind Gordon's entire livelihood. As Bones Bourcier put it:

You probably know what happened next: on the afternoon when a few thousand fans converged on tiny little Haubstadt, their hero, Jeff Gordon, winner of the first stock car race ever held at the Indianapolis Motor Speedway, was riding alongside Mickey Mouse in a theme-park parade a thousand miles away. Suffice it to say that the disposition of many a Tri-County spectator did not exactly match the weather in Orlando, which was sunny. (44)

Jeff Gordon made the decision he felt was best, especially in relation to the scope of both events. It would be easier to reschedule the Tri-County appearance than it would be the Disney World parade. For NASCAR's sake, it was important to capitalize on the immediate post-race rush of press attention. Wait a week for the Disney World event, and another Winston Cup race would be in the national media spotlight. Regardless of rationale or reason, the Haubstadt affair "turned into a giant public relations headache, providing endless fodder for the letters-to-the-editor pages in the trade papers. Folks who had traveled from far and wide to . . . chat with Jeff Gordon, blasted him to bits for not showing up" (Bourcier, "Gordon" 44).

Many upset with Gordon felt it was because he "had forgotten where he came from, that he had changed," comments that offended the young driver because they suggested his "roots" meant nothing. Jeff Gordon responded to their opinions in an interview, being quoted as saying, "Nobody knows how much I do remember where I came from. There have been a lot of people who helped me get where I am. Those people who truly helped me get here, they know how much that means to me. They know I haven't forgotten them" (qtd. in Bourcier, "Gordon" 44).

Such emotional response from a community says something about their notion of social responsibility. When neighbors need our help, it is our inherent responsibility to offer assistance. This is part of the Midwestern rural stereotype. Like all forms of stereotypes, the character traits are assumed and assigned, based loosely on a highly generalized interpretation of the people and region involved. Nevertheless, Gordon's trip to Disney World was interpreted by some as being non-communal—something not done in a close-knit society like that of the Midwest, despite his commitment to NASCAR, a major international sanctioning body with its own obligations to corporate America.

Today's NASCAR drivers are marketed and promoted by major corporations, and the corporate image projected is often the one turned into contemporary folklore. Take, for example, the image of Dale Earnhardt. His father, the late Ralph Earnhardt, was a peer of Curtis Turner and Junior Johnson; his rough-and-tumble reputation made him a successful and revered driver throughout the Southeast. Dale grew up in this environment, watching his father beat and bang against the best of them on his way to a NASCAR Modified championship. Dale Earnhardt knew that he was going to be a race car driver like his father, and that is precisely what he became.

Dale Earnhardt's climb to championship status, however, was a tough one. The stories of his struggle used to be part of the man's personal history, part of Earnhardt's personal narrative. Failed marriages, working a variety of day jobs, and living in near poverty while trying to make it as a stock car driver were all stories of Dale Earnhardt's life experiences. Now those stories are a part of Winston Cup folklore, reflecting the challenges, hardships, and sacrifices required of a national champion. Look at Winston Cup racing, and you find stories of the obstacles all drivers had to clear.

Stories of challenge and hardship like these have circulated throughout the grandstands and garage stalls, many carried by the media and interpreted by those who hear or read them. Personal narrative is the fuel that drives the wheels of emerging folklore, and the lessons we learn from such stories make up the fabric of the NASCAR Winston Cup Series. Many times these stories will conjure up images that stock car fans will identify with, providing them with a connection that brings the spectator one step closer to the sport.

One aspect of NASCAR Winston Cup racing fans can identify with is its emphasis on nicknames. Using nicknames projects an air of familiarity, of being an insider and knowing things the "average" fan does not. "Nicknames," Dixon Wecter wrote, "show the informality of our hero-worship" (13). Hence, Harry Gant becomes known to fans as "Handsome Harry," David Pearson becomes "the Silver Fox," and Richard Petty—even before earning his 200 career victories and seven Winston Cup titles—becomes "King Richard." Other nicknames Americans consider popular, according to Dixon Wecter, are those "that suggest homely origins," like Bill Elliott's recognition as "Awesome Bill from Dawsonville" (14). Nicknames can also have a sarcastic or critical connotation, again as a means of showing intimacy with the sport. This explains how a history of aggressive driving can earn Ernie Irvan the moniker "Swervin' Irvan," or Jimmy Spencer the name "Mr. Excitement." In cases like these, the nicknames usually come from within the sport—often dubbed by fellow participants—and are introduced to the public through the media.

Nicknames also show the evolution of a driver's reputation with fans. A driver's image with his peers or the fans is often reflected by his nickname, and that nickname will change as his attitudes do. The evolution of Dale Earnhardt makes a good example. Earnhardt, at one point in his career, was known as "Ironhead" because of his implied stubbornness, a trait that supposedly caused him to generate accidents. As Earnhardt matured as a driver, his nickname changed to "the Intimidator," because of his effect on his opponents. When GM Goodwrench became Earnhardt's primary sponsor in 1988, he became known as "the Man in Black" because of his team's new color scheme—a label that reflects a Western "outlaw" image, not unlike the image of legendary country singer Johnny Cash.

Throughout his career, however, Earnhardt became recognized for more than his nicknames, positive or negative. Dale Earnhardt also became known as a symbol. The notion of Dale Earnhardt as cultural icon began during his relationship with Wrangler Blue Jeans, his primary sponsor from 1981 through 1987, in a series of magazine advertisements based on traditional American character traits. These print advertisements presented Earnhardt as more than a stock car driver; they presented him as a symbol in American cultural mythology.

One advertisement from 1981 referred to Earnhardt as "a born perfectionist." The photographs show him at work, his Pontiac leading the field into a banked corner, and at rest, polishing a restored 1938 automobile. At the bottom of the Wrangler advertisement is text that addresses Dale's character—his desire to be the best. "On the track," the ad copy declares, "Dale won't settle for second place. Off the track, he won't settle for second best." The advertisement focuses on Dale Earnhardt's drive for success and achievement, a quality admired in American culture. Wrangler even applies its company slogan—"One Tough Customer"—to Earnhardt, using it at the very bottom of the page. Thematically, this print advertisement identifies an important cultural trait and personifies it through the image of Dale Earnhardt.

Another Wrangler advertisement using Dale Earnhardt as a cultural symbol is one from 1983 featuring Dale and two of his children. This print ad focuses on Dale's emphasis on self-reliance, and the role individualism has played in his life. "My daddy would help me when I needed help," Earnhardt is quoted as saying, "But he didn't hold my hand," says the Wrangler advertisement. The children, one of Dale's sons and one of his daughters, are sitting in front of him, and the copy continues with Earnhardt's view of parenting American-style: "My daddy encouraged me to be my own man. And that's how I hope to raise my kids. I want them to learn self-confidence and independence."

These distinctly American character traits—ones rooted in the spirit of the men and women who traveled West to settle the frontier, are then related to Earnhardt's success. The 1983 Wrangler ad copy continues: "Confidence and independence—Dale shows the stuff champions are made of every time he climbs behind the wheel." We should not be surprised at such platitudes of American individualism, especially in an advertisement for blue jeans, a piece of quintessential American clothing. Once again, Dale Earnhardt represents a critical component in the shaping and defining of the American character.

Another component of American character is hard work. This is the stuff of Horatio Alger, Jr., and his inspirational tales of "luck and pluck." Wrangler saw these same qualities in Dale Earnhardt during the 1983 Winston Cup season, when Dale was driving a Ford Thunderbird for Bud Moore. Wrangler created a print advertisement to address the work ethic inherent in not only Earnhardt, but in all Americans who wore blue jeans. This Wrangler advertisement of 1983 pictures Earnhardt working out on a universal gym—this at a time when stock car drivers were just acknowledging the benefits of physical training. The text is to the point: a strong work ethic makes for a successful and admirable American. "Bud Moore has a great crew working on the car," the driver explains, "But when it comes to keeping Dale Earnhardt in working condition, I've got to depend on myself. And it takes a lot of discipline and perseverance to work out as often as I have to."

The company's text once again, as it did in the earlier advertisements, celebrates Dale's dedication, stating that "Dale shows the stuff champions are made of. . . ." This is an expression of Earnhardt's personal fortitude and his strict work ethic, not unusual in a man who has already been identified as a "born perfectionist" just two years earlier. Since the audience already knows of his belief in self-reliance, seeing Dale working out to become a stronger stock car driver puts the "rugged" in his symbolism as a "rugged individual."

Individualism was the focus of a later print advertisement done by Wrangler during its tenure with Dale Earnhardt. In 1986, after Earnhardt had been hired to drive for Richard Childress, Wrangler created an ad that blended a number of cultural images central to the recognition and interpretation of American character traits. A picture of Earnhardt and Childress flanking country singer Willie Nelson was at the center of the advertisement, all three men wearing Wrangler caps and Nelson with his index finger pointing straight up in the air. Earnhardt and Childress are supporting Nelson's hand as if in a sign of solidarity. The ad copy reads: "Wrangler Jeans and these three men have a lot in common. They're all authentic, down-to-earth and hard working. They have a lot of fans in common, too, and their fans stand for the same values."

The association of these men—two stock car racers and one country singer—is a direct appeal to people who identify with either of the two occupations. Since country music and stock car racing are kindred spirits, the shared audience provides Wrangler with more bang for its advertising buck. This advertisement does, however, address another aspect of American hero-worship, that being our culture's fascination with rebels. In the words of Dixon Wecter, "The American temper has a marked sympathy for rebels, non-conformists, and cross-grained dissenters" (25).

Willie Nelson is a perfect example of Wecter's statement; his reputation is that of a noble outlaw. "The outlaw movement" in country music, according to Patrick Carr, "was 'about' all sorts of things. It was about style and image: Willie [Nelson] wanting to drop all pretense" (32). Here was a man who charmed both fans and critics with his music, yet angered some Americans by his failure to pay taxes. Nelson, like Dale Earnhardt, is a "lovable rogue," a hero whose "mores . . . may vary with his times" (Wecter 484). Wrangler wanted its customers to identify with these men—men who were "authentic," not just celebrities. The identification of fans with personalities like these is important since consumers recognize men like Dale Earnhardt and Willie Nelson as independent thinkers. Shaking the status quo is what Nelson did to the staid world of country music, and what Earnhardt did (with Childress's help) to the old guard of the NASCAR Winston Cup Series. The ad's tag line, "A legend in jeans," says it all. These three men are just that—legends in jeans who represent the traditional "down-to-earth" spirit and work ethic of the American character.

More recent advertisements present Dale Earnhardt in a slightly different light, perhaps as a commentary to his maturation as a husband, father, and a race car driver. Stetson hats, one of Earnhardt's secondary sponsors, ran a print advertisement on the rear page of *Stock Car Racing* magazine in March of 1994, to mark his sixth Winston Cup title in 1993. The ads showed Earnhardt wearing a black Stetson and holding the championship trophy. Despite no revealing text, the ad's intent was clear—Dale Earnhardt, like the frontiersman, had conquered the toughest territory in America, the 17 speedways of the NASCAR Winston Cup Series.

While browsing in a NASCAR collectibles store in Ohio, I came across another testimony to Dale Earnhardt's role as a symbol of American individualism. In a rack of T-shirts, I found one marketed for Earnhardt with a Western motif—the silhouettes of cowboys on horseback. On the back, the shirt read "Cowboys and Engines," an obvious attempt at connecting the iconography of Dale Earnhardt and the cultural mythology of the American West.

Earnhardt's role as an American folk hero has even been used in television commercials. One ad for the Chevrolet Monte Carlo, shown on TBS in October 1996, features Darrell Waltrip—himself a NASCAR legend—sharing a story about Earnhardt with Terry Labonte and Jeff Gordon. The commercial shows Gordon sheepishly asking Labonte if he finds Earnhardt "intimidating," a reference to Dale's popular nickname. When Labonte mentions Dale's black Monte Carlo, fitting Earnhardt's image, Waltrip admits, "But remember one thing, when he first started, his car was pink."

"Pink?" Gordon asks naively, in disbelief. With an advertisement like this, Dale Earnhardt is perceived of as a legend, the subject of stories, rumors, and racing history. Jeff Gordon and Terry Labonte, in their own right, are depicted as young and in awe of their predecessors—even though both are former Winston Cup champions. What separates Earnhardt from Gordon and Labonte in this commercial is the mystique of his character, the popular image of Earnhardt as the "Man in Black." This is the stuff folk heroes are made of.

The image of Dale Earnhardt is also symbolic of attitudes within America. Ed Hinton wrote about "the general surliness of our society, a public with an attitude that mirrors Earnhardt's attitude" ("Attitude" 71). This, according to Charlotte Motor Speedway's president and general manager H.A. "Humpy" Wheeler, might explain Earnhardt's appeal to a larger, more casual racing audience:

"Earnhardt is the resurrected Confederate soldier. . . . Where [Richard] Petty was always compliant, Earnhardt will stand his ground and say, "I'm not going to do that." And the people who love him are the people who are told, every day, what to do and what not to do, and they've got all those rules and regulations to go by. That just draws them closer to him. (qtd. in Hinton, "Attitude" 71-72)

Earnhardt's attitude toward the Winston Cup lifestyle makes him a symbol of individualism in a sport where following sponsors' (and NASCAR's) orders is expected. The rebellious nature of Earnhardt, a reminder of stock car racing's other free spirits, Curtis Turner and Tim Richmond, provides race fans with a model to emulate—at least subconsciously—in times of personal and occupational stress and uncertainty. In this sense, Dale Earnhardt is much more than a Winston Cup driver and media celebrity; he projects cultural meaning through his behavior in the world of professional sport. He is a central figure in the history of NASCAR and its evolution into one of America's most popular spectator sports.

The history of the NASCAR Winston Cup Series in and of itself is expressive of numerous issues: development of the automobile, Prohibition, labor organizations, advertising, and mass media to name a few. More important, however, the sport of stock car racing expresses other, more deeply rooted elements of American life. It is an activity that operates as a text—a guidebook that embodies some basic rules for American living and some fundamental ideas that help us cope with the responsibilities and problems of American civilization.

Rituals, in and of themselves, are celebratory acts. Frank E. Manning, in his book *The Celebration of Society: Perspectives on Contempo-*

rary Cultural Performance, identifies celebrations as having four "central features":

First, celebration is performance; it is, or entails, the dramatic presentation of cultural symbols. Second, celebration is entertainment; it is done for enjoyment . . . however much it is tinctured, consciously or unconsciously, with ideological significance or pragmatic intent. Third, celebration is public. . . Celebration socializes personal meanings, enacting them on the street, on the stage, in the stadium. . . Fourth, celebration is participatory. (4)

The act of celebration involves two elements—play and ritual. An act of play has license to alter our social order, while a ritual regulates and maintains the social order we know (Manning 7). A sport like bullfighting is highly ritualistic, symbolizing the inequality of the struggle between man and nature, and has its origin in the religious ceremonies of ancient Crete (Guttmann 29). The ritual of bullfighting reaffirms a social order—that man is superior to animals—and regulates interaction between the two species by permitting the man to taunt, stalk, and eventually kill the bull he is facing.

In this sense, a Winston Cup stock car race is an example of ritual. NASCAR creates a "social order," then "regulates" the behavior of those competing according to protocol. Race cars are inspected by NASCAR officials, declared legal (or illegal) for competition according to written rules, allowed to practice and qualify at certain times of the day, and policed during the race by officials representing the governing organization. Teams that fail to qualify by making a fast trial run are allowed entry into races by NASCAR based on the number of points the car owner has accumulated. These provisional starting spots demonstrate the social order created by NASCAR. Car owners who have earned more points than their competitors are given preferential status by the governing body and allowed into a starting field, while owners whose cars have struggled throughout a season are told to go home if their qualifying times are not fast enough. The social order of NASCAR rewards past success, and puts unsuccessful teams at a lower level of consideration.

Throughout all of this, a ritual is followed at each Winston Cup event. An order of ceremony is maintained, not unlike that of other professional sporting events. Drivers in a particular race are introduced to the fans, the National Anthem is sung or played, there is a ceremonial call to action (usually "Gentlemen, start your engines!"), and there is a victory celebration where the winning team is cheered by the spectators and greeted by members of the media. Given the dangerous nature of automobile racing, a prayer for safety is often included as part of the opening ceremonies. Through all of these ritualistic customs, we can see the dominant force at work behind the scenes of stock car racing. The cultural symbols are obvious, especially given the religious and political emphasis within American society.

According to Frank E. Manning, "When those who control celebration are also those who dominate the social order, there is a tendency to ritualize that dominance in order to sustain and legitimize it" (7). The ritualistic pattern of Winston Cup stock car racing serves as an example of Manning's theory. A pre-race prayer is not unusual in a nation where Christianity is the dominant religious force. The National Anthem is common at the start of many events in America, a country founded on the principles of patriotism. Maintaining ritualistic practices such as these helps to legitimize the dominant social order.

"Ritual," says Manning, "is a metastatement of truth, delivering a moral critique of society, an understanding of what ought to be" (22). Winston Cup racing, in this way, appeals to the desires of its fans, giving them symbolic actions that contain all-important cultural meanings. *Sports Illustrated* writer Ed Hinton asked Humpy Wheeler why Earnhardt has become so popular with NASCAR's national base of fans. Wheeler explained:

I think everybody in the country is angry about having to drive in urban areas. They hate the traffic with a passion. Earnhardt drives through traffic too. And he won't put up with anything. He's going to get through. And that's what *they* (the fans) want to do—but they can't. So Earnhardt is playing out their fantasies. (qtd. in Hinton, "Attitude" 71)

Dale Earnhardt symbolizes an American motorist's anger over urban traffic. The cultural meaning projected by Earnhardt tearing his way through door-to-door, bumper-to-bumper speedway congestion is heartfelt by an audience who will curse crowded highways during rush hour on their way to work (and while trying to leave the speedway parking lot once the race is over). The competition of Winston Cup stock car racing "defines, dramatizes, and thereby renders meaningful, central frustrations of the audience" (Manning 12).

Competition, in terms of mobility, is the key to life. The most elementary form of competition is the simple foot race, pitting individuals against each other for the honor of being considered the fastest, or the one with the greatest endurance. A contemporary ancestor of such racing is the marathon, named after the city in Greece from where a messenger carried news on foot to Athens. In this situation, running was a means of communication, to send and receive messages during the Persian War.

Today its function is as a community event, especially in large cities like Boston or New York, where thousands of citizens participate on a variety of competitive levels, from the professional to the novice. Because transportation by foot was the first means of travel, it is no great surprise that foot racing would be an initial form of competition.

As human beings developed alternative means of transportation technology, so too they developed alternative forms of competition, again with an emphasis on speed and endurance. These new types of racing also placed importance on handling and stability, important when negotiating tight corners around pylons or course markers. A large part of early spectator sports history concerned such events as these, especially during the era of the Roman Empire. This era was the time of the great coliseums—the Hippodrome resembling the modern speedway used by automobiles today.[3]

No matter what the means of transportation, the same basic focus for competition holds true: people are obsessed with speed. These earliest types of sports competition, when compared to sports seen today, have remained essentially the same over the centuries. The vehicles for movement have changed dramatically—even when studied over the course of the past century. What has not changed is that basic aspect of competition—the spark of conflict that rises when an instigator levels a challenge against an opponent. It becomes a matter of ego versus ego, of person versus person.

The non-competing public finds a role to play as spectators. Their place is near the playing field, but not directly on it. It is their duty to serve as an audience, showing praise, support, or disdain while awaiting the possibility of a tragedy that will lift the competition into the arena of sheer spectacle. In ancient Rome the spectacle was chariot racing within the confines of the track; in 20th-century America it is the superspeedway at Daytona or Indianapolis where modified automobiles run on the "ragged edge" that separates disaster from victory, riches, and fame. The victor becomes a hero.

Americans raise individuals to heights of national recognition and try to emulate them. In some cases, we are inspired by figures who have achieved something that we ultimately want to achieve ourselves, as in the case of a movie star or a professional athlete. In other cases, we admire people whose lives and personalities reflect our own.

Automobile racing, in general, is a sport of personalities and machinery. It is a sport of almost limitless variables. The driver is the figure at the center of the team, even though his or her role is actually fairly secondary. Today's stock car drivers work with high-dollar contracts and press agents. Media attention is constant, with newspapers, magazines, television, and radio all muscling in for a piece of the sport. Stock car racing used to be a matter of family and community; today it is a matter of a family being associated with Fortune 500 companies and CEOs. Sponsorship has become the key to racing success, as all too many independent drivers have learned the hard way.

The subculture of the NASCAR Winston Cup Series lives off deep roots. Its legions of fans are legendary and seriously loyal to drivers, automobile manufacturers, and sponsors. These are the people who purchase the tickets and the T-shirts, the caps, and the collectibles. They write letters to racing publications when they feel their driver has been wronged. They buy personal messages to offer support and/or praise when their driver needs a pat on the back. These are the people who comprise the backbone of Winston Cup stock car racing.

NASCAR and its many racing teams recognize this fact. Stock car drivers realize that fans make it possible for them to race for a living. The sponsors realize that fans will buy their products, with almost blind loyalty, simply because of their Winston Cup connections. This is the reason why stock car drivers still give their autographs for free, while "mainstream" athletes charge for their signatures at card shows or memorabilia exhibitions. Stock car drivers realize that fans make their race cars go 'round, that dedicated and happy fans make the NASCAR Winston Cup Series a real force within the realm of professional sports.

Media exposure has helped stock car racing evolve into a true professional sport. Putting the races—and the racers—in front of a national audience has given the Winston Cup Series a release from its Southern heritage. NASCAR racing has, from its earliest days, attracted competitors from above the Mason-Dixon Line. Some of the sport's first drivers came from places like Defiance, Ohio. and Great Bend, Kansas (Fielden 1: 7). In spite of this, history convinces us that stock car racing thrived on people based in the American Southeast. Such is the impact of cultural mythology.

Fig. 21. The Sandwich Construction Company is perhaps the best known stock car-theme restaurant in America. Given the many teams located nearby, the "Sandwich" is often frequented by racers and race fans alike. (Photo by Mark Howell)

136

Fig. 22. Inside the Stock Car Cafe in Cornelius, North Carolina, diners are treated to a variety of NASCAR material culture, including sheet metal from actual race cars and an interesting assortment of posters, photographs, and corporate promotional items. (Photo by Mark Howell)

137

Fig. 23. The North Carolina Auto Racing Hall of Fame is located in the Lakeside Industrial Park in Mooresville. Surrounded by Winston Cup and Busch Grand National race shops, the Hall of Fame provides visitors with a close look into the history of stock car racing. The facility also sells fine pieces of stock car art through its gift shop. (Photo by Mark Howell)

Fig. 24. Pit crews stand at attention along pit road during the playing of the National Anthem. A fairly new part of Winston Cup tradition, it originated out of complaints that some crews failed to pause and honor America. This seems to signify recognition of pit crews as athletes, since it requires them to occupy specific places on the track and stand apart from the regular audience. (Photo by Virginia Howell)

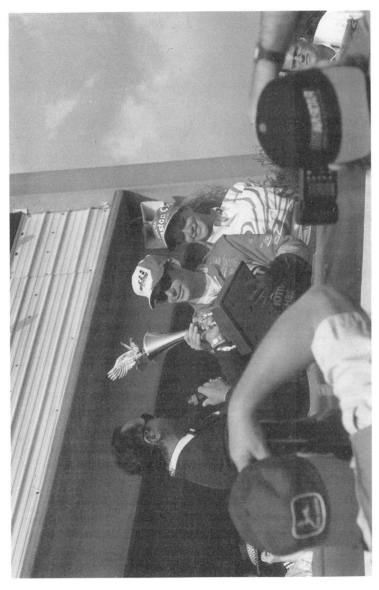

Fig. 25. Jeff Gordon celebrates his win in the UAW-GM Teamwork 500 at Pocono by accepting the champion's trophy. Miss Winston, a regular part of the Winner's Circle ritual, stands to the right of Gordon. (Photo by Mark Howell)

140

Fig. 26. The garage area at Rockingham is filled with corporate names, logos, and colors. Madison Avenue is well represented in Winston Cup racing. (Photo by Mark Howell)

141

Fig. 27. Contingency sponsors provide Winston Cup competitors with parts, publicity, and added dollars. These stickers are placed according to a specific pattern and represent bonus money for every race. (Photo by Mark Howell)

Fig. 28. A Legacy Car, like this one, offers Winston Cup looks on a low-dollar budget. This car resembles a Ford Thunderbird, yet it is powered by a Mazda motor. A car such as this allows the stock car fan to try his hand at an affordable division with minimal financial or personal risk. (Photo by Mark Howell)

143

Fig. 29. Today's Winston Cup pit stall includes some high-tech equipment. Most teams use a pit tool box, known as a "war wagon," that is loaded with satellite television reception, VCRs, video cameras to tape pit stops from overhead, and a computer workstation. (Photo by Mark Howell)

Fig. 30. A show car program is an effective way to generate consumer interest in a sponsor's product. Show cars are actual Winston Cup stock cars that have been pulled from a team's active lineup. They tour the nation and allow fans to have an upclose-and-personal encounter with the machines they watch on the track each week. (Photo by Mark Howell)

145

7

Seeing Is Believing:
A Personal Ethnography
of NASCAR's Winston Cup Series
and Stock Car Racing in America

The popularity of the NASCAR Winston Cup Series can be attributed to its accessibility, its closeness to the public. Unlike other professional sports, stock car racing tries to maintain ties to its fans. The involvement of corporate sponsors is partly responsible for this open door policy; contact with the fans means contact with consumers. NASCAR fans are likely to spend their money on products because a particular company supports a Winston Cup team. Because of this, keeping drivers and cars in front of the public is critical to the sport's success. Making contact with the public—whether they are racing fans or not—is a way to generate brand-name identification and customer loyalty, a goal for sponsors investing money in Winston Cup teams.

Studying the Winston Cup Series meant studying these encounters between race teams and the public, both at the speedway as well as in the marketplace. During the writing of this book, I spent many days within the sport of stock car racing. At times I just observed racing as an interested bystander. Sometimes I was an active participant, going behind the scenes in one capacity or another. Ethnography is the "study of lived experiences, involving description and interpretation" (Denzin 141). This approach supplied me with the information needed to do a cultural analysis of the sport.

I have no conscious recollection of when stock car racing was introduced to me; it has always been there. As racing fans themselves, my father and mother are the ones who first taught me about the sport. My childhood included days spent in the grandstands at Pocono International Raceway and along the dusty wooden benches of Herb Harvey's dirt track in Lemon, Pennsylvania. The sights and sounds of stock cars, and the idea that people built these machines and operated them, always thrilled me. How exciting, I thought, to make an automobile that would go so fast and sound so loud. The little cars I played with would never be so fast.

147

As I grew older, I realized that racing was the life for me (right after I decided against becoming an astronaut and a forest ranger). By the time I was in middle school, I discovered that automobile racing could be used effectively in my studies. My reports for math and English class suddenly became important: a graphing project was my chance to show relative speeds between different types of race cars, the book about grand prix racing I read for fun suddenly became good material for detailed review. I was hooked on automobiles and the men who made them go.

By my freshman year of high school, the hook was reeling me in. I decided to build a Street Stock and race it at some of the short tracks around our area, namely at a paved, half-mile oval in Owego, New York, called Shangri-La Speedway. My parents and I had been going to Shangri-La on a regular basis after being introduced to the track by my cousins. The NASCAR-sanctioned speedway hosted Street Stocks and Modifieds, and I had every intention of becoming the Street Stock champion there before moving on to Late Model Sportsman cars. This was my road to the Grand National division—what we call the Winston Cup Series today.

My road to Daytona was simple, efficient, and paved with youthful ignorance. I mentioned my career plans to my parents one evening at the supper table. They heard me out, listening to my carefully thought-out strategy with open minds and complete silence. Only after I finished speaking did they offer their input. "We've always said you can do whatever you want with your life," my father began, "but all we ask is that you get a college education. Get a four-year degree, and your mom and I will give you our blessings for whatever you decide to do."

My parents' decision was the best one they could have made. I became more focused on school, especially since college was in my plans. My class schedule in high school aimed me toward a university, and suddenly putting my "career" as a stock car racer on hold was not so difficult. It was one Saturday night in 1981, however, that demonstrated how good my parents' decision really was. The night opened my eyes to racing in a way that no magazine, newspaper, or television broadcast ever could. It was a night when I went racing at Shangri-La Speedway.

It was April, and I was just turning 16 years old. A good friend of mine, Larry Polachek, was working after school with a bunch of guys who were running a NASCAR Modified. Larry and I grew up together—he and his family lived up the road from us—and he and I were classmates in school. Larry's father worked at a place called Quality Metal Products; it was a shop where they did precision metal working, and Larry would go up there in the evenings to watch these guys work on their race car. Larry would travel with the team occasionally, going with them to places like Martinsville Speedway in Virginia, where he met drivers like Richie Evans.[1] One day he asked me if I would like to go with the team on their regular Saturday night trip to Owego. I mentioned it to my parents, and they decided to go along as well. That weekend, Larry, my parents, and I drove to Shangri-La Speedway, where I was to learn about short track racing from the other side of the fence.

Larry and I entered the pit area at Shangri-La and went over to where the Quality Metal Products team had set up. They were getting the car ready for practice and the team's driver, a young man with glasses in a white firesuit, was moving about the car making last minute adjustments and changes. Once things looked right, the young man climbed into the car's tight cockpit, strapped himself in, put on his helmet, and fired the big Chevrolet engine to life. The bright orange car rolled away and, over the din of the car's motor, Larry leaned over to me and shouted, "That's the guy I've been telling you about! That's Brett Bodine!"

Brett was starting to make his move toward big-time stock car racing. He began his career driving at a small race track his family owned near Chemung, New York. His older brother, Geoff, had come up through the Modified ranks and had gone on to flirt with the Grand National division. Geoff had just run a Grand National race that month at Darlington, where he finished in thirtieth place driving a Pontiac owned by Dick Bahre (Fielden 4: 331). Brett, like Geoff had done, was using Modifieds as a means of gaining driving experience.

On that Saturday night at Shangri-La, Brett was flying, the car responding to all the tweaking and adjusting the crew was doing. By the time the qualifying races were finished, Brett had made the feature. The slower cars for the night were loading up to go home, and Brett was in line to make some money. As an up-and-coming young talent, I assessed the situation and decided that this was the way to go. I made the right choice, this short track stuff was all right. A couple of years at the local level, and I would be on my way to the top. I would be running against the big guns on the Grand National level in no time. Brett was showing me just how easy it could be done.

We were ready for the feature race. The crew made some final adjustments to the car according to Brett's suggestions. Tires were checked and changed, gasoline was put in the fuel cell, and the crowd cheered as the track announcer announced that the cars could line up for the main event. The lights shined brightly down onto pit road from above the grandstands as Brett climbed aboard for his final run of the night. With everything ready, the car roared to life and rolled away. Larry and I positioned ourselves for the start, and the crowd stood in unison as the Modifieds prepared for battle. Standing in the pits, with the lights and the cheers and the noise of engines, I was beside myself. Man, I thought, this was the life! This was exactly what I wanted to do.

The race was only about four laps old when my mind suddenly changed. Brett tangled with a slower car as they headed down the front straightaway. The two cars slid toward the outside wall and hit the concrete hard, Brett's bright orange Modified going into the wall backwards and sliding along the retaining fence toward turn one. That quickly, our night had come to an end. All the hard work during the week, all the hard work and adjusting that evening, all of Brett's driving and attention during practice and qualifying—it all came to an end with one harsh spin and a dull thud against the wall.

Brett was okay, but the car was undrivable. A tow truck dragged the carcass of Brett's car back to our pit space, dumping it there before us in a heap. One of the crew handed me a flashlight and said, "Let's see what's left." I began going over the car, taking a mental inventory of what was damaged, what was destroyed, and what might be salvaged. Larry and the crew—despite their dejected and fatigued expressions— were doing the same thing. The race continued as we combed over the bent and torn race car.

It had been a bad accident, but once the green flag dropped for the restart, the fans suddenly forgot about it. They continued to yell and cheer as the Modifieds kept on running. Any excitement was lost on us; we were watching beams from flashlights as they danced across broken suspension parts and crumpled sheet metal. The car was in need of major repair, and there would be another race the next weekend. As the crew circled the car, and as I crawled under the back end to inspect the fuel cell for damage or broken gas lines, the next week's shop schedule was obvious: bring the dead back to life and get ready to go racing all over again. It suddenly became a long and cold night at Shangri-La.

As we drove home that night, having met up with my parents after the feature, Larry and I shared our stories about what had happened and how frustrating it was. I suddenly realized, as we glided down the tree-lined roads of the Southern Tier, that this was the career I had wanted to pursue. The accident and subsequent cleanup were rough and emotional, and I had absolutely no stake whatsoever in the race car, the sponsor, or in Brett's career. What if I had been the one slamming backwards into the wall? What if I was the one who had to make all the repairs? What if I was the one whose livelihood was riding on how I finished that night? Brett was probably lucky to make enough money to cover his fuel costs—what about his rent or electric bill? As we rode on through the night, I found myself calmed by the fact that my parents wanted me to go to college, not to another speedway the next weekend. Another race could mean another accident with another week's worth of repairs. College was a chance for me to evaluate my talents and dreams, and decide if racing was really what I wanted to do.

As you can see, I found another calling while in college. That calling never kept me far from automobiles or stock car racing, although it drew me away from the race track and into the library, where I explored the role of motorsports within American culture. I drove some amateur events as a member of the Sports Car Club of America, where I could race my "stock car" (a 1976 Ford Elite) without ringing up too many bills for parts and tires. While I went off to college and graduate school, Brett Bodine went off to make his career as a driver down South. By the time I was finishing my master's degree, Brett was winning his first Winston Cup race. As I was finishing my doctorate, Brett was buying his own race team and setting out as one of NASCAR's newest breed—the driver/car owner. Given our careers, I never guessed our paths would cross again.

Gathering data for this book took me all over the country, with much of my time spent in the area surrounding Charlotte, North Carolina. Despite NASCAR's Florida roots, and the fact that the sanctioning body's main offices are located there, Charlotte is the hub of stock car racing. Race shops are scattered throughout the region, and businesses that cater to stock car racing are all over the area. Doing fieldwork in North Carolina, I thought I might run into Brett at either a race, or a shop, or perhaps a restaurant near his home. I never ran into him while in Charlotte; we wound up crossing paths while Brett was doing a personal appearance in Toledo, Ohio, where I was living at the time.

The sport of NASCAR stock car racing is a hectic, often chaotic, and always transitory environment. Even when drivers are in the midst of the season, they have to do appearances away from the race track for their sponsors. It was June 1996. The Winston Cup Series had just run at Dover, Delaware, and there was a week off before the next race at Pocono. I was going to do research at the Pocono event, so I spent a few days at home working on my manuscript before hitting the road. One morning while reading the newspaper and having a cup of coffee, I came across a short article about a fund-raising event for the United Way. Owens-Corning, a Toledo-based company that manufactures insulation and other building materials, was sponsoring an evening of music and community fun. The Cub Scouts were holding their Pinewood Derby, there was going to be a car show and a concert of 1950s music, and Brett Bodine was scheduled to make an appearance with the Team Lowe's show car.

I got to the Stranahan Auditorium early as a light sprinkle began to fall from the overcast skies. A number of restored cars from the 1950s and a few street rods were on display at the front of the building. A local radio station was doing remote broadcasts as people began to arrive for the evening's festivities. The rain began falling quickly, so I moved inside. My plan was to observe and record a Winston Cup driver doing a "typical" personal appearance, if there was such a thing. With NASCAR's explosion in popularity, it seemed hard to imagine that any interaction with the public could be interpreted as being "normal." It would be fun to watch Brett as a Winston Cup driver—meeting his fans, signing autographs, and promoting his sponsors—away from the pressures and hassles of a speedway.

I entered the main hall where a number of activities were already set up. There were tables displaying the line-up for that evening's races, row after row of Pinewood Derby cars all brightly painted and decorated. The smell of Tony Packo's hot dogs and chili was wafting through the air as volunteers moved tables, hung banners, and set up a variety of door prizes donated to be given away. There was a large garage door on the far wall of the main hall, so I started to work my way in that direction. As I approached the door, the growl of an engine exploding to life could be heard outside. The sound was unmistakable; it was the sound of a Winston Cup stock car.

Heads snapped toward the garage door as it slowly opened to reveal the familiar blue and yellow of Brett's Team Lowe's Ford Thunderbird. The show car rolled through the open door, the weather outside having cleared enough to keep the car from getting drenched. As the car entered the room, there was a sense of excitement. Volunteers handling the food stands emerged from the kitchen to take a look, and security guards from the building walked over to watch the car as it came to a stop.

Volunteers working Brett's appearance moved into action, setting up tables and chairs for the staff who would be selling Team Lowe's souvenirs. One table would be for Brett to use as he signed autographs and met with the public. An added feature would be photographs with Brett, taken by a volunteer with a Polaroid camera. From the number of people already there wearing T-shirts, hats, and jackets emblazoned with Winston Cup cars and names, it looked as though Brett Bodine had done the first part of his job—he had attracted a crowd to the United Way fund-raiser. The number of race fans increased rapidly as the event was set to officially begin, their cameras and pens in hand to greet the NASCAR driver.

One race fan waiting for Brett Bodine was a little boy who appeared to be around four years of age. He wore a Remington Arms Racing T-shirt with a picture of Morgan Shepherd's Ford on it, and a Ford Racing baseball cap. He came to meet Brett loaded for bear: he had a diecast car in its package and a photograph card to be signed, his hat was decked out in enamel pins for various Ford race teams, and he carried his Fisher-Price camera to record his meeting with the driver. His excitement was obvious as he moved from the show car to his father and back to the show car repeatedly. I stood next to the boy's father as the crowd continued to gather. "He's a Ford fan," the man said, "Brett'll be the first driver he's ever met. He knows all the Ford drivers and sponsors, but Brett's the first one he's met in person."

Brett Bodine arrived a few minutes before the doors were set to open. He came in through the kitchen, its doors opening into the main hall near the show car. With Brett was a representative from Sports Marketing Enterprises, Dean Kessel, who oversaw the public relations events for Team Lowe's.[2] Brett wore a red sport shirt and slacks, but soon changed into his driving suit and shoes. This not only added to Brett's appearance as a stock car driver, but it would also put his sponsors' names upfront in every photograph taken and every television interview done that evening.

The first fan to greet Brett was the little boy in the Ford regalia. He showed the driver the items he brought, and Brett looked at each one. Brett talked with the little boy about racing—asking him questions and listening to the boy's responses—and the pair posed for snapshots. The boy also took a photograph of Brett on the camera he was carrying, and Bodine made sure he autographed everything the boy wanted signed. It was a big night for the little Ford fan; he walked away hand-in-hand with his father, having made a new and very special friend.

The local media swarmed around Brett as he positioned himself near the show car, which was actually a Team Lowe's race car that had been removed from active duty. Its nose was that of a 1995 Thunderbird, and it did not have the roof flaps that are now mandatory on all Winston Cup machines. To the casual fan, it looked like a race car, and what mattered most was that it had the sponsors' names in all the right places. As Brett set up to meet the public, I visited with Dean Kessel. He explained the strategy of sponsorship placement to me according to the Team Lowe's situation.

Since Lowe's Companies, Incorporated, specializes in the retail sale of materials for home improvement, the firm handles numerous brands of merchandise. Some of these brands include: MTD Yard Machines, Owens-Corning, Sylvania lighting fixtures, Southeast wood treating, and Valspar Paints. To balance these separate companies on the Lowe's race car, the companies choose specific weeks when their name will receive "top billing" on the fenders, deck lid (trunk lid), and rear panel (where the tail lights would be on a production-model car). The Lowe's name is always seen above the wheel well on the quarter panels, but the other corporate names rotate their position on the remainder of the fender. Since Owens-Corning is a business based in Toledo, Ohio, Dean explained, their name would receive priority placement at races in the Midwest, like the two run at Michigan International Speedway. When the circuit moved to New York, to run at Watkins Glen, then Sylvania's name would be given the most visible spot on the car beneath the Lowe's name.

Dean Kessel and I stood and talked for a while as Brett went about his business. He told me a story about the importance of corporate sponsorship placement. During Speedweeks at Daytona International Speedway in 1996, Brett had had a rough time. He wrecked two cars against the wall during practice, one of which nosed into the fence and caught fire. In *USA Today,* a color picture of Brett's car aflame against the wall was printed on the first page of the sports section. Clearly visible was the MTD Yard Machines name, which was on the rear, or "TV," panel. This is a high-visibility area on the car, especially when in-car and on-car cameras are filming the racers running ahead of them. The exposure MTD Yard Machines received from that photograph—on the front page of the sports section of a nationally distributed newspaper—was priceless. Buying such placement would have been almost impossible, but because of their involvement with Winston Cup racing and Team Lowe's, they received an advertising benefit beyond imagination. If you were to figure in television coverage of Brett's mishap, and the time MTD's name spent on camera, the benefits together would be worth hundreds of thousands of dollars.

The sponsor at the top of the list on this night was Owens-Corning, which had been supplying volunteers for the event and making Brett Bodine feel at home. As the crowd moved through, Brett visited with each person. The volunteers made sure the fans were given souvenir promotional postcards with Brett's picture on them, and they helped to insure that people could buy the souvenirs they wanted, like Owens-Corning posters or photographs of themselves with Brett next to the show car. The volunteers also made sure that Brett was comfortable as well, bringing him soft drinks and anything else he needed during his two-hour appearance.

Several Owens-Corning executives stopped by to say hello to Brett, including Glen H. Hiner, the chairman and chief executive officer. Many opted for photographs with the Winston Cup driver. Regardless of who stepped up to the table, whether an executive, a little child, or a diehard NASCAR fan, Brett Bodine treated each like a personal friend. He spoke with them, answered any questions, and made sure he gave them whatever they wanted. Photographs were for sale that evening, but Brett often posed for snapshots taken by the fans themselves. In most cases, children were subjects. The youngster would stand next to Brett, he would squat down and put his arm around the little fan, and the happy parent would get a keepsake to commemorate his child's big night. This is the stuff that separates stock car drivers from their professional athlete counterparts. NASCAR drivers know that the fans are the ones who make the sport so popular. Not once did Brett charge someone for his autograph, not once did he simply sign an item and hand it back with his head down in silence—he treated each fan with respect, grace, and sincerity.

What struck me about doing a personal appearance like this was the length of time drivers spend "on the job." Two hours seemed like a long time to be signing and posing and talking. There were times when the crowds would subside a bit, and Brett could catch his breath. He would have a cold drink, get up and walk around, and visit with hangers-on like me. Brett and I spoke about the "good ol' days" when he drove for Quality Metal Products and was climbing the ladder toward the big time. We swapped names and stories, and it made me feel good that Brett had achieved his goal—he had become a NASCAR Winston Cup driver and car owner. There were no championships, and only one win so far, but at least Brett Bodine was there—he had made it, and that was more than most Saturday night racers could say for themselves.

There is no such thing as an overnight success, especially within the world of professional sports. With time comes experience, and few sports require more years of experience than automobile racing. Just like the years Brett Bodine spent running the short tracks of the Northeast, drivers find themselves paying their dues, serving their apprenticeships with car owners, crew chiefs, and sponsors in hopes of getting a shot at the big time, regardless of where that "big time" takes them. For some, it is Formula One and the circuits of Europe. For others, it is the Indianapolis 500. For most in America, it is the NASCAR Winston Cup Series, where winning just one race is an accomplishment. As the sport grows, and as corporate sponsorship becomes more important, many drivers/car owners are looking ahead to the future, grooming the next generation of Brett Bodines, Darrell Waltrips, and Bill Elliotts.

An apprenticeship can groom a driver for a future in racing, while allowing the current driver to hand-pick his successor. Bill Elliott has turned his earnings, his equipment, and his success into a launching pad for his team, using his resources to train Ron Barfield, a young driver from Florence, South Carolina. Barfield drives Fords for Bill Elliott and his partner, Charles Hardy, in ARCA competition and in the NASCAR

Craftsman Truck Series. My father and I had the chance to meet Barfield while at Pocono in 1996, where he told us about his relationship with Elliott, who at the time was recovering from a broken leg he had suffered at Talladega.

Ron Barfield had moved from Florence to Dawsonville, Georgia into a house supplied to him by Elliott. His Ford Thunderbird ARCA car and his Ford F-150 NASCAR pickup truck were maintained by Elliott's crewmen with sponsorship by New Holland farm equipment. Bill Elliott allowed Barfield and the crew to use his team's private jet for their transportation to and from the speedway. When my father inquired about Elliott's love of airplanes, Barfield replied that Bill owned several of them and that he had been flying around Georgia with Elliott earlier that week. As Bill Elliott's protégé, Ron Barfield was supplied with everything needed to equip a first-rate racing team. The results of Elliott's generosity were readily seen as Barfield finished third in the ARCA race at Pocono and won the ARCA event at Michigan just one week later.

Other Winston Cup drivers have been trying this apprenticeship arrangement to better prepare for the future. Dale Earnhardt has been working with protégés of sorts. He hired Jeff Green, brother of 1994 Busch Grand National champion David Green, to drive his GM Goodwrench Grand National car on a full-time basis. Earnhardt then replaced Jeff Green with an up-and-coming driver named Steve Park, who showed great talent in Busch North and Craftsman Truck races during the summer of 1996. Jeff Green, during his tenure with Dale Earnhardt, received an introduction to Winston Cup competition. Earnhardt's personally-owned team debuted a Chevrolet, sponsored by *Racing for Kids* magazine, at Pocono in 1996 in the UAW-GM Teamwork 500.

My research trip to Pocono during the summer of 1996 introduced me to some interesting developments in the relationship between tobacco companies, the world of professional sport, and the consumer. Despite the accessibility of stock car racing, it is surprising how hungry fans are about the sport. Walking along pit road the morning of a Winston Cup event, you see people studying pit equipment and race cars with great interest, taking photographs and asking questions while seeking autographs and brushes with their favorite drivers. The "open door" policy of NASCAR facilitates the fan's education. Knowledgeable fans are long-term and loyal fans, so it benefits the Winston Cup Series to educate and acculturate its fans as quickly and as much as possible. By fostering a spectator's understanding of the sport, the spectator grows to feel more comfortable, more connected, and more involved in it.

Such "hands-on" activities can also bridge the gap between corporate sponsors and the consumers they hope to attract. The R.J. Reynolds

Tobacco Company is trying one such attraction, the "Winston Track-house," at Winston Cup races across America. For fans, the attraction provides an opportunity to get close to the sport they love. For R.J. Reynolds, the attraction provides an opportunity to get close to consumers whose dollars are up for grabs—and that includes those race fans who do not smoke or use tobacco products.

I first saw the Winston Trackhouse at the UAW-GM Teamwork 500 at Pocono, Pennsylvania. The attraction was in the process of being assembled when I first arrived at the track earlier that race week. It was difficult to miss the long, billowing red tents and the white Winston banner calling all to come and see the show. My first introduction to the Trackhouse came from a young man who had approached my father and me while we were enjoying a cup of coffee during a break in Winston Cup practice one morning.

We had just found a seat at a table under cover near a concession stand. As we sat and began to relax from hours on our feet, a handsome young man approached us with a large duffel bag slung over one shoulder. "Excuse me, gentlemen," he began, "but do either of you two smoke?"

My father answered for the both of us. "No," he replied, "we don't smoke. Never have smoked, and don't plan to start now."

The young man, dressed in a white T-shirt and shorts, smiled and gave us an affirmative nod of the head. "Good for you," he said, "and make sure you don't start." I noticed the graphics on his T-shirt as being Winston slogans used to promote their involvement in racing. "You work for R.J. Reynolds?" I asked.

"I represent them at races," the man explained. He went on to say he worked as a professional model, and that his agency had booked him to work at the speedway for R.J. Reynolds. It was his job to locate smokers and approach them about the brand they used. He continued, "If you say you don't smoke, I'm supposed to say something like 'Good . . . and make sure you don't start!'" In the duffel bag, he carried loose packages of cigarettes and coupons for purchase discounts. I introduced myself and my father, and I explained what we were doing at the races. When I started to inquire about his duties with R.J. Reynolds, the young man— whose name was Darrin—sat down to join us for a while.

As my father and I talked with Darrin, whose "day job" was as a stockbroker in Ithaca, New York, he explained that it was his job to gather data from smokers he met at the speedway. The questions seemed to be focused on demographics and brand choice. In return, Darrin would give the survey-takers free cigarettes and coupons for RJR's products. As we talked, I could not help but think about something I saw while doing research at Martinsville Speedway during the spring of 1992. While working at the Hanes 500, I saw Miss Winston repeatedly walking up and down the rows of car haulers, handing out packages of cigarettes to mechanics, drivers, and other people connected to NASCAR or its racing teams. The same was true at the Michigan race I attended that same summer. This seemed to be part of Miss Winston's job—distributing her company's products while visiting with people and promoting the racing series.

Darrin was doing the same thing, only his duties seemed to be more concerned with gathering statistical information. Before he resumed his work, I asked Darrin about the Winston attraction located in the infield. "That's the Trackhouse," he said, "it's something you should go and see." We walked toward the tents and were amazed by what we saw. The Winston Trackhouse's exterior was something akin to a medieval carnival; souvenir stands and radio-controlled racing games caught curious passersby, and the outside attractions near the tents were crowded with sunburned and interested onlookers.

One of the most popular outside attractions was the "Winston Cup Tire Change Challenge," where would-be pit crewmen tested their skills against a Goodyear Racing Eagle, an impact wrench, and an electronic timer. The idea of the simulation was for the "crewman" to remove five lug nuts and the tire (mounted on an actual wheel rim), then replace the wheel and tighten the lug nuts without missing any or leaving any loose. Penalty seconds were added to the crewman's final time for any and all loose lug nuts, just as they would be in the Unocal Pit Crew Championships held each fall at Rockingham, North Carolina. Very few attempts were successful, as fans learned just how difficult being a tire changer could be. Most people relegated themselves to standing by and watching, obviously intimidated by the task at hand.

Another simulator was stationed near the tire change test; a "Reaction Timer" based on NHRA drag racing challenged fans to out-accelerate a series of staging lights on a miniaturized "Christmas tree" starting tower. This test was being regularly overlooked, despite its more realistic success rate. The least anyone could do was "jump" or "red light" the start, rather than looking somewhat foolish fumbling with an impact wrench, lug nuts, and wheel rim. Given the fact the Trackhouse was stationed at a Winston Cup venue, it was not unusual for fans to be interested in attempting a tire change instead of a clean NHRA start.

The interior of the Winston Trackhouse was more subdued—more like a museum than the midway at a county fair. Fans could get a close-up look at a Winston Cup pit stall, complete with nitrogen tanks, tires mounted with lug nuts, and pit wagons loaded with the latest in computer and video equipment, just like the ones seen on pit road. At one end of the main tent was a stage where special guests would come for question and answer sessions. Directly in front of the stage was a series of video kiosks, each one in the shape of a package of cigarettes. The video monitors showed continuous footage of the Winston Cup champions—each monitor focused on a particular number of years, and each film displayed highlights of races and driver interviews. In the middle, on a platform, was a life-sized replica of the 1995 Winston Cup championship trophy. Next to these video kiosks, at one end of the stage, was Jeff Gordon's No. 24 Dupont Chevrolet. The show car commemorated Gordon's reign as the 1995 Winston Cup champion.

At the other end of the main tent, there was a theater attraction free of charge to visitors. The show was a promotional film made by R.J. Reynolds about the Winston Cup Series. As a cultural text, the film was a masterpiece. Shots of American flags and race fans were quick-cut with in-car camera footage of stock cars in action. The soundtrack was loud and exciting, building the tension on-screen as closeups of cars banging into one another kept flashing by in bright colors. Interspersed throughout the film were platitudes celebrating the aggressive, all-American nature of Winston Cup racing. The written text on-screen echoed the slogans seen on Winston shirts all around the speedway: "The only dancing done in our sport is 3-wide at 200 mph" and "Around here, actions still speak louder than words." Darrin and the other promotional people had these slogans on their shirts, which were part of print advertisements for Winston's "No Bull" campaign. At one point, the film became somewhat interactive, as footage of a car hitting a water barrier at Richmond was followed by water splashing at the audience from both sides of the screen.

The most striking part of this film was its attention to Winston Cup racing's stereotypical class distinction. Scenes of blue-collar fans partying in the infield and sitting atop recreational vehicles were scattered among shots of the American flag waving in the wind. This connection between working class spectators and symbols of patriotism and nationalism are not coincidental—the distinction is meant to be easily understood. Winston cigarettes were trying to present themselves as the cigarette of the common man, the everyday hard-working American. This same idea was carried through by the print advertisements run in racing publications, which showed photographs of fans cheering from the infield or the grandstands. The attention to class reinforced stock car racing's reputation as a sport of community, an event where people get together and live as one for an afternoon or entire weekend. The film certainly supported this idea.

After the film, many people headed to the far end of the main tent. Just outside the far end was a souvenir stand, where T-shirts carrying the slogans seen in the film were being sold. Right next to the souvenir stand was the Winston Simulator, a box-like cabin poised on hydraulic arms. It served as a large video viewing room with stereo sound and seating for about 30 people. One of the RJR staff overseeing the Trackhouse said the simulator gave fans a realistic "ride" in some high-speed vehicles, including a fighter jet, the Smokin' Joe's hydroplane, the Smokin' Joe's NHRA top fuel dragster, and the Smokin' Joe's Winston Cup stock car. The simulator's cabin moved in synchronization with the footage being shown on-screen, much to the delight of fans who staggered from it following their interactive experience.

What struck me about the Winston Trackhouse was its ability to draw on all of the RJR products connected with motorsports competition. With a few changes, this attraction could be customized to fit any Winston-related racing event. The emphasis here was the Winston Cup Series, but NHRA drag racing could have been adapted just as easily. Souvenirs being sold covered all aspects of R.J. Reynold's Tobacco, and added publicity came from the cigarette stands located in front of the Trackhouse site.

This same scene is replayed at every Winston Cup Series race. Souvenir row is one of the most popular places for fans attending a NASCAR event. Thousands of spectators wander around through the rows of trailers before and after the races, and most do more than simply wander and browse. Most are active consumers, purchasing a variety of items that promote the name of their favorite driver or their favorite corporate sponsor. Their purchases are not limited to small items; it is not unusual to see fans spend $50 for a jacket or a special shirt. Most racing jackets cost better than $80, and if the customer throws in a matching hat, he or she will be looking at a purchase of $100. A couple of souvenirs bought at the racetrack will quickly rival the cost of the fan's ticket, and in some cases the souvenirs will be worth more.

Souvenir row is not for the faint of heart, nor for the faint of credit card. The trailers along souvenir row sell anything including clothing, photographs, toys, hats, food items (like Bill Elliott Barbeque Sauce), patches, bumper stickers, pins, clocks, glassware, life-sized cardboard standing cutouts, jewelry, jackets, and baby paraphernalia (bibs, rattles, bottles, and socks). For the fans, it means an opportunity to buy treasured souvenirs while the Winston Cup Series is in town. For the drivers, it means they receive a percentage of the trailer's total season sales as added income.

When you consider that a driver can receive $40,000 just for having his photograph placed on a trading card, it is no small wonder that the souvenir business is a lucrative sideline for the drivers and their race teams to pursue, as Peter Golenbock noted in his 1993 book, *American Zoom: Stock Car Racing—From the Dirt Tracks to Daytona.* The memorabilia business makes about $2 billion each year (8-9).

Golenbock, while visiting "souvenir row" at the 1992 Daytona 500, made the following observation:

It is estimated that in addition to shelling out for the ticket at Daytona, each fan in attendance will spend about $200 on mementos. After I spent fifteen minutes by one of Dale Earnhardt's trailers, I knew the estimate was too low. A steady queue of eager fans were waving their money toward the venders, vying for attention, snapping up Earnhardt souvenirs as though they were priceless treasures. (8)

To the fans, their purchases *are* priceless treasures. Such items represent a connection between the fan and his or her beloved driver and/or team. Notice that Golenbock mentions he spent time by *one* of the Dale Earnhardt souvenir trailers. At races like those run at Daytona, Talladega, Atlanta, and Michigan, it is possible to have multiple souvenir vendors representing a single driver.

Dale Earnhardt is the king of souvenir sales in Winston Cup racing. According to Robin Hartford, *U.S. News and World Report* reported in the spring of 1996 that "Sports Image sells approximately 5,000 Dale Earnhardt T-shirts at every Winston Cup event. . . . If 5,000 shirts were sold at $20 each, that is $100,000 on T-shirts alone" ("Collectibles" 98). Multiply that $100,000 by the 31-race NASCAR schedule (not counting specialty races like the Busch Clash or the Winston all-star race), and you have annual T-shirt sales alone of $3,100,000. Figure in other souvenir products, like caps, jackets, bumper stickers, and pocket knives, and you are looking at sales totals most retail businesses would die for. In 1993, Dale Earnhardt "grossed an estimated $42 million in souvenir sales alone," and when he tied Richard Petty's record of seven Winston Cup championships, estimates stated that Earnhardt's "souvenir sales surpassed $50 million" (Hinton, "Attitude" 70). Earnhardt is connected to over 700 souvenir items, and he even went so far as to buy Sports Image—the company that handles most of his souvenirs—and install himself as its chief executive officer (Hinton, "Attitude" 71).

In the case of a driver with an adult-oriented sponsor, such as Ricky Craven's sponsorship by Budweiser, Rusty Wallace and his sponsorship from the Miller Brewing Company, or Ken Schrader and his Skoal sponsorship by U.S. Tobacco, there will often be a trailer selling items with the sponsor's logos separate from a trailer selling mementos carrying the driver's name and image. These preventive measures are taken to insure that young race fans are protected from souvenirs that advertise a particular driver's connection with alcohol or tobacco products.

During the autumn of 1994, I was able to travel with the Smokin' Joe's racing team to the AC-Delco 500 at Rockingham. I had gone to Charlotte, North Carolina, for a conference. My travel plans were simple: I was going to present a paper, spend some time with family and friends while in town, then return home a few days later. Just before leaving for North Carolina, I received a telephone call from my sister-in-law. She had been talking to some friends about my upcoming visit. One of these friends, Andy Macvicar, was working at the time as a welder for the Smokin' Joe's team. Andy suggested that I could attend the race as his guest. Plans were arranged, permission was granted by Travis Carter, and everything was set for my day at the races.

Sunday, the day of the race, dawned rainy and foggy. I picked up Andy at 6:00 A.M. and we drove south on Interstate 77 from Statesville to Mooresville. We were to meet two other pit crew members there at a Hardee's near the Lakeside Industrial Park, where several other Winston Cup teams were based. Andy and I met his teammates; we grabbed a quick breakfast for the road, climbed aboard the team's brand new Ford Super Cab diesel pickup, and the four of us headed east toward Rockingham.

Rockingham is a 90-minute drive from Charlotte. During the trip, we all discussed the previous day's events: a Grand National race and the Unocal World Pit Crew Championships. Morale was pretty high on the Smokin' Joe's team since they had placed third in the pit crew competition. The team's car was going to start Sunday's race from the 34th position, so the crew would have to continue their fast pit work if the car was going to move up through the field. Everyone felt confident about what the day had in store.

The only real question seemed to be the weather. As we approached Rockingham, the sky became darker and more threatening. Sporadic rain struck the truck's windshield as we reached the Rockingham town limits. The forecast was calling for clearing skies and warm temperatures. As we entered the gates to the speedway, it looked as though our day might become a washout.

Andy and I entered the NASCAR credential building and I signed in to receive my infield pass. Once we entered the infield, I then had to visit another NASCAR office in order to receive my garage credentials. Security is tight around the pit and garage areas, especially at a smaller facility like Rockingham. Despite the early hour—it was only a little after 8:00 A.M.—there were already a couple hundred race fans clustered around the gates to the garages. Most carried pens and programs, hoping to catch a driver and get his picture or autograph. The scene was unusually chaotic as I waited to receive my NASCAR clearance.

As I turned around to leave the credential office, I saw the reason for the chaos. Mark Martin, driver of the Valvoline Ford Thunderbird, was attempting to enter the garage gates. Fans had mobbed him as he walked toward the chain-link fence that separated the cars from the fans. Such a scene did little to upset the driver. Martin stopped and visited with the fans who were crowding close, signing autographs and talking as the people swirled around him with cameras in hand. He smiled graciously and signed everything from postcards to T-shirts. All the while, he continued toward the garage area. I, too, headed for the garages, following in the path left by Martin and some of his pit crew.

Once inside the garage area at Rockingham, things settled down a little. The "garages" were really just connected shelters that resembled carports. They had no doors or walls, and they offered little protection in the event of a driving rainstorm.[3] Under each stall was a Winston Cup stock car. Their hoods and deck lids were up, and many were perched on top of jackstands, their wheels and tires piled off to one side. Each car was surrounded by its mechanics and crew personnel. The crews were studying sheets of checklists that were taped to each car's fenders. Some of the mechanics were underneath the chassis, while others were peering and working under the hoods. Every now and then a car would roar to life and idle, allowing its mechanics to work on its throttle and carburetor. Other team members were going around the cars with rags and bottles of cleaner, shining fenders and doors so the cars would look good once they were ready to be lined up along pit road.

The stock cars were not the only things receiving attention, however. As I walked along the area where the car haulers were parked, I noticed numerous meetings going on between crew chiefs, car owners, sponsors, and media people. Some of the crew chiefs were conducting interviews, some were talking with personnel from other teams. The environment within the garage area was very communal—very open and casual—and very unlike that of any other professional sport. There was a familial atmosphere, even though these teams would be racing each other like the hammers of hell in a couple of hours. It was this sense of community that caught my attention.

The NASCAR Winston Cup Series functions very much like a small town, with its own form of government and its own form of law enforcement. Rules and regulations are at the center of the sport, as witnessed by the long line of race cars going through technical inspection. Rule violations unseen by the naked eye are cause for teams to work and rework, double-checking and correcting heights, angles, tolerances, lengths, and widths. The officials overseeing the series police the sport closely and carefully, making sure that each race car meets NASCAR's standards and specifications. Adhering to strict rules has made NASCAR competition famous for close racing through parity, a quality that has elevated NASCAR above other forms of motorsport.

While walking through the NASCAR garage area, I heard music coming from a small gathering near one end of the stalls. Groups of people were heading toward the gathering, so I followed along to satisfy my curiosity. The music was coming from a bluegrass gospel group that was playing as part of the Motor Racing Outreach, the "church" of the Winston Cup Series. A large group of people, including many of the stock car drivers and their families, was sitting in front of the bandstand. Darrell Waltrip and his wife, Stevie, were there, as was Jeff Gordon and his then-fiancée, Brooke. Bill Elliott and his wife, Cindy, stood along one side of the crowd, as did several pit crew members who were taking time off from their pre-race preparations. The congregation contained about 150 people altogether.

A special moment occurred when Ernie Irvan and his wife, Kim, arrived for worship. Irvan was recovering from a near-fatal accident he suffered on August 20, 1994, while practicing for a race at Michigan International Speedway. It had been only two months since his wreck, yet Irvan had recovered enough to attend the race at Rockingham and offer advice to Kenny Wallace, his replacement driver. The crowd at the MRO worship service watched with relief and comfort as Ernie and Kim took their seats, everyone thankful that the driver was back in the NASCAR fold after cheating death in the Irish Hills.

Death is a part of automobile racing, and the Winston Cup Series had—by the fall of 1994—already experienced more than most people could fathom during a two-year period. Since April of 1993, four Winston Cup drivers had been killed. Ironically enough, only two of the four fatalities—the deaths of Neil Bonnett and Rodney Orr at Daytona in February of 1994—happened in a stock car. The 1993 deaths of Winston Cup champion Alan Kulwicki and Davey Allison occurred in aviation mishaps, but these four losses combined had sent the NASCAR family reeling. Ernie Irvan's victory over death gave the Winston Cup community something to celebrate; the human spirit was greater than the spectre of death, and Irvan was a living testimony to the power of life.

Such a service as the one I witnessed at Rockingham demonstrated to me that this group of professional athletes possesses an amazing amount of faith and spiritual strength. Part of it has to do with the regional distinction of the sport's participants. Many in the stock car racing family come from rural families where religion has been a major part of their lives. Another aspect of stock car racing is based on faith in others. A driver climbs behind the wheel of a 200 mile per hour race car that has been built and prepared by a team of mechanics and welders. The driver himself has little to do with the car's preparation; his life rests in the trust he has in the people around him. On the track, the driver has to rely on the skills and judgment of the other drivers and *their* mechanics—a 20- or 30-car "freight train" drafting around Talladega rides on the efforts of hundreds of people. Faith in their fellow competitors is an essential virtue for NASCAR Winston Cup participants and their families.

Another essential for Winston Cup participants is corporate sponsorship, and it was an obvious element during the pre-race activity at Rockingham. Pre-race tours for sponsors and their guests are a regular part of a NASCAR Sunday. Garage areas overflow with representatives from the world of industry and business. A meeting for the Smokin' Joe's race team held prior to the 1994 AC-Delco 500 that day reflected such involvement. It was nearing race time, and the Smokin' Joe's crew, outfitted in their yellow, green, and purple uniforms, were finishing sandwiches and cold drinks before heading out onto pit road.

Travis Carter was speaking informally to his team members. A man in a white sweater stood quietly off to one side, just a few feet behind Carter. The man was T. Wayne Robertson, an executive with the R.J. Reynolds Tobacco Company whose Camel cigarette brand sponsored Carter's race car. Travis Carter introduced Robertson, saying that he wanted to speak briefly to everyone before the race began. Robertson stepped forward and congratulated the pit crew for their good work in the pit crew competition held the day before. Finishing third out of 29 teams was something for the team to be proud of. The 1994 season, overall, had been a rough one for the Smokin' Joe's racing team; driver Hut Stricklin was going to leave the fold and an increase in regular Winston Cup competitors had made qualifying a gamble. As a result, the Smokin' Joe's Ford Thunderbird had failed to make the starting field for two events. The third place pit crew award felt good following a season of struggle.

T. Wayne Robertson complimented the pit crew on their hard work and determination. The team members seemed to relish the praise being given to them. Most sponsors, given the kind of year Camel had experienced, would have come into a meeting like this with a speech full of hellfire and brimstone. Those kinds of speeches had already been given around the Winston Cup garage area. You could sense them in the air, and people on certain teams seemed to be doing their work with added vigor and troubled expressions on their faces. It was that time of year— late in the season after a grueling stretch of races with little time off— and sponsors were making their 1995 plans and decisions.

Robertson's speech had nothing to do with anger or threats; his was to announce a gift for every member of the Smokin' Joe's team. Because of their strong finish in the pit crew competition, R.J. Reynolds was going to award each team member with a Smokin' Joe's leather jacket worth about $1,200. It was important for the firm to demonstrate its support because, according to Robertson, R.J. Reynolds was dedicated to helping its team achieve greatness in the coming seasons. A driver change—unmentioned during the team meeting—would bring Jimmy Spencer back to Travis Carter's stock car team for 1995. Victory, it seemed, was just around the corner, and the people at R.J. Reynolds had a special interest in this team.

The company's interest was focused on this team's success for a couple of reasons. First, the Smokin' Joe's Thunderbird was an advertising vehicle—literally—for a product that had come under attack for its questionable marketing techniques. "Joe Camel" had been called a bad influence on children by both parents and government, a cartoon "spokesman" who made smoking look cool, wrote Ellen Neuborne in *USA Today*. The race team was also intimately connected to the firm that was responsible for underwriting the entire Winston Cup Series. What might be seen as a conflict of interest by some was considered a promotional tool by others close to the sport, said Deb Williams in *Winston Cup Scene* ("RJR Team Sponsor" 21). Providing a race car, and a racing series for that car, gave R.J. Reynolds maximum public exposure.

T. Wayne Robertson completed his comments and the crew took their places along pit road. I found a safe place out of the way and proceeded to observe the events as they unfolded that afternoon. The clouds and rain of early morning had burned off under oppressive sunshine as the damp Sunday turned hot. The change in weather made for a long day as Stricklin was involved in various mishaps, including a collision on the backstretch near where the car was being pitted. Minor adjustments turned into major repairs, and the race blurred into the rest of the dismal 1994 season. When the checkered flag fell, Dale Earnhardt had won his 63rd Winston Cup race, his seventh Winston Cup championship, and the Smokin' Joe's crew packed up for the 90-mile ride home after coming in 27th and winning $13,200.

The car, extra parts, and tool boxes were loaded in the Smokin' Joe's hauler, and everyone grabbed a cold drink or two for the road.

Andy and I threw some new tires mounted on rims into the bed of the Ford Super Cab pickup, grabbed a couple more cold drinks to dissipate the heat of the long October afternoon, and climbed aboard the Ford to head back to Mooresville. As we started out of the infield, starting and stopping in the congested post-race traffic, people began yelling at us. A small boy, no more than ten years old, was running barefoot along the access road that took us to the tunnel under the race track. He shouted at us: "Hey! Hey! Gimme one o' them tires! I want one o' them tires!"

"Can't do it," one of the Smokin' Joe's crewmen with us yelled back. "Those're brand new tires!" The small boy, already carrying a cracked windshield almost bigger than he was, continued to shout at us, "Just one? Come on . . . . gimme one!" We picked up our speed a little bit, and managed to escape the persistent youngster's pleas for "just one" tire. As we approached the tunnel out of the infield, a golf cart being driven by one of the Budweiser crew suddenly appeared to my left near the window of the truck. The golf-cart driver motioned for us to let him in. Since Travis Carter's race team began as a sister team to the operations run by Junior Johnson, this was like letting an older sibling use the telephone before you. A gap opened between our pickup and the white Ford van—another Smokin' Joe's team vehicle—directly ahead of us. The golf cart dipped in between the two Fords, and seated on the back of it was Bill Elliott and his wife, Cindy.

Elliott and his wife were trying to get out of the facility as easily and quickly as possible. Many drivers have airplanes to catch, or fly themselves. Some drivers have appointments or engagements to get to, others are just anxious to get home and enjoy some peace and quiet. Elliott and his wife held on tight as the little golf cart bounced through the tunnel and emerged into a sea of fans all heading to their cars. We could hear the shouts of people as they realized it was Bill Elliott zooming past them on the back of a golf cart. Elliott waved to the crowds quickly, so as to not lose his grip on the cart. Had he fallen out, he would have been mobbed by passersby. We continued along behind, closing the gap between the Elliotts and our truck, hoping to break a hole past the fans and out toward the main road.

As we crawled along in post-race traffic, people continued to shout at us about the tires in the bed of the truck. NASCAR souvenirs are big business, especially used items like tires and sheet metal, and it was easy to see these were the real thing, given that three of the four men in the truck were wearing Smokin' Joe's uniforms and the truck had a No. 23 sticker in the rear window. The yelling and propositioning got to be a little much as we slowly worked our way toward open road. Once we cleared the traffic jam, it was clear driving back to Mooresville.

On the way home—after stopping for a quick snack and some more cold drinks—we discussed the day's events and the prospects for the next year. Winston Cup gossip gave way to Winston Cup strategy, and the Smokin' Joe's team was anxious to see Jimmy Spencer behind the wheel. It had been a long season, and a fresh start in 1995 seemed like the best medicine to ease the team's long slump. Spencer was hanging around the Smokin' Joe's car hauler before the start of the race, talking with Travis Carter and T. Wayne Robertson. The easiest way to try and improve a race team is to change drivers, and it looked like Stricklin would be looking for another ride.

Jimmy Spencer and Hut Stricklin are both still running the Winston Cup Series. Stricklin replaced Steve Kinser early during the 1995 season in the No. 26 Quaker State Ford Thunderbird owned by NHRA drag racing champion Kenny Bernstein. Stricklin then enjoyed a decent 1996 season in the No. 8 Stavola Brothers Ford, sponsored by Circuit City electronics stores. Jimmy Spencer, on the other hand, has driven the Smokin' Joe's Thunderbird since he joined the team in 1995.

Spencer, from Berwick, Pennsylvania, drove NASCAR Modifieds throughout the Northeast en route to the Busch Grand National and Winston Cup circuits. Like Brett Bodine, Spencer drove at Shangri-La Speedway in New York to earn "seat time," that all-important experience behind the wheel. He earned two Winston Cup victories in 1994 while driving Junior Johnson's McDonald's-sponsored Ford Thunderbirds. The wins came in the summer races at Daytona and Talladega. In 1996, Spencer enjoyed a good season, notching nine top ten finishes by the fall race at Rockingham. Despite the team's run of success, the Smokin' Joe's Ford had yet to win a race with Jimmy Spencer behind the wheel. By the time the Winston Cup Series swung back to Michigan International Speedway, Spencer was getting national attention for his solid race performances and consistent finishes.

To accentuate Jimmy Spencer's strong 1996 season, PASS Sports featured him as their special guest on *This Week in NASCAR,* a weekly live television program shot "on location" from a venue near that week's speedway. Spencer's visit was going to be televised at the Motorsports Hall of Fame and Museum in Novi, Michigan. Having a connection to the Hall of Fame and Museum, I volunteered to help with the broadcast. I was stationed in the museum's collection of race cars to keep people from interrupting the program as it took place.

About 20 minutes before the program went on the air, I saw Jimmy Spencer walking around the museum looking at the cars on display. It was Thursday evening. Spencer and the Smokin' Joe's team had spent the day at Michigan practicing, working on setups, and going through the first round of qualifying. As he moved through the museum, Spencer looked tired from his busy day. One of the production crew approached him with a microphone and battery pack, which were hooked to Spencer's shirt and blue jeans. All at once, the museum became very quiet. The program, hosted by Allen Bestwick, was moments away from beginning.

It would be a little while before Jimmy Spencer would be needed on stage, so he continued to tour the car collection. Sensing his nervousness, I shadowed Spencer in hopes of being able to make his pre-interview wait a little more relaxed. A replica of Henry Ford's 999 sat at one side of the museum's center display, and I launched into a brief lecture about the car's important role in automobile racing history. I spoke of Barney Oldfield, and how he made Henry Ford famous, and Spencer smiled and replied, "Barney Oldfield . . . I know that name. I've heard of him."

Then we got talking about the Northeast, and Spencer's past as a Modified driver. I mentioned seeing Jimmy drive at Shangri-La, and he smiled and admitted that the Modifieds were a great way to gain experience, and that the division's competition was always some of the best in the nation. We talked about his family's history in stock car racing, and the fact that I grew up about 20 miles from his hometown of Berwick, Pennsylvania. Spencer seemed surprised that he was talking to someone from back home, someone who had followed his career as he worked his way toward the Winston Cup Series. I asked him about Travis Carter and how everyone on the team was doing, and explained that I had been a guest of the team at Rockingham in 1994. Spencer said that all was going well, when a production assistant called the driver away for his television interview.

Once the show began, Spencer and Bestwick talked about the museum, his career, and the upcoming race at Michigan. It was interesting to watch the broadcast develop as the evening wore on. Fans from the speedway had driven to Novi to attend the show, and many of them stayed afterward to meet Spencer and get his autograph. As the crew dismantled the set, Allen Bestwick and I talked for a while following the broadcast. He proved to be just as amiable and open as Jimmy Spencer.

What this evening at the Motorsports Hall of Fame and Museum proved was that the life of a Winston Cup stock car driver is one of constant motion and attention to responsibilities. One day in the life of Jimmy Spencer, driver of the Smokin' Joe's No. 23 Ford Thunderbird, involved a variety of activities: from practicing and qualifying to doing television interviews and meeting with fans. Every one of these activities had a primary focus—promoting NASCAR, the Winston Cup Series, and the products of the R.J. Reynolds Tobacco Company. Whether he was wearing a firesuit and driving a stock car, or shaking hands and signing autographs, Spencer's day was spent in the public spotlight. As Spencer and the Smokin' Joe's public relations representative drove away from the Motorsports Hall of Fame and Museum that night, I could not help but think that the cycle would begin all over again the next morning, and the morning after that, and the morning after that. As the taillights of their Ford Taurus drifted off into the darkness, I wondered if Jimmy Spencer—or any of his NASCAR compatriates—would ever care to have it any other way.

While doing research in North Carolina, my wife, Bonnie, and I decided to drive out to Taylorsville, where Harry Gant, retired driver of the famous No. 33 Skoal Bandit Chevrolet, lives. We had met Harry Gant in 1987, after eating lunch at the steak house he owns there and visiting the Skoal team's race shop. On this trip, we met his two daughters who manage his fan club out of a small building near Harry's house. We also visited several memorabilia shops this time that did not exist in 1987. At one of the stores, the owner was telling a customer about a robbery that had occurred a few nights earlier. Apparently someone broke into a man's home and stole only his racing memorabilia collection, which was valued at close to $1,000. This seemed odd, but it proved how big and powerful the collecting business had become in just a few years.

Such artifacts constitute history in a physical form. Other elements of material culture allow for stock car racing to present itself as a type of living history. The restoration and display of race cars is one way that this happens. My friend, Alex Beam, of Davidson, North Carolina, is one such restorer and collector.

Alex and some of his fellow race car collectors were going to conduct an exhibition race at Cherokee Speedway, a half-mile high banked dirt oval located about 60 miles south of Charlotte in the town of Gaffney, South Carolina. These car collectors created the Southern Vintage Stock Car Racing Association, and they traveled to race tracks throughout the south to run one Saturday night a month during the racing season. Alex invited Bonnie and me to see him in Gaffney for the exhibition event.

The SVSCRA put their cars on display for the fans outside the main grandstand. All types of stock cars were represented, from a number of restored 1939 and 1940 Fords to an open-wheeled, winged dirt car from Georgia that ran during the 1950s and 1960s. These cars are truly living history, representing an era of American home-spun automotive technology. The vehicles are more than just machines driven by legendary men like Curtis Turner, Ned Jarrett, and Ralph Earnhardt. These cars are reminders of a simpler time in American motorsports, a time when hard work, sweat, and a seat-of-the-pants approach to engineering meant more than computer assisted designing and wind tunnels. Restoring race cars such as these teaches young fans about the sport's past, and allows older fans to relive a few of their own memories.

Cherokee Speedway reminded us of its racing history that evening once the late models took to the track for their feature event. As the cars began to line up, Bonnie and I noticed the spectators pulling shop glasses and swim goggles out of their purses and carry bags. We wondered about this, but it did not take long for us to figure out why they carried such things. Once the late models made their first pass through turn four and the green flag dropped, a cloud of thick red clay dust rose from the track and blanketed us for the next 25 laps. We went home, literally, as rednecks. For days afterward, we found red clay residue in places we never imagined possible.

Following our trip to Cherokee Speedway, I drove north from Statesville on I-77 to North Wilkesboro. North Wilkesboro is one of the most historic regions in the sport of stock car racing, the area where moonshine runners like Junior Johnson sharpened their driving skills against the federal agents who tried desperately to catch them. This area has kept the atmosphere of its past. You can almost feel the eyes of federal agents watching you from the woods. The roads are thin strips of asphalt running through the hills, winding along through the valleys. A trip through this region is an emotional—almost a spiritual—experience. History would come alive for me that rainy day. I was going to meet Junior Johnson, a fifty-race winner and the owner of two Winston Cup race cars. Johnson's shops, at that time, produced the Budweiser Ford Thunderbirds of Bill Elliott, and the Maxwell House Ford Thunderbirds driven by Sterling Marlin.

One of Alex Beam's fellow stock car collectors, Billy Biscoe, worked for Junior at his shops in Ronda, about 12 miles from North Wilkesboro. The shops were located in Ingle Hollow, which appeared—at first—to be little more than a dip in the road. A small sign greeted visitors at the bottom of the hollow. Behind the sign, which read "Junior Johnson and Associates," was a rather plain structure that housed a reception area and the teams' main offices.

After meeting Junior Johnson in the team's reception area, I entered the compound where his teams were unloading their car haulers and preparing for that weekend's race at Pocono. Junior's hunting dogs were running in and out of the workshops while the crews were finishing the cars that would compete that week. A family of race fans was touring the facilities and photographing each other next to the battle-scarred Ford Thunderbirds that ran in California. A relaxed and contented Junior Johnson roamed the compound, talking with crewmen and holding hounds for the visiting children to pet. The teams were also relaxed, despite the rushed schedule they were following. Their car haulers had just returned that morning from California, and they were to leave that evening for Pennsylvania, giving the teams just a few hours to unload, do inventory, and reload parts and tools for the next race. Even with this busy schedule, Billy Biscoe was still able to show me around the facilities.

Billy used to work for Richard Petty as part of his pit crew, but the rigors of constant traveling burned him out. He worked on Junior Johnson's permanent shop crew because it enabled him to stay home on race weekends and spend more time with his family. As a race car collector and restorer, Billy was enthusiastic about his work. He placed a top priority on accuracy in restoration, using original parts, when possible, and making sure that any reproduced parts meet all original specifications. Billy was proud of his work, and proud of his role within the NASCAR Winston Cup Series.

Billy gave me a private tour of the shops. He showed me a 1940 Ford coupe that sat behind the building where Bill Elliott's stock cars were kept. The coupe was painted black and apparently all original, as some of its body parts—like its running boards—were showing some age. I asked Billy the obvious question: was this a moonshiner's car? Billy told me to look underneath the rear axle. I did, and found two sets of leaf springs instead of just one. This car had been double-sprung, so it would ride level on town streets when it was loaded with moonshine. Billy then opened the trunk and showed me its false bottom, which would easily carry 70 or 80 quart jars of corn liquor. He then pulled up the back seat, which also had a false bottom for carrying jars. When fully loaded, this car could carry almost 200 mason jars of moonshine and still generate enough horsepower to outrun most federal agents. Here, again, was another example of an automobile as living history, albeit part of the outlaw past of the rural American South.

The 1940 Ford, according to Billy, was the car of choice for most moonshiners. This particular automobile at Junior's was owned by a local man who had about nine such cars and a shop full of other moonshine memorabilia. Billy said Junior often drove the Ford around Ronda on his days off. No one was sure if this particular coupe was one that Junior actually used to run moonshine, since most former bootleggers, according to Billy, are apprehensive to discuss the stereotyped romanticism of the "good" old days.

Billy then showed me the body and paint shop. He and some of the team's body men explained how wind tunnel testing is converted into physical developments on a stock car. They showed me how you can shape a car's sheet metal with body putty to recreate improved aerodynamics discovered during pre-season wind tunnel tests. Just by adding body putty in specific areas, like around the top of the front quarter panels where the windshield's posts meet the rest of the body, a team can reproduce the side force discovered in a wind tunnel to improve the car's stability at prolonged high speeds. I was amazed at how a dusty body shop in the hills of North Carolina could implement such "high tech" information generated by the Ford engineers in Michigan.

Billy said that Ford engineers called almost every day with new information they wanted to be tried on the race cars. Usually these ideas must be fine-tuned because the engineers do not have a real stock car at their disposal. What shows up on a computer screen and how it fits on a race car are, according to Billy, often two different things. Usually the shop crews have to suggest adjustments and/or changes because they know—just from hearing where the development is located—if the idea will not work. Because this happened on a regular basis, Junior Johnson developed a state-of-the-art machine shop. This shop had computer-operated equipment that could actually create any motor or suspension part from scratch. If any standard part needed to be modified or adjusted, the machine shop staff could customize the part to meet such demands. According to Billy, this machine shop was probably the best one of its kind on the Winston Cup circuit.

Billy then gave me a tour of the fabrication building, where the cars were actually built before specific engine and suspension components were added. The frames and roll cages were purchased in Charlotte already put together. This eliminated some work for the teams because, according to Billy, these parts were always the same for every stock car. The crew then installed a full-sized "dummy" engine, transmission, and rear end assembly to make sure the stock car had sufficient tolerances and was aligned properly. Then sheet metal was cut, shaped, and welded into place to form the basic body style. A fiberglass nose piece was added to finish the front, and the driver's seat was installed to determine comfort and alignment.

From there, Billy took me into the teams' dynamometer rooms. A standard dynamometer—used to test engines for horsepower and torque amounts—was already in place. A new dynamometer was in the process of being built with the cooperation of the Ford Motor Company. This new experimental dynamometer would be used to test a motor for its "rolling" capabilities, as would be found if the car were on a racetrack.

The new "dyno" was computerized and arranged with a cockpit, including an accelerator, brake and clutch pedals, and a four-speed gear shifter. The "dashboard," complete with all gauges, would monitor and record the engine's performance while at the car's rolling weight, or the amount of pressure exerted on an engine by a car as if under racing conditions. The rolling weight was created by a large stone wheel, resembling a millstone, located outside the building. The stone literally rolled, being suspended on an axle, and produced stress on the engine. This stress, and its effect on the engine, was measured by the computer and printed for engineers and mechanics to analyze. Once completed, it would be the most accurate way to test an engine's performance without the added expenses of testing at a racetrack. This kind of research, according to Billy, came from Detroit's revitalized interest in stock car racing and how it could improve standard passenger cars. Ford allowed Junior Johnson to test new innovations while creating an exciting marketing machine that was proven to increase sales.

Race shops like the ones discussed above are fascinating, and often ignored, reserves of material culture research. There is so much more to stock car racing—or any kind of motorsport, for that matter—than painting a number on the machine, pulling on a crash helmet, and heading for the starting line. In the early days of stock car racing, that was about the extent of race preparation. Today's race shops are less like garages and more like factories. A facility like that at Junior Johnson and Associates was capable of turning out virtually anything needed for a Winston Cup stock car. To do such work requires special equipment, like the rolling dynamometer mentioned earlier. Not only does this kind of machine demonstrate the advances of automotive technology, but it shows us just how far the sport of stock car racing has come in its 50-year history. The sport often associated with bootleggers and the rural South is now the sport of Detroit engineers and state-of-the-art computer science.

The best place to see NASCAR's move toward the 21st century is at Lakeside Industrial Park in Mooresville, North Carolina. Mooresville is known as "Race City, USA" because of its large concentration of Winston Cup and Busch Grand National shops. In addition, there are other racing-based enterprises like the North Carolina Auto Racing Hall of Fame, a growing museum, and Simpson World, a state-of-the-art gift shop. Lakeside is great for NASCAR tourists because everything is within walking distance. Some of the drivers whose shops are found in Lakeside include Ricky Rudd, Rusty Wallace, Jeff Burton, Robby Gordon, Bobby Hillin, Johnny Benson, Jr., Jeremy Mayfield, and Rick Mast. Many of the shops have viewing areas or tours available and are open year round.

Because of the large numbers of visitors NASCAR shops attract, some teams have developed their own museums, like those found at Petty Enterprises, Rick Hendrick Racing, and Darwal Racing. I visited the museums at Petty Enterprises and Darwal Racing, and was impressed with how these teams were able to encapsulate rich histories of racing in entertaining and educational ways.

We chose a rainy day to drive the 60 miles from Statesville to Level Cross. I was going to photograph the 1969 Ford Torino that Richard Petty drove to eight wins following his split that season from Plymouth. Alex Beam, my friend in Davidson, bought the car from Richard. He then loaned it back to Petty, so he could display it in his museum. The car is one of the most famous in NASCAR stock car racing history, especially considering the Petty family's ties to both Dodge and Plymouth over the years.

Richard's museum is well stocked with Plymouths and Dodges. The building is fairly small. Visitors to the museum may actually see Richard and his crew as they work in the race shop, depending on the day of the week. The day we visited the museum, we saw both Richard and his father, Lee, walking around the cars being maintained and repaired in the garages, which are inaccessible to the general public.

Darrell Waltrip's museum at his Darwal Racing shop is a showcase of a long and successful career in stock car racing. Various cars from throughout Darrell's career are on display, as are many awards, including his Winston Cup championship trophies and his Most Popular Driver award. From inside the display rooms, visitors are able to look into the race shop and watch the Darwal crew going about their work. In addition, there is a souvenir area where Darrell Waltrip and Western Auto memorabilia is sold. Darwal Racing is located near the Charlotte Motor Speedway.

The benchmark for speedways on today's Winston Cup schedule is the Charlotte Motor Speedway in North Carolina. It has become the centerpiece of the Winston Cup community, surrounded by the shops and businesses that thrive on this sport. Daytona Beach may be the home of NASCAR, but Charlotte is where many of the sport's participants go to work.

Charlotte Motor Speedway is a facility that blends everyday life with automobile racing and business. Luxury condominiums line the front straightaway of the track, and the Speedway Club, a restaurant noted for its style and elegance, sits high above the start/finish line. Offices are located within the main structure of the speedway's grandstands, and a bustling gift shop attracts customers every day of the week, whether there is racing going on or not. Two smaller racetracks are located on the speedway's grounds, and the CMS Industrial Park is located nearby.

In 1992, we went behind the speedway to the CMS Industrial Park, where racing teams have built facilities that measure 28,000 square feet and larger, and visited Bobby Allison Motorsports. This is the shop Bobby opened following his recovery from the 1988 accident at Pocono that ended his driving career. Here we received a warm and friendly welcome. The team's receptionist talked with us and took us on a private tour to see where their Raybestos Chevrolet Luminas were built and maintained.

The standard shop tour simply skirts the area where finished cars are prepared for races, but our tour included the engine assembly room, the dynamometer room, the fabrication shop (where we got to see a new Lumina being fitted with sheet metal), and the painting room (where another car was getting the team's colors). It was a testament to the level of professionalism and seriousness required of competitive Winston Cup teams. Another team located in the CMS Industrial Park is Geoff Bodine Racing, in what was Alan Kulwicki's facility when he won the 1992 Winston Cup championship. Bodine, who is sponsored by QVC, is building a museum and gift shop that will be open in the near future.

Future development of Charlotte Motor Speedway is currently being planned. A $640 million addition will be instituted around the speedway as part of a growth project called "Plan 2000." The first phase will involve the construction of a 197-acre golf club across from the speedway's location along Route 29. Some of the other features included in "Plan 2000" are "a hotel, exposition center, office buildings, and a light industrial complex" (Cooper 72). The speedway will also add 91,400 seats, raising its capacity to 205,333 spectators and making it one of America's largest racing facilities—second only to the Indianapolis Motor Speedway (Cooper 72). With added tourist traffic coming to the Charlotte area, provisions are constantly being added to meet the growing needs of the fans.

An expanding area of Winston Cup material culture is the growth of restaurants that exhibit a stock car motif. One of these restaurants—The Sagebrush—is located in Statesville, North Carolina, just off of Interstate 40. It is decorated with hoods, doors, and trunks from old stock cars, and the walls are covered with photographs of drivers. It has a honky-tonk atmosphere, yet it makes families feel right at home. Such a restaurant, and its unique decor, is pretty much like the typical "sports bar," only this particular business caters to the regional distinction of its sporting heritage. I visited a few restaurants like The Sagebrush during my travels throughout North Carolina.

On June 11, 1992, I met and had dinner with Deb Williams, who is now the editor of *Winston Cup Scene,* the largest weekly stock car racing publication in America. Deb has also covered stock car racing for *USA Today* when an event was large enough to warrant more than one writer.

Because I was going to meet Deb in Charlotte, we decided to have dinner at the Sandwich Construction Company, a popular racing restaurant down Route 29 from CMS. The place is decorated with all sorts of stock car memorabilia, most of which was donated by teams who eat there often. Menu items are starred to show which are the drivers' favorites, and several race teams are represented with a variety of autographed photographs. Because of its close proximity to Charlotte Motor Speedway, the Sandwich Construction Company is sometimes used as an informal setting for television broadcasts like mid-season reports and post-season reviews done by networks like ESPN.

The Sandwich Construction Company is now expanding its stock car-themed restaurants into new regions of the country. These new restaurants are called The Stock Car Cafe, and they—like the original Sandwich Construction Company—blend food and fun with a NASCAR motif. I visited the Stock Car Cafe in Cornelius, North Carolina, and found it to be a great atmosphere for racing fans looking for an informal night out on the town. Other Stock Car Cafes are located in Bristol, Tennessee, and Myrtle Beach, South Carolina. NASCAR is opening its own chain of restaurants as well. Called NASCAR Cafe, these eateries will feature a stock car decor with casual dining aimed toward race fans of all ages.

Another informal, yet racing-intensive, restaurant may be found in Hickory, near the community's famed racetrack of the same name. The restaurant is known as Montana's Steak House, and it is a combination of Swiss chalet, honky tonk, and race shop. What makes the Montana Steak House so interesting is its museum-like approach to the displaying of its artifacts. Each hood or bent quarter panel is labeled with the driver of the car from which it came. In some cases, the accident that caused the damage is given as a means of validation. Its atmosphere is pleasant and regional as certain booths have been "dedicated" to drivers, depicting them through the display of memorabilia from throughout their careers.

Such establishments as those discussed above focus on the remnants of stock cars much as a hunter would consider a trophy suitable for hanging as a decoration. In one sense, the bent and scarred hood from a Winston Cup race car is just that—a trophy to be displayed and admired. In another way, however, the crumpled pieces of sheet metal torn from wrecked race cars represent some other important issue within material culture. These pieces are symbolic of stock car racing and its role within the histories of these particular communities.

The ethnography of NASCAR is the ethnography of modern corporate America. To repeat Norman Denzin's definition of ethnography, it is the "study of lived experiences, involving description and interpretation." Based on my fieldwork, it was no surprise that so much of the foundation beneath the Winston Cup Series comes from the blending of professional sport and professional business. It would be foolish to try and separate corporate sponsorship from the sport of Winston Cup stock car racing. Whether a person visits racing museums, collects diecast cars, watches races, or eats supper at The Sagebrush, he or she will find constant reminders of the intimate relationship between corporate America and the NASCAR Winston Cup Series. It is worth repeating Neil Bonnett's adage that stock cars run on money; such an expensive fuel source is what keeps the Winston Cup Series and major corporations joined at the purse strings.

8

Is Bigger Always Better?
The Future of the NASCAR Winston Cup Series

The sport is flourishing and expanding by leaps and bounds. . . . It's a fan-driven sport, a money-driven sport, a corporate-driven sport, it's inevitable that these things are going to happen. . . . I don't like change myself . . . but this is the way life is, you have to go with it.
—Rick Mast, driver of the No. 75 Remington Arms Ford Thunderbird, on the rapid growth and evolution of the Winston Cup Series.

On Sunday, September 29, 1996, the NASCAR Winston Cup Series put into practice what had been speculated for months. Participants within the sport, members of the media, race promoters, speedway owners, and fans had been talking about this day with tones of optimism, sadness, anger, and foreboding. The future of Winston Cup racing was finally set into motion; the series' final event at North Wilkesboro Speedway in North Carolina was run that day, closing an important chapter in NASCAR's history.

North Wilkesboro began hosting races on May 16, 1947, when Fonty Flock won a Modified race in a car dubbed the Easter Egg, because of its purple paint job ("End of an Era"). NASCAR became part of North Wilkesboro history when Bob Flock beat Lee Petty by 100 yards on an October afternoon to win the first Strictly Stock race ever held at the facility (Fielden 1: 16). It was a track that bridged the gap in stock car racing's evolution—the arena where moonshiners became race car drivers. As North Wilkesboro's page in history turned, it marked yet another stage of the sport's evolution—the point when short tracks gave way to the larger, more recognized, and more lucrative superspeedways.

Tradition fell by the wayside as North Wilkesboro prepared for its final Winston Cup event. Many drivers had mixed feelings about the historic facility not being on the 1997 schedule. Former North Wilkesboro winner Geoff Bodine, owner and driver of the QVC Ford Thunderbird, remarked that he was "disappointed that this track isn't going to be on the schedule any longer . . . it's one the really neatest short tracks that we race on."

Dale Earnhardt, another winner at North Wilkesboro, put the schedule change in terms of stock car racing's business aspect, saying that many sponsors "put a lot of money into the sport, so we need to run a place where everybody can get in the show." Superspeedways, like the new tracks in California and Texas, make qualifying less of a gamble because their size makes larger fields possible. The bigger the track, the bigger the starting grid, and the more sponsors who get time in front of fans. NASCAR's growth, in the eyes of Dale Earnhardt, is smart business.

Kyle Petty, who—like Dale Earnhardt—is part of a racing family, commented on the role that North Wilkesboro played in his personal life, saying:

For me, I guess it's a double-edged sword. I hate to see it go because I've been coming here for so long with my father; I've seen him win a million races here. I've never been fortunate enough to win a race here myself. . . . This is one of the racetracks where I get to stay at home and sleep in my own bed at night and drive here [to the speedway].

Such freedom would disappear since the two new events replacing North Wilkesboro on the schedule would require increased travel time and expense.

Darrell Waltrip, a three-time Winston Cup champion and one of the longest running drivers currently campaigning in the series, saw the closing of North Wilkesboro in terms of attracting new attention to the sport. Prior to the race, Waltrip was quoted as saying:

We don't want to leave our roots behind. We don't want to forsake the people who helped us get where we are. But time marches on. We call it progress. That's what this is. It's the progress and growth of the sport. We have a lot of tracks—[North] Wilkesboro, Martinsville, Charlotte, Bristol [Tennessee], Rockingham—that are in the same market. This market is saturated with tracks. Forget growth. We need to diversify. We're racing within miles of each other every week right now. We're using the same fans week in and week out. We need to diversify for that reason alone and spread the sport out. We need to attract new fans, and also give the fans that are in this [mid-Atlantic] market a break. ("NASCAR Notes")

The Holly Farms 400 that day was typical of races at North Wilkesboro—close and explosive competition among 37 cars. The interval between the pole position to the final starter was only one quarter of a second. Packed grandstands (and millions of television viewers) watched with delight as Jeff Gordon battled against Dale Earnhardt, Jeff Burton, and Dale Jarrett for first place. The "two Dales" symbolized NASCAR's past and present, both men being talented second-generation drivers who grew up with the sport. The "two Jeffs" represented NASCAR's future; both drive for "superteams," the three-car operations becoming more common in Winston Cup racing.[1]

Jeff Gordon started the race from the outside of the front row and was leading the field by the end of the first lap. Gordon was being pursued by Bobby Hamilton in the No. 43 STP Pontiac owned by Richard Petty, the winningest driver in the history of the speedway—the new face of NASCAR being chased by a familiar car from the sport's past. This "changing of the guard" had been occurring for some time, since Jeff Gordon's emergence on the circuit as a driver to be reckoned with. What made this change so apparent during the final race at North Wilkesboro was the fact that Gordon was the defending Winston Cup champion, already a nine-time winner during the 1996 season, and the current leader in the points standings.

Just one week earlier, Jeff Gordon celebrated a win at Martinsville Speedway, where he defeated Terry Labonte, his teammate and the man running second in the points chase. Like a scene from a Zane Grey novel, Jeff Gordon—"The Kid"—was in a showdown with "Texas Terry" Labonte, a cool and collected driver from Corpus Christi. In Charlotte, one week after the race at North Wilkesboro, "Texas Terry" would gain the upper hand on "The Kid" by winning the UAW-GM Quality 500. Gordon would finish far behind Labonte in a race that would close the Winston Cup points chase down to a gap of just one point with three races to go. "Texas Terry" and "The Kid" were gunning toward Atlanta in November of 1996, where their final showdown would begin shortly after high noon.

The final showdown in 1996 would go to "Texas Terry" in an emotional 500-mile duel among the top five in points. Gordon, Jarrett, Mark Martin, and Dale Earnhardt would all take their shots at Labonte, but none would get close enough to knock the points leader off his pedestal. By the time the checkered flag flew at Atlanta, the Labonte brothers would be making victory laps before 140,000 screaming fans. Older brother Terry claimed the Winston Cup championship, younger brother Bobby won the NAPA 500 race, and two droughts came to an end. It had been 40 races since Bobby Labonte had won a Winston Cup race, and 12 years since Terry Labonte had earned a Winston Cup points title. "Man, it is great to go out a winner at last," Bobby Labonte said after the race, "this is the coolest thing I've ever done in my life" (qtd. in Waid, "Labontes").

For his work at Atlanta, Bobby Labonte would earn $274,000, including a $136,800 bonus from Unocal for winning from the pole (Waid, "Labontes"). Terry Labonte would make over $3.4 million for his work during the 1996 Winston Cup season—$1.5 million of that coming from Winston cigarettes in honor of winning the championship. As the two brothers from Texas circled the speedway in a side-by-side victory lap, it marked a significant moment in the evolution of the NASCAR Winston Cup Series. Here were two brothers at the peak of their success in an occupation based on acculturation and experience. Their two cars were indicative of the sport's changing influence: Bobby's carried the colors of Interstate Batteries, an aftermarket automotive parts supplier, while Terry's was bedecked in the bright graphics of Kellogg's Corn Flakes, a sponsor more at home in America's kitchens than America's garages and workshops. Most significant was what happened following the victory lap; Terry "The Iceman" Labonte sat quietly in his Chevrolet, his voice cracking with emotion as the "cool" customer was crowned a humble champion. The years of struggle, months of media attention, and days of pressure culminated in a moment of reflection and tears. From the last race at North Wilkesboro to the season finale at Atlanta, the end of the 1996 Winston Cup Series was symbolic of all that was happening to the sport of big-time stock car racing.

The final race at North Wilkesboro was a metaphor for all that is changing in the world of Winston Cup racing. Just as the moonshine cars of Wilkes County gave way to custom-built stock cars from nearby Mooresville and Charlotte, the rugged old short tracks gave way to newer, more profitable venues in Texas and New Hampshire. People raised in Wilkes County watched as their two Winston Cup races—part of their history, their community, and their economy—were sent to regions north and west. The last Sunday in September 1996 was bittersweet, even if the racing that day was exciting and all too familiar. As Wilkes County native Junior Johnson, who ran moonshine throughout the region and won races at the speedway, commented:

I think that this being the last race at North Wilkesboro is just absolutely a shame. You see a race track like that, that's probably the backbone of the whole sport being where it is today, going by the wayside, that's very sad. . . . It's sad it all has to come to an end. A lot of good, fond memories are going to die with it. ("End of an Era")

This statement indicates some of the concerns raised over expanding the length and the geographic focus of the NASCAR Winston Cup

Series. Time and money are two valuable commodities on the Winston Cup circuit, especially late in the midsummer stretch of continuous races. Being able to eat and sleep at your own home is a luxury most team members are unable to enjoy very often. When the series comes to a "local" track, like North Wilkesboro (which is only a 30-50 minute drive from most race shops), participants are able to spend some much-needed time at home with family. Adding a trip to Texas, and additional trips to New Hampshire and California will put pressure on an already stressful schedule for drivers, mechanics, and media people alike.

Increasing the travel load means increasing the financial load as well. Teams with Fortune 500-level sponsors will have little problem adding new airfares, lodging, and meals to their travel budgets. Teams with smaller sponsorship budgets might have a problem footing the bill for additional travel costs. Whereas North Wilkesboro could ease the financial pressure on a smaller team, going to Texas might keep that smaller team from trying to compete in the first place. Not making the trip means not making the field, and not making the field means not racing on national television where the sponsors get returns on their investments. North Wilkesboro's removal from the 1997 Winston Cup schedule was a sign that NASCAR racing's future was one of growth and change, not stability and security.

On the Wednesday prior to North Wilkesboro, Gordon was a guest on *Late Night with David Letterman*. It was the second appearance in less than a year for Gordon, who talked about crashing at Talladega with Ricky Craven, Mark Martin, and Ricky Rudd in a multicar wreck that left Craven injured for several weeks. The young driver traded quips with Letterman in a relaxed and articulate manner. Now, just four days later, Gordon was in the NASCAR record book as the last man to win at North Wilkesboro Speedway.

Gordon's appearances on network television, his Winston Cup championship, his dominance of the 1996 season, and his win at North Wilkesboro signaled NASCAR's giant step into the mainstream of professional sports. Gordon's victory in the final Winston Cup race at North Wilkesboro served as a means of putting NASCAR in a cultural context. The historic relevence of the past gave way to the promise of the future. As Jeff Gordon, Rick Hendrick, Ray Evernham, and all the "Rainbow Warriors" celebrated their 10th win of 1996, many of the fans who came to see the race stood quietly in the grandstands and infield, absorbing what was happening. From the perspective of a television viewer, the thousands assembled seemed to watch the celebration in Victory Lane with a sense of loss. Many stayed after the race ended, as though paying their last respects to the era that had just passed on.

The demise of Winston Cup racing at North Wilkesboro comes at the hands of a new facility: Texas Motor Speedway near the Dallas/Fort Worth area. This is a superspeedway built with spectators, television, and big money in mind. The birth and development of Texas Motor Speedway marks the next generation of NASCAR Winston Cup racing, an era in which the sport may rise above its past to meet the demands of its future—a new market west of the Mississippi River. These new venues—Texas, Las Vegas, and Los Angeles—are where Winston Cup racing is headed.

To meet the demands of new markets and an increase in new speedways, the Winston Cup Series is facing the possibility of expanding its already crowded schedule. A larger racing schedule is a NASCAR fan's dream come true, and it means more exposure for the sponsors involved with race teams. The problem is fitting more races into the regular Winston Cup season—a schedule that already has teams running for 14 consecutive weekends from mid-June until early October. To the drivers, a few more events mean more seat time, a few more days "at the office" where they can do what they like to do best. For the pit crews and mechanics, however, an increase in races represents a decrease in free time. As driver Rick Mast put it:

It bothers me in that the workers, the guys that prepare the cars, are really taxed to the limit right now, seven in the morning to seven at night and seven days a week. When you start adding more races it makes the work harder for the guys in the shop. From a driver's standpoint it really doesn't matter, we just show up and drive the cars. We have sponsor stuff but for the guys working on the cars, it's hard. There are just so many days in a week. ("Mast Chat Session")

Given the demands placed on teams by new racing markets, it seems inevitable that some kind of compromise will have to be made between speedway management and NASCAR.

But who will make the sacrifices needed to support a growing Winston Cup Series? Currently, 34 out of 52 weekends are being used for some form of Winston Cup event, either points-paying races, exhibition events like the Suzuka race in Japan, or special events like the Busch Clash (Berggren, "Winston Cup" 16). Might expanding the Winston Cup schedule mean dividing the series into two leagues like baseball does? How would such a split be made, and how would a national champion be determined in such a system? If the Winston Cup Series goes to 36 or 37 races a season, teams might consider doubling their shop staffs and pit crews to ease the strain on teams already trying to maintain cars for the current 32 race schedule. These possible compromises are just part of the solution, however, provided more speedways are not built or renovated for Winston Cup competition. The new facility in Las Vegas has a Busch Grand National date already scheduled, but what about future Winston Cup races at that track, and what about Quad-Cities International Raceway Park in Illinois—what if it wants one (or two) Winston Cup dates? Perhaps the best way to fit new markets into the Winston Cup Series is, as historian Bob Latford has suggested, to put races up for bid. In the words of Dick Berggren:

A higher purse and sanction fee would go a long ways [*sic*] toward sending dates to tracks. Each track that now gets any dates at all would continue to get one date under Latford's plan. Those bidding highest get a second date. Money bid and the nature of the event would both count. Bigger, higher paying and more spectacular would be better. ("Winston Cup" 28)

One of the biggest of these new racing markets is Asia. Prior to the 1995 awards banquet in New York City, NASCAR announced that it had arranged a schedule of three demonstration races to be held on a 1.4-mile road course in Suzuka, Japan. Held on November 24, 1996, the first event included an international field of competitors made up of drivers from the Winston Cup, Busch Grand National, Winston West, and Craftsman Truck divisions. In addition to the field of American drivers, four Japanese drivers were added to the roster to provide a regional connection. To prepare the Japanese drivers for their stock car debut, NASCAR held a special practice session at Watkins Glen under the direction of Winston Cup Director Gary Nelson, and another acclimation session at Charlotte as part of the Richard Petty Driving Experience.

Considering the way Japanese automobile makers took over the American market in the 1970s following the oil crises of 1972 and 1979, it seemed rather surprising that an all-American sport like Winston Cup racing would consider taking its show on the road to the Land of the Rising Sun. It was not that long ago that a friend of mine returned from a business trip to find a "Buy American!" note stuck under a windshield wiper of her Honda Accord as it sat in the long-term parking lot at Detroit Metro Airport. It was good to hear NASCAR President Bill France, Jr., speaking enthusiastically about the prospect of introducing Winston Cup racing to a vast new market, but what exactly was the new market being approached? Is it a new market of potential NASCAR fans, or is it a new market of potential R.J. Reynolds customers targeted in response to a crackdown on tobacco companies in America by the federal government?

The R.J. Reynolds Tobacco Company—like other tobacco firms—is quickly getting a foothold in the lucrative Asian cigarette market. Smoking is on the rise in Asia, and American tobacco companies like Philip Morris are discovering that "success in these countries has caused foreign profits to be up nearly 17 percent while the domestic American market fell by nearly half" (qtd. in Shenon). As cigarette sales drop in the United States because of a decrease in American smokers and an increase in health awareness, the cigarette market expands in Asia and taking NASCAR to Japan becomes a logical move. R.J. Reynolds can maintain its identity with NASCAR as stock car racing finds a legion of fans overseas; the sport's growing popularity will generate loyal Winston Cup followers who care more about sponsors and benefactors than about interfering government agencies. Just as RJR served as a connection between Southern culture and a national audience, the company is poised to connect American culture with an Asian audience fascinated by this truly American sport.

The 1996 NASCAR Winston Cup season included a renewed debate over the sport's connection with cigarette companies. President Clinton lashed out against the use of tobacco brands as sponsorship, especially as it affects children, when he approved regulations by the Food and Drug Administration (FDA) that recognized nicotine to be an addictive drug. President Clinton's approval gave the FDA "the authority to curb the sale and promotion of tobacco as part of a crackdown on teen-age smoking" ("Tobacco Sponsorship").

Specifics within the federal guidelines called for "no more brand-name sponsorship" of professional sports, and no further production or sale of "T-shirts and hats bearing cigarette brands or logos, what Health and Human Services Secretary Donna Shalala calls 'walking advertisements'" ("Tobacco Sponsorship"). Along with the ban in sponsorship, print advertisements in magazines would be limited to black and white, text-only displays. The backlash from the motorsports community (and primarily those in NASCAR) upon hearing these restrictions, was fast and furious.

NASCAR and the R.J. Reynolds Tobacco Company both issued public statements in response to the President's approval of the FDA guidelines. NASCAR found the move to be just like earlier debates over the same issue, when the federal government started targeting tobacco's involvement in sports. A legal response seemed to be in order, as NASCAR declared: "it appears to us that lawsuits filed last year by various advertising and tobacco interests will now move forward. With litigation, it is entirely possible that the courts may stay implementation of the regulations, pending judicial review. It looks like now it is in the hands of the courts" (qtd. in "Tobacco Sponsorship"). Given the federal government's intent to stop tobacco sponsorship, NASCAR braced itself for a long litigious battle. The only way to fight law was through the law.

From an economic standpoint, this issue between President Clinton, the FDA, the tobacco companies, and NASCAR is based on tens of millions of dollars—money spent on sponsorship, legislation, advertising, and time lost because of tobacco-related illnesses. The situation raises questions about taxes, special interest groups, and the fact that 1996 was a presidential election year.

Americans' distrust of bureaucracy and oppressive government is nothing new. This is what led to the American Revolution. It dates back to the days of the Whiskey Rebellion and it runs through the entire history of America. From Prohibition, to banning cigarette advertisements on television, to censorship of written or recorded material, and now to abortion rights—these have all been major issues concerning the involvement of big government. This emphasis on individual rights was what prompted moonshiners to make and sell their own corn liquor. Big government meant too many rules, too many taxes, and too much legislation affecting too many people.

At the core of the FDA/R.J. Reynolds/NASCAR controversy was the fact that tobacco companies were the sponsors involved. The emphasis was on children and the fact they were most likely to be affected by tobacco's involvement in sports. However, statistics show that "about 4% of the people watching Winston Cup on TV are 19 and younger. Which should kind of make you wonder, since there really aren't a lot of kids involved here [in Winston Cup racing], how the new rules eliminating tobacco's sponsorship of racing could have any impact at all" (Berggren, "Big Government" 115). Legislation was already in place to stop children from getting cigarettes and snuff. "There are already laws on the books . . . that prohibit the sale of tobacco to minors," Dick Berggren has written, "yet, the laws we already have are not enforced and as proof, the government's own statistics have it that 3,000 kids start smoking every day" ("Big Government" 16).

One of the attacks against R.J. Reynolds was directed at its Camel cigarettes brand, which used "Joe Camel," a cartoon character as a spokesman. It was targeted by former Surgeon General Joycelyn Elders—and other like-minded people—as a negative emblem capable of enticing adolescents into smoking. Travis Carter's Ford Thunderbirds carry the sponsorship of "Smokin' Joe's Racing," a fictional business representing the Camel brand. Many insiders believed that such a sponsorship arrangement would constitute a conflict of interest. Carter's team was announced on October 29, 1993, but it was not until January 19,

1994, that a public announcement had to be made to settle the rumors that were circulating concerning the team's financial backing. The primary concern, however, from the aspect of cultural significance, is not simply the rumored conflict of interest at R.J. Reynolds.

A larger, perhaps more socially directed issue, is the way in which the Camel sponsorship is presented to Winston Cup fans. The article heralding the new team stated that "the Carter/Stricklin car won't carry the Camel name on the hood and quarter panels. 'Smokin' Joe's Racing' will be the sponsor's identification" (Williams, "RJR"). Once again, the problem of adult-oriented products sponsoring a vehicle in America's most popular and well-attended division of automobile racing presented a concern.

When we first saw the race car in 1993, it was easy to overlook the corporate connection to Camel cigarettes. At a quick glance, one saw the "Smokin' Joe's" displayed prominently on the rear quarter panels of the Ford Thunderbird. A closer look, however, presented a more direct relationship between "Smokin' Joe" and the Camel brand. The "Smokin' Joe's Racing" found on the car's hood looked innocent. Closer examination revealed an image within the letters—specifically the letter "J" in "Joe's"—that resembled the profile of "Joe Camel" himself. Some corporate folklore gives a Freudian reading of the Camel character, stating that Joe's head and facial features were designed to subliminally represent a man's genitals. The image we saw on the car's hood, however, was not so profane or obvious. This image of Joe's head was merely a profile, complete with a lit cigarette sticking out of the "mouth."

A more obvious image connecting the car to Camel cigarettes was the silhouette of a small camel beneath the Ford logo at the front of the hood. Difficult to see because of its small size, the camel rode on the car's front bumper, placed between the small grilles that carry air through duct work to cool the front brakes. This sign was clearly tied to Camel cigarettes, but its size and location made it easy to ignore. If the car was sitting still and seen from the front, or being filmed by an in-car camera running immediately ahead of it on the racetrack, a viewer could see the image and recognize what it meant. Again, at a quick glance, the small camel was easy to overlook.

This paint scheme was shown in a pre-season advertising campaign, which promoted the team's competitive debut during "Speedweeks" at Daytona International Speedway in 1994. In the advertisement, the viewer saw the new stock car at speed, turning a corner on a fictional racetrack. Standing to the left side, near our line of sight, was the infamous "Joe Camel" cartoon character, dressed in a black leather jacket. Joe was wearing a white T-shirt, smoking a Camel cigarette, and pointing over his left shoulder at the oncoming race car. The viewer saw the front of the car, "Smokin' Joe's Racing" displayed on the hood. The advertisement's copy carried a large heading that read, "Daytona's Gonna Be Smokin'." Smaller sized copy down below the stock car read: "Forget horsepower. CAMELPOWER is here. Smokin' Joe's Racing Team is rolling out at the Daytona 500. So look for it. Because when this car hits the track, things are gonna be smokin'" (*Winston Cup Scene* 13 Jan. 1994: back page). Even though the race car had no direct reference to Camel on it, there were evident clues that connected Carter's car to its tobacco-based sponsor.

Since the team's competitive debut in 1994, the graphics on the No. 23 Thunderbird have changed. As of 1996, there was still no direct connection to Camel cigarettes per se, but the picture of a camel on the hood and rear quarter panels was still indicative of R.J. Reynolds' involvement. The camel now wears a checkered scarf, signifying its tie to racing, but the profile of Joe Camel has been completely removed. The small camel on the front of the car, near the Ford oval logo by the grill, is also gone. Lacking much in the way of written text, the Smokin' Joe's Thunderbird is predominately decorated with a simple camel sillouette and an attractive yellow, purple, and green color scheme. These changes were instituted to downplay the negative publicity of the "Joe Camel" controversy.[2]

So who should sponsor Winston Cup race teams given its new, more diverse audience? Country music acts like Diamond Rio and David Lee Murphy each sponsor cars that appeal to many of the NASCAR fans who enjoy country music. McDonald's, Burger King, and The Cartoon Network have special appeal to children. Prodigy online computer services and Hayes Modems capture the rapidly growing numbers of computer literate fans. Joe Gibbs Racing has NFL Properties as an associate sponsor on their No. 18 Interstate Batteries Pontiac, a package that attracts football fans. One of the most unusual Winston Cup sponsors to date combines qualities of all these aforementioned teams: fast food, computers, and football have one common denominator, and that is American colleges.

The university connection to Winston Cup racing originated with school programs pertaining to motorsports technology. Luzerne County Community College in Pennsylvania and Clemson University in South Carolina allow students to study chassis design, engine development, and motorsports engineering (Hembree, "Mousetrap" 27). The idea is for students to gain classroom training and hands-on experience and earn a degree in a form of motorsports technology that will land them a position with a racing team.

Princeton University took strides toward the NASCAR community when it invited Jeff Gordon and his crew chief, Ray Evernham, to talk with first-year engineering students about working and racing in the Winston Cup Series. Evernham addressed the human element in engineering, and was quoted as saying that

the dean wanted the class to understand that even though they were going into engineering, there's still a human element in everything they do. Racing is something that can motivate young people. Engineers are motivated by high performance. There's no better way to draw a comparison between the human element and engineering. You can engineer the whole car, and it still comes down to the human element. ("A Day in the Ivy League")

According to Evernham, about 90 percent of the people present had seen a NASCAR Winston Cup event, and many had interesting competition-based suggestions. Evernham, in a story released by Winston Cup Online, added:

they had a lot of questions about restrictor plate racing, and they really had a lot of good solutions. I was going to give them [NASCAR Winston Cup Director] Gary Nelson's [phone] number, but I didn't. . . . They suggested some gearing solutions and engine control systems, engine fuel management, electronic ignition management. . . . We had some good aerodynamic questions, questions about driving training, about computer stuff, materials used to build cars. Those are the guys who are going to build the future. It's pretty good to know they're race fans. ("A Day in the Ivy League")

The number of Winston Cup fans found on college campuses is often higher than people would think, mainly because they associate college sports with football. Football is a good way for universities to obtain national publicity, but the season offers limited visibility. From August through December, and through the beginning of January—if a school makes it to a New Year's bowl game—a university's football program can get attention from the media. What makes the NASCAR Winston Cup season so appealing is its longevity—from February through late November. Stock car teams occupy most of a calendar year, and their schedule takes them to all regions of the United States.

The length of the NASCAR Winston Cup schedule makes it a perfect promotional tool for universities, because not only are all of the races televised, but an active show car program can take the university's name to areas where there might not even be a speedway or a Winston Cup event. Corporate sponsors have utilized this exposure for years, but it has only been since the fall of 1996 that American colleges have picked up on the potential advantages of being associated with a NASCAR team.

The University of Nebraska was the first school to align itself with a Winston Cup race team. Signing on as the sponsor of Lake Speed's No. 9 Ford Thunderbird, Nebraska's name and school colors will be seen all across America on live national television over 32 times. The University of Nebraska's association with Speed and his car owner, Harry Melling, was instigated by funds donated by Trev Alberts, a former Nebraska player who now plays for the Indianapolis Colts. Having a donor like Alberts is crucial for a college thinking about the same kind of arrangement, because if people assume the university itself is spending funds on engines, pit crew expenses, and tires, other donors and alumni might have second thoughts about where their money is going.

The University of Nebraska program is externally funded. In addition to Albert's investment, additional money comes from Nebraska-based corporate sponsors. According to Gordon Grigg, who arranged Nebraska's deal with Melling's team, "The sponsorship will benefit three parts of the university—academic, athletic, and general scholarships. . . . There's a lot more involved than just the standard endorsement program" ("A Very Unusual Sponsorship"). Other racing team revenue, like money made from merchandising and souvenir sales, will go back into various areas of the school. A foundation named after Trev Alberts, for example, will get four percent of merchandise sales. The most significant benefit for the University of Nebraska is a promotional program that will generate almost year-round attention.

A marketing and promotional program with nearly constant exposure is already being examined by other colleges around the country. Grigg, who works for Empire Management Group, stated that a number of schools are seriously considering having their own Winston Cup race teams, including Clemson, Michigan, Colorado, Penn State, and the University of Tennessee ("A Very Unusual Sponsorship"). Schools like these attract students from all over America, so having a promotional program that automatically runs from Florida to California and from Texas to New Hampshire virtually guarantees contact with potential students, either through television, print media, or actual race attendance.

For college-bound NASCAR fans, seeing schools that are involved with Winston Cup racing might be enough to influence a student's decision about where to go for an education. A school with NASCAR ties might also inspire a student to work harder in order to become a part of that particular university. For students with no aspirations to attend college, a Winston Cup program just might be enough to change the student's mind and place him or her on a path to higher learning. A university like Clemson, with a strong commitment to engineering, might use its Winston Cup program as a means of giving students practical work experience. What better way to try automotive engineering than to work one summer or one semester with a NASCAR team?

An additional advantage to working through a university is access to computer equipment and such resources as the Internet, which was designed as a way for scholars to share research and information across the country and around the world. There are numerous NASCAR-related sites on the World Wide Web, including the official NASCAR web site, which provides up-to-the-minute news and event reports, and even supplies live qualifying coverage and chat sessions with drivers. There are also web sites for many Winston Cup sponsors and teams, as well as home pages for speedways and driver fan clubs.

Another use of the Internet in connection to the NASCAR Winston Cup Series is a more recent phenomenon involving interactive computer games. One of the hottest games among computer users is NASCAR Racing by Papyrus Design Group, Incorporated, which is part of Sierra On-Line Incorporated.[3] This game has spawned a subculture of virtual Winston Cup competitors who race on computer models of actual speedways from their own homes. Because of the game's popularity, the NASCAR Racing league, "an actual new division of NASCAR," has been organized for 1997. The league will have "online racers compete against other humans instead of the game's computer-simulated opponents" (Kanaley). What has made this game so popular is its detail. The game simulates television coverage by including in-car camera footage and instant replays of great passes or terrible wrecks. Pit stops are incorporated in the game, as are replicas of actual Winston Cup cars and drivers. You have the freedom to do anything a real stock car driver might do without the fear or potential of getting hurt. As Nim Cross, a 30-year-old virtual driver from York, Pennsylvania, explained in the *Philadelphia Inquirer,* "'I've found myself not breathing, shaking, all kinds of things. I have to remind myself to breathe, it's very intense'" (qtd. in Kanaley).

One of the reasons for the popularity of the computer game NASCAR Racing is that it provides users with a safe and affordable racing experience. Far from the speed and danger of real Winston Cup racing, the computer game allows people to take an active role in their fantasy of being a real NASCAR driver for a fraction of the cost. Whereas starting your own Winston Cup team can cost about $4 million (Shaw), the NASCAR Racing game costs only $60. There are other forms of NASCAR-type racing available, such as the popular arcade game Daytona USA by Sega, but it does not provide as much interaction as the computer game. The arcade game has a car the "driver" sits in with a steering wheel and a gearshift. There are no pit stops, and no adjustments of the car's chassis may be made. Even race lengths are limited; one "run" I made with Daytona USA lasted only eight laps around a rather generic-looking speedway, unlike the highly detailed tracks based on actual Winston Cup venues found in NASCAR Racing.

Involvement is a central part of the NASCAR Winston Cup Series, whether you are a driver trying to win the points championship, a mechanic hoping to become a crew chief, or a fan just wanting to live in the NASCAR environment. Notice fans in the garage area or on pit road following a race. Many wear clothing decorated with the car, the name, or the sponsor of their favorite driver. Some are wearing matching caps or jackets, but all are drifting around looking for action: a driver signing autographs, a team loading its car hauler, a particular car at the Unocal gas pumps, something that fits their location and their connection to the sport. Watch post-race interviews with drivers and crew chiefs, and notice the behavior of fans standing in the background. To the average viewer, these people may come across as obnoxious. They will often stand directly behind the person being interviewed, making sure they are clearly seen by the camera's lens.

After the AC-Delco 400 at Rockingham in 1996, a post-race interview with Bobby Hamilton was backdropped by a young man in a Dick Trickle T-shirt and a Ford Quality Care Racing cap. As Hamilton was interviewed by Glenn Jarrett of The Nashville Network, the bedecked young man moved into camera range and pointed at his cap. When the camera moved in to a closeup of Hamilton, the young man removed his cap and thrust it once again into the camera's view. From a cultural perspective, this person's actions are less obtrusive than they seem. He is merely trying to be a part of the NASCAR environment by showing his allegiance to Ford, Dale Jarrett, and Dick Trickle. The young man is playing a role; he is no longer a passive fan in the stands, but an active participant in the center of the excitement. By drawing attention to himself, the young man draws attention to an assumed position of status.

Such is true for the men and women who run Winston Cup races on their home computers. It is not enough to simply enjoy the game of NASCAR Racing; it becomes more meaningful to actually compete against other individuals. Instead of living vicariously through the drivers and teams racing for real, it becomes more important to live the experience yourself; it is a matter of status. This intensifies the experience by making you feel connected, as if you really were a driver or a team member living and working within the NASCAR community.

The need to feel connected, the need to actually live as a part of the Winston Cup environment, is apparent in NASCAR's newest marketing strategy. During the fall of 1996, NASCAR announced its entry into the aftermarket automobile parts business. Given the respect that automobile enthusiasts have for the NASCAR name, and considering that parts used by stock car teams are largely based on production-type parts used on street-driven cars, making a line of NASCAR-brand parts and fluids capitalizes on the need to use what the professionals use and endorse.

NASCAR's reputation for being "a driving force in quality and performance" is one that fosters faith in motorists and racing fans alike ("NASCAR Set to Drive"). The connection between NASCAR and parts for production-type automobiles draws on the idea of stock cars being "stock," as they were in the early days of the sport. Just as Hudson, Chevrolet, and Ford turned on-track victories into off-track sales, the firms allied with NASCAR's aftermarket program are hoping to ride on the sport's coattails and find a consumer audience that identifies with the Winston Cup Series and its participants.

According to George Pyne, NASCAR's vice president of licensing and merchandising, "More than seventy percent of NASCAR fans say they are loyal to sponsors. . . . We are working with the automotive aftermarket to bring NASCAR fans and other aftermarket customers high quality products while providing innovative marketing opportunities for the manufacturers and retailers" ("NASCAR Set to Drive"). These "innovative marketing opportunities" work on the relationship between regular motorists and their Winston Cup heroes. The thing that connects racers and their fans is the fact that all automobiles—whether they negotiate turnpikes or Talladega—use oil filters, ignition parts, brake pads, and motor oil.

Because of this direct connection, the relationship between NASCAR teams and NASCAR fans narrows greatly; the motor oil used by Robert Yates the car owner is now the same motor oil used by Roberta Yates the third-grade school teacher. This kind of a marketing approach is nothing new. Auto suppliers have been using such advertising for years—just recall the years when STP was "The Racer's Edge." What has changed is that now NASCAR has put its seal of approval on standard aftermarket products. The parts once endorsed by drivers or teams are now directly endorsed by the sanctioning body itself. This, in a way, makes the automobile enthusiast a participant in the world of Winston Cup racing.

This need to belong, to share a common understanding and bond with Winston Cup participants is what makes fans so loyal to the sport. Unlike other professional athletes, NASCAR drivers and mechanics are usually very open and accessible. By allowing fans behind the scenes and exposing them to the sport through a variety of mediums, people develop a familiarity with it which often leads them to believe that racing is easier than it seems. Tom Cruise, who was intrigued by the sport after filming *Days of Thunder,* pursued the thought of having a car built for him to drive in the Daytona 500, to which the late Harry Hyde responded "Hell no!" (qtd. in Hager 52). It is one thing to have the money and desire to race a Winston Cup stock car; it is another to have the skill and experience necessary to do it. Because of this, a series of driving schools have opened to properly and safely introduce people to the Winston Cup experience. A few hundred dollars and a couple of days can allow a race fan to "really feel the power and speed that has made Winston Cup racing the most popular form of racing in the world" (Richard Petty Driving Experience pamphlet).

The Fast Track High Performance Driving School lets students drive or ride around speedways like Charlotte, Atlanta, and Bristol, while the Richard Petty Driving Experience allows students to run a Winston Cup stock car at either Charlotte, Atlanta, or Las Vegas. These schools do more than teach people how to drive Winston Cup stock cars on actual speedways; they are a means by which fans can challenge themselves to unknown limits and excitement, leaving them with a much better appreciation of what drivers actually go through on Sunday afternoons, and allowing Winston Cup fans to bridge the gap between participant and spectator.

Ironically, despite NASCAR's dedication to keeping racing affordable, the sport has still left most Winston Cup hopefuls on the outside looking in. Unlike the early days of NASCAR, when a showroom model car could be driven in Strictly Stock events, today's Winston Cup "wannabes" find themselves priced out of competition. The economics of big time racing have impacted lower levels of regional and local competition as well, making it difficult for the average race fan to try his hand at the sport. To meet the demands of frustrated stock car drivers, two forms of race cars have been designed to make stock car racing available to enthusiasts on limited budgets.

These two divisions, the Legends Cars and the Legacy Cars, offer actual racing experiences in relatively controlled and safe environments. The Legends Cars, built by 600 Racing, Incorporated, of the Charlotte Motor Speedway, use 1200 cc Yamaha FJ motorcycle engines, Toyota rear ends, and fiberglass bodies shaped like "the great Modifieds driven by the sport's earliest stars during the formative years of NASCAR" (promotional brochure). These bodies are shaped like Fords and Chevrolets from the late 1930s and early 1940s. This is a 5/8-scale car that offers "anyone the thrill of big time professional auto racing on a hobby-ists's budget." The main feature of these cars is their NASCAR-like dedication to standardization. A company pamphlet reads:

. . . all Legends Cars are built to identical specifications and all cars are to remain that way. A strict rulebook and thorough technical inspections are the ways that SPEC CAR (national sanctioning body for Legends Cars) can keep the cost of racing to a bare minimum. Winning comes down to driver ability rather than the size of his of her wallet.

This is the fundamental ideology behind NASCAR Winston Cup racing. By keeping the rules tight and the cars standardized, the emphasis of competition shifts from high dollar technology to culturally significant qualities like hard work, dedication, and old-fashioned resourcefulness. The key to the Legends Cars, according to a promotional brochure, is "minimal maintenance, maximum thrills, pleasure, and enjoyment," something a fan wants from stock car racing without the years of personal and financial sacrifice.

The Legends Cars have recently been challenged by a new form of affordable racing out of Salisbury, North Carolina. Allison Brothers Race Cars, Incorporated, are now constructing what they call Legacy Cars, which resemble the Legends Cars in size but more closely resemble Winston Cup cars in shape. Legacy Cars utilize a 2000 cc Mazda engine, a quick change rear end, and an adjustable front end suspension. This hardware is wrapped in a fiberglass body that is shaped like a 1996 Ford Thunderbird or Chevrolet Monte Carlo. I first saw one of these cars at Larry Hedrick's race shop in Statesville during the summer of 1996. Hedrick was taking delivery of two Legacy Cars for him and his driver at the time, Ricky Craven, to race for fun. These cars are a true legacy of NASCAR stock cars since they are manufactured by Donnie Allison's sons. Donnie (the brother of Bobby Allison) is a former NASCAR driver who was named Rookie of the Year in 1967 and won 10 Winston Cup events during his career.

The Legends Cars and the Legacy Cars do more, however, than resemble the past and present of NASCAR. These cars reaffirm the two predominant images of NASCAR and its cultural significance. The Legends Cars remind us of NASCAR's "good ol' days," when bootleggers became stock car drivers and were transformed into national heroes. A Legend Car can be ordered in the shape of a 1937 Chevrolet Coupe or a 1940 Ford Coupe, cars that were revered for their moonshine-hauling abilities. NASCAR's current image is that of the Winston Cup Series and its brutish yet sleek machines. The Legacy Cars remind us about what

NASCAR is today, the hand-built racers that look "stock" but are not. These opposite images—the moonshiner's Modified and the aerodynamic Cup car—are how American culture perceives the NASCAR Winston Cup Series.

The NASCAR Winston Cup Series is a complex sport. It is more than just "good ol' boys" in hopped-up cars tearing around in circles for hours on a hot Southern Sunday afternoon, as has been the popular perception of the sport. A detailed examination of the Winston Cup Series teaches us that there is more to the sport than meets the eye. Since its origin in 1947, NASCAR has created a professional sport that addresses significant social concerns. Like cars lined up two-by-two on a starting grid, the NASCAR Winston Cup Series involves money and power, heroes and villains, technology and television, rituals and symbols, and fact and fiction. It is a sport of rich history and meaning. The culture at the center of the Winston Cup Series is American culture. It embodies the traits and qualities that are essential to what we know as the American character: individualism, self-reliance, dedication to community, hard work, and common faith. NASCAR racing is essentially an all-American sport, from the cars and the drivers to the fans in the stands. From the patriotic rituals to the competition on the track, the Winston Cup Series celebrates the spirit of America.

Part of this American spirit comes from our ancestral restlessness and a constant need for challenge. The settling of the frontier reflected our addiction to mobility and expansion, as does our exploration of outer space. The advent of the automobile facilitated this addiction, carrying us toward the future in the name of progress. This is what drives race teams to continually push for faster cars and better lap times, for pole positions and championship trophies. It is also what compels corporate America to spend millions of dollars a year on sponsorship, marketing, and promotion. Expansion is part of our nature as Americans. Therefore, it is an expected and essential part of NASCAR's future. To expect anything less is to deny the hard work of those who have made stock car racing what it is today.

History has taught us, however, that bigger is not always better. When dealing with the unknown, there is always the possibility of failure. By NASCAR and Madison Avenue increasing the quantity of races, money, and responsibilities, we do not want to lose touch with the quality of the sport—its dedication to professionalism, safety, and exciting competition. Above all, NASCAR must not lose touch with its fans, the people who attend the races, buy the souvenirs, and support the race teams' sponsors. Fans already spend upwards of $60 per person for a day at the races. They count on the accessibility of drivers, not just at the speedway but at their local grocery stores or shopping malls. Let the NASCAR Winston Cup Series and its participants develop an attitude, and watch the fans walk away feeling betrayed. Fans are already buying "preferred seat licenses" at the new Texas Motor Speedway that allow spectators to have permanent rights to the seats they wish to purchase tickets for—over and above the price of the actual seats themselves (Ballard, "Bruton Smith"). Roger Penske is doing the same thing for his brand new speedway near Los Angeles ("Penske Announces"). The question looms large before us, however: how much is too much? How many added expenses can fans afford to pay? NASCAR makes efforts to keep costs low for its competitors, but what about the costs for those who buy the tickets, souvenirs, and sponsors' products? Only the future will answer these questions.

NASCAR Winston Cup racing is a sport that may be interpreted on two distinct levels: tangible and intangible. A demonstration race in Japan is tangible, the future of the sport is not. In writing this book, it was my goal to study the cultural significance of the Winston Cup Series and to inform people about a sport long ignored and stereotyped. What I found was a professional sport emerging as an important part of our national consciousness. It is a sport that has been embraced by the media and by corporate America, accepted and recognized by both as a reflection of American culture and a reaffirmation of the vital relationship between athletics and big business. This relationship is always changing and although it will be difficult to keep up with the pace of progress, I will continue my study of NASCAR and its growth with hopes to further analyze its effect on our culture. This book is but one lap completed in a very long race; I can only hope to keep my foot on the floor and continue moving ahead.

Appendix A
1997 Winston Cup Schedule

Date	Track	Event
Feb. 9	Daytona	Busch Clash*
Feb. 16	Daytona	Daytona 500
Feb. 23	Rockingham	GM Goodwrench 400
Mar. 2	Richmond	Pontiac Excitement 400
Mar. 9	Atlanta	Primestar 500
Mar. 23	Darlington	TranSouth 400
Apr. 6	Texas	Texas 500
Apr. 13	Bristol	Food City 500
Apr. 20	Martinsville	Goody's 500
Apr. 27	Talladega	Winston Select 500
May 4	Sears Point	Save Mart Supermarkets 300
May 17	Charlotte	The Winston Select*
May 25	Charlotte	Coca-Cola 600
June 1	Dover	Miller 500
June 8	Pocono	Pocono 500
June 15	Michigan	Miller 400
June 22	California	California 500
July 5	Daytona	Pepsi 400
July 13	New Hampshire	Jiffy Lube 300
July 20	Pocono	Pennsylvania 500
Aug. 2	Indianapolis	Brickyard 400
Aug. 10	Watkins Glen	Bud at the Glen
Aug. 17	Michigan	ITW Devilbiss 400
Aug. 23	Bristol	Goody's 500
Aug. 31	Darlington	Mountain Dew Southern 500
Sep. 6	Richmond	Miller 400
Sep. 14	New Hampshire	New England 300
Sep. 21	Dover Downs	MBNA 400
Sep. 28	Martinsville	Hanes 500
Oct. 5	Charlotte	UAW-GM Quality 500
Oct. 12	Talladega	DieHard 500
Oct. 26	Rockingham	AC Delco 500
Nov. 2	Phoenix	Dura Lube 500
Nov. 16	Atlanta	NAPA 500
Nov. 23	Japan	Exhibition Race*

* Non-Points race
From Speedworld, 13 Nov. 1996
Available: http://www.speedworld.net

Appendix B

Winston Cup Race Tracks and Locations

Atlanta Motor Speedway
U.S. Highway 19 & 41
Hampton, GA 30228
1.522 mile oval
(1.54 miles by Fall of 1997)

Bristol International Raceway
2801 P.O. Box 3966 Highway 11 E
Bristol, TN 37625
0.533 mile oval

Charlotte Motor Speedway
Highway 29 North & Morehead Rd.
Concord, NC 28025
1.5 mile oval

Darlington Raceway
1301 Harry Byrd Highway
(Highway 151-34)
Darlington, SC 29532
1.366 mile egg-shaped oval

Daytona International Speedway
1801 W. International Speedway Blvd.
Daytona Beach, FL 32114-1243
2.5 mile tri-oval

Dover Downs International Speedway
1131 North DuPont Highway
Dover, DE 19901
1 mile oval

Indianapolis Motor Speedway
4790 W. 16th Street
Indianapolis, IN 46222
2.5 mile oval

Martinsville Speedway
Speedway Road, U.S. 200 South
Martinsville, VA 24112
0.526 mile oval

Michigan Speedway
12626 U.S. 12
Brooklyn, MI 49230-9068
2 mile oval

New Hampshire International Speedway
Route 106
Louden, NH 03301
1.058 mile oval

North Carolina Motor Speedway
US Highway 1 North
Rockingham, NC 28379
1.017 mile oval

North Wilkesboro Speedway
381 Speedway Lane
North Wilkesboro, NC 28659
.625 mile oval

Phoenix International Raceway
7602 South 115th Ave.
Avondale, AZ 85323
1 mile oval

Pocono Raceway
Long Pond Road
Long Pond, PA 18334
2.5 mile tri-oval

Richmond International Raceway
602 East Laburnam Avenue
Richmond, VA 23222
.750 mile D-shaped oval

Sears Point Raceway
Highways 37 & 121
Sonoma, CA 95476
2.5 mile road course

Talledega Superspeedway
3366 Speedway Boulevard
Talledega, AL 35160
2.66 mile tri-oval

Watkins Glen International
500 Country Route 16
Watkins Glen, NY 14891
2.45 mile road course

New Tracks
Texas Motor Speedway
2421 Westport Pkwy, Suite 500
Fort Worth, TX 76177
1.5 mile oval

California Speedway
9300 Cherry Ave.
Fontana, CA 92335
2 mile tri-oval

Las Vegas Motor Speedway:
7000 Las Vegas Blvd.
Las Vegas, NV 89115
1.5 mile oval

Quad-Cities International Raceway Park:
P.O. Box 477
East Moline, IL 61244
1.5 mile D-shaped oval

Appendix C

1997 NASCAR Winston Cup Team Listing

# Driver	Sponsor	Make	Team/Owner
1. Morgan Shepherd	Delco Remy	Pontiac	Richard Jackson
2. Rusty Wallace	Miller Lite	Ford	Penske Racing
3. Dale Earnhardt	GM Goodwrench Service	Chevrolet	RCR
4. Sterling Marlin	Kodak Film	Chevrolet	Morgan-McClure
5. Terry Labonte	Kellogg's Corn Flakes	Chevrolet	Hendrick Mtsp.
6. Mark Martin	Valvoline	Ford	Roush Racing
7. Geoff Bodine	QVC Network	Ford	Bodine Racing
8. Hut Stricklin	Circuit City	Ford	Stavola Bros.
9. Lake Speed	Univ. of Nebraska	Ford	Melling Racing
10. Ricky Rudd	Tide	Ford	RPM
11. Brett Bodine	Frontier/Catalyst Comm.	Ford	BDR
12. ?	?	Ford	Bobby Allison
15. Larry Pearson	?	Ford	Bud Moore Eng.
16. Ted Musgrave	Family Channel/Primestar	Ford	Roush Racing
17. Darrell Waltrip	Parts America	Chevrolet	DarWal, Inc.
18. Bobby Labonte	Interstate	Pontiac	Joe Gibbs Racing
19. Gary Bradberry	HealthSource	Ford	Tri-Star
20. Greg Sacks	Hardee's	Ford	Ranier/Walsh
21. Michael Waltrip	Citgo	Ford	Wood Brothers
22. Ward Burton	MBNA America	Pontiac	Bill Davis
23. Jimmy Spencer	Smokin' Joes	Ford	Travis Carter
24. Jeff Gordon	DuPont	Chevrolet	Hendrick Mtsp.
25. Ricky Craven	Budweiser	Chevrolet	Hendrick Mtsp.
27. Elton Sawyer	?	Ford	David Blair
28. Ernie Irvan	Texaco/Havoline	Ford	Yates Racing
29. Robert Pressley	Cartoon Network	Chevrolet	Diamond Ridge
30. Johnny Benson	Pennzoil	Pontiac	Bahari' Racing
31. Mike Skinner	Lowe's Home Improve.	Chevrolet	RCR Enterprises
33. Ken Schrader	Skoal	Chevrolet	Andy Petree
36. Derrike Cope	Skittles	Pontiac	Nelson Bowers

37. Jeremy Mayfield	RC Cola/K-Mart	Ford	Kranefuss-Haas
40. Robby Gordon	Coors Light	Chevrolet	SABCO
41. Steve Grissom	Kodiak	Chevrolet	Hedrick Racing
42. Joe Nemechek	Bell South Mobility	Chevrolet	SABCO
43. Bobby Hamilton	STP	Pontiac	Petty Ent.
44. Kyle Petty	Hot Wheels	Pontiac	Petty Ent. 2
46. Wally Dallenbach	First Union	Chevrolet	SABCO
71. Dave Marcis	Realtree	Chevrolet	Marcis Racing
75. Rick Mast	Remington Arms	Ford	Mock Motorsports
77. Bobby Hillin	Jasper/Federal Mogul	Ford	Jasper Mtsp.
78. Billy Standridge	MCA/Diamond Rio	Chevrolet	Standridge Mtsp.
81. Kenny Wallace	Square D	Ford	Filmar Racing
88. Dale Jarrett	Ford Quality Care	Ford	Yates Racing
90. Dick Trickle	Heilig-Meyers	Ford	Junie Donleavy
91. Mike Wallace	Spam	Chevrolet	Pro-Tech
94. Bill Elliott	McDonald's	Ford	Elliott Racing
96. David Green	Caterpillar	Chevrolet	McCall Racing
97. Chad Little	John Deere	Pontiac	RYP Racing
98. John Andretti	RCA	Ford	Cale Yarborough
99. Jeff Burton	Exide Batteries	Ford	Roush Racing

From Speedworld, 13 Nov. 1996
Available: http://www.speedworld.net

Appendix D

NASCAR Winston Cup Champions
1949-1996

1949	Red Byron	1973	Benny Parsons
1950	Bill Rexford	1974	Richard Petty
1951	Herb Thomas	1975	Richard Petty
1952	Tim Flock	1976	Cale Yarborough
1953	Herb Thomas	1977	Cale Yarborough
1954	Lee Petty	1978	Cale Yarborough
1955	Tim Flock	1979	Richard Petty
1956	Buck Baker	1980	Dale Earnhardt
1957	Buck Baker	1981	Darrell Waltrip
1958	Lee Petty	1982	Darrell Waltrip
1959	Lee Petty	1983	Bobby Allison
1960	Rex White	1984	Terry Labonte
1961	Ned Jarrett	1985	Darrell Waltrip
1962	Joe Weatherly	1986	Dale Earnhardt
1963	Joe Weatherly	1987	Dale Earnhardt
1964	Richard Petty	1988	Bill Elliott
1965	Ned Jarrett	1989	Rusty Wallace
1966	David Pearson	1990	Dale Earnhardt
1967	Richard Petty	1991	Dale Earnhardt
1968	David Pearson	1992	Alan Kulwicki
1969	David Pearson	1993	Dale Earnhardt
1970	Bobby Isaac	1994	Dale Earnhardt
1971	Richard Petty*	1995	Jeff Gordon
1972	Richard Petty	1996	Terry Labonte

* Denotes the first year of R.J. Reynolds' involvement and the beginning of the Winston Cup championship. Prior winners were known as Grand National Champions.

Source: *The Official NASCAR 1996 Preview and Press Guide.*

Appendix E

Manufacturers' Champions
1949-1996

1949	Oldsmobile	1973	Mercury
1950	Oldsmobile	1974	Chevrolet
1951	Oldsmobile	1975	Dodge
1952	Hudson	1976	Chevrolet
1953	Hudson	1977	Chevrolet
1954	Hudson	1978	Oldsmobile
1955	Chrysler	1979	Chevrolet
1956	Chrysler	1980	Chevrolet
1957	Ford	1981	Buick
1958	Chevrolet	1982	Buick
1959	Chevrolet	1983	Chevrolet
1960	Ford	1984	Chevrolet
1961	Pontiac	1985	tie: Ford and Chevrolet
1962	Pontiac	1986	Chevrolet
1963	Ford	1987	Chevrolet
1964	Ford	1988	Ford
1965	Ford	1989	Chevrolet
1966	Dodge	1990	Chevrolet
1967	Plymouth	1991	Chevrolet
1968	Ford	1992	Ford
1969	Ford	1993	Pontiac
1970	Plymouth	1994	Ford
1971	Plymouth	1995	Chevrolet
1972	Chevrolet	1996	Chevrolet

Source: *The Official NASCAR 1996 Preview and Press Guide*

Appendix F

Outstanding NASCAR Winston Cup Career Victories

Former Drivers

Driver	No. of Victories in Career
Richard Petty	200
David Pearson	105
Bobby Allison	84
Cale Yarborough	83
Lee Petty	54
Ned Jarrett	50
Junior Johnson	50
Tim Flock	40
Fireball Roberts	32 *
Fred Lorenzen	26
Benny Parsons	21
Davey Allison	19 *
Buddy Baker	19
Neil Bonnett	18 *
Harry Gant	18
Curtis Turner	17 *
Tim Richmond	13 *
A.J. Foyt	7
Alan Kulwicki	5 *
Bob Flock	4 *
Parnelli Jones	4
Elmo Langley	2 *
Mario Andretti	1
Johnny Rutherford	1
Wendell Scott	1 *

Current Drivers

Darrell Waltrip	84
Dale Earnhardt	70
Rusty Wallace	47
Bill Elliott	40
Jeff Gordon	21
Mark Martin	18

Geoff Bodine	18
Terry Labonte	18
Ricky Rudd	17
Ernie Irvan	14
Kyle Petty	8
Dale Jarrett	8
Sterling Marlin	6
Dave Marcis	5
Ken Schrader	4
Morgan Shepherd	4
Bobby Labonte	4
Derrike Cope	2
Jimmy Spencer	2
Brett Bodine	1
Ward Burton	1
Bobby Hillin, Jr.	1
Phil Parsons	1
Jody Ridley	1
Greg Sacks	1
Lake Speed	1
Bobby Hamilton	1

* = deceased

Source: *The Official NASCAR 1996 Preview and Press Guide* (updated through March 3, 1997).

Appendix G

NASCAR Winston Cup Series'
Most Popular Drivers

This annual award, sponsored by the National Motorsports Press Association, is voted on by the fans. Starting in 1995, a 900 telephone number was used to tally votes.

1956	Curtis Turner	1977	Richard Petty
1957	Glenn "Fireball" Roberts	1978	Richard Petty
1958	Glen Wood	1979	David Pearson
1959	Junior Johnson	1980	Bobby Allison
1960	Rex White	1981	Bobby Allison
1961	Joe Weatherly	1982	Bobby Allison
1962	Richard Petty	1983	Bobby Allison
1963	Fred Lorenzen	1984	Bill Elliott
1964	Richard Petty	1985	Bill Elliott
1965	Fred Lorenzen	1986	Bill Elliott
1966	Darel Dieringer	1987	Bill Elliott
1967	Cale Yarborough	1988	Bill Elliott
1968	Richard Petty	1989	Darrell Waltrip
1969	Bobby Isaac	1990	Darrell Waltrip
1970	Richard Petty	1991	Bill Elliott
1971	Bobby Allison	1992	Bill Elliott
1972	Bobby Allison	1993	Bill Elliott
1973	Bobby Allison	1994	Bill Elliott
1974	Richard Petty	1995	Bill Elliott
1975	Richard Petty	1996	Bill Elliott
1976	Richard Petty		

Source: *The Official NASCAR 1996 Preview and Press Guide.*

Appendix H

NASCAR Rookies of the Year
1996–1958

Year	Driver	Year	Driver
1996	Johnny Benson, Jr.	1976	Skip Manning
1995	Ricky Craven	1975	Bruce Hill
1994	Jeff Burton	1974	Earl Ross
1993	Jeff Gordon	1973	Lennie Pond
1992	Jimmy Hensley	1972	Larry Smith
1991	Bobby Hamilton	1971	Walter Ballard
1990	Rob Moroso	1970	Bill Dennis
1989	Dick Trickle	1969	Dick Brooks
1988	Ken Bouchard	1968	Pete Hamilton
1987	Davey Allison	1967	Donnie Allison
1986	Alan Kulwicki	1966	James Hylton
1985	Ken Schrader	1965	Sam McQuagg
1984	Rusty Wallace	1964	Doug Cooper
1983	Sterling Marlin	1963	Billy Wade
1982	Geoff Bodine	1962	Tom Cox
1981	Ron Bouchard	1961	Woody Wilson
1980	Jody Ridley	1960	David Pearson
1979	Dale Earnhardt	1959	Richard Petty
1978	Ronnie Thomas	1958	Shorty Rollins
1977	Ricky Rudd		

Source: *The Official NASCAR 1996 Preview and Press Guide.*

Appendix I

How Points Are Distributed
in the Winston Cup Series

The number of points awarded is the same for each and every race, regardless of how long the race is for that day. There is a five point difference for the top five finishers of a race, a four point difference for those who finish sixth through tenth, and a three point difference for those who finish beyond tenth place, regardless of how many drivers actually start.

The only way a driver can receive bonus points is by leading a lap. Five extra points are awarded to every driver who leads one lap. At the end of the race, the driver who has led the most laps gets an additional five points.

Relief drivers do not receive points. Points are only awarded to the driver who starts the race, but one lap must be completed in order for that driver to collect points. The points earned by the relief driver then go to the starting driver.

In case of a tie, the number of wins that season is used to break the tie between two drivers. If that is the same, the number of second, third and successive places are used to break the tie.

The owner receives points as well. The point system is the same, except that it does not matter who the driver is. The only time owners' points are used in a race is if qualifying is canceled, if two drivers have the same top qualifying time, and as preference for provisional starting spots. They are also considered in the distribution of NASCAR plan money.

Finish	Points Earned
1	175
2	170
3	165
4	160
5	155
6	150
7	146
8	142
9	138
10	134
11	130
12	127

13	124
14	121
15	118
16	115
17	112
18	109
19	106
20	103
21	100
22	97
23	94
24	91
25	88
26	85
27	82
28	79
29	76
30	73
31	70
32	67
33	64
34	61
35	58
36	55
37	52
38	49
39	46
40	43

Source: *The Official NASCAR 1996 Preview and Press Guide.*

Appendix J

NASCAR Winston Cup Series Race Shops

NASCAR racing is known for its "open door" policy. Access to drivers, race cars, and mechanics has always been part of the sport's popularity. Many shops offer fans the chance to see their favorite cars being built, prepared, or repaired. Some shops, like those operated by Rick Hendrick or Darrell Waltrip, have museums and gift shops inside. Each shop has its own protocol for visitors, such as special tour hours or restricted areas for viewing work activities, so be flexible, especially on Wednesdays or Thursdays during the season when teams might be loading haulers and getting ready to travel.

Occasionally you will get to see drivers at the shops, especially if the driver also owns the race team. Mondays or Tuesdays are often the best time to see drivers at the shops. Visitors are allowed into this professional work environment as a courtesy. If you receive a cool reception or little opportunity to tour the facility, remember that serious work is going on behind the scenes. Most teams are very gracious and willing to respond to your questions or requests.

The following listings are in numerical order according to car. Because owners maintain car numbers, names of drivers have been relegated to the end of each listing. Wherever possible, known driver changes have been made. For more detailed information regarding visits to race shops, please consult *The Fan's Guide to Racing Shops: 1996 Edition,* published by The Digital Desktop, Charlotte, North Carolina.

1. Precision Products Racing
    1633 NC Highway 16 North, Denver, NC
    Car Owner: Richard Jackson
    Mailing Address: P.O. Box 569, Denver, NC 28037
    Driver: Morgan Shepherd

2. Penske Racing South
    136 Knob Hill Road, Mooresville, NC (Lakeside Industrial Park)
    Car Owners: Roger Penske, Don Miller, and Rusty Wallace
    Mailing Address: 136 Knob Hill Road, Mooresville, NC 28115
    Driver: Rusty Wallace

3. RCR Enterprises
    Industrial Drive, Welcome, NC
    Car Owner: Richard Childress
    Mailing Address: P.O. Box 1189, Welcome, NC 27374
    Driver: Dale Earnhardt

4. Morgan-McClure Motorsports
    25139 Lee Highway, Abingdon, VA
    Car Owner: Morgan-McClure
    Mailing Address: Rt. 10 Box 780, Abingdon, VA 24210
    Driver: Sterling Marlin
    NOTE: This team will have a new shop sometime during the summer of
    1997.

5. Hendrick Motorsports
    5315 Stowe Lane, Harrisburg, NC
    Car Owner: Rick Hendrick
    Mailing Address: P.O. Box 9, Harrisburg, NC 28075
    Driver: Terry Labonte
    NOTE: Hendrick's shops have a museum and gift shop for visitors.

6. Roush Racing
    5835 Highway 49 South, Liberty, SC
    Car Owner: Jack Roush
    Mailing Address: P.O. Box 1089, Liberty, NC 27298
    Driver: Mark Martin

7. Geoff Bodine Racing
    6007 Victory Lane, Harrisburg, NC
    Car Owner: Geoff Bodine
    Mailing Address: 6007 Victory Lane, Harrisburg, NC 28075
    NOTE: Bodine is planning to build a gift shop and museum at his shop
    site in the near future.

8. Stavola Brothers Racing
    2240 NC Highway 49, Harrisburg, NC
    Car Owners: Bill and Mickey Stavola
    Mailing Address: P.O. Box 339, Harrisburg, NC 28075
    Driver: Hut Stricklin

10. Rudd Performance Motorsports
     292 Rolling Hills Road, Mooresville, NC (Lakeside Industrial Park)
     Car Owner: Ricky Rudd
     Mailing Address: P.O. Box 6010, Mooresville, NC 28115
     Driver: Ricky Rudd

11. BDR Racing
     304 Performance Rd., Mooresville, NC
     Driver: Brett Bodine

12. Bobby Allison Motorsports
     5254 Pit Road South, Harrisburg, NC
     Car Owner: Bobby Allison Motorsports Team, Inc.
     Mailing Address: 5254 Pit Road South, Harrisburg, NC 28075
     Driver: TBA

14. Dale Earnhardt Inc.
     1675 Coddle Creek Hwy., Moorseville, NC
     Driver: Ron Hornaday, Jr.
     NOTE: This team may have a new shop sometime during 1997.

16. Roush Racing
     Location: see No. 6 above
     Car Owner: see No. 6 above
     Mailing Address: see No. 6 above
     Driver: Ted Musgrave

17. Darrell Waltrip Motorsports
     6780 Hudspeth Road, Harrisburg, NC
     Car Owner: Darrell Waltrip
     Mailing Address: P.O. Box 293, Harrisburg, NC 28075
     Driver: Darrell Waltrip
     NOTE: Waltrip has a small museum and gift shop on the premises.

18. Joe Gibbs Racing
     9900 Twin Lakes Parkway, Charlotte, NC
     Car Owner: Joe Gibbs
     Mailing Address: 9900 Twin Lakes Parkway, Charlotte, NC 28269
     Driver: Bobby Labonte

19. Tri Star Motorsports
    103 Center Lane, Huntersville, NC
    Car Owner: Mark Smith
    Mailing Address: 103 Center Lane, Huntersville, NC 28078
    Driver: Gary Bradberry

20. Ranier-Walsh Racing
    510 Performance Rd., Mooresville, NC
    Driver: Greg Sacks

21. Wood Brothers Racing
    21 Performance Drive, Stuart, VA
    Car Owners: The Glen Wood Co.
    Mailing Address: Rt. 2, Box 77, Stuart, VA 24171
    Driver: Michael Waltrip

22. Bill Davis Racing
    301 Old Thomasville Road, High Point, NC
    Car Owner: Bill Davis
    Mailing Address: 301 Old Thomasville Rd., High Point, NC 27260
    Driver: Ward Burton

23. Travis Carter Enterprises
    Highway 421, Hamptonville, NC
    Driver: Jimmy Spencer
    NOTE: This team will relocate to Statesville, NC, during the fall of 1997.
    The new shop will be near the intersection of I-77 and I-40.

24. Hendrick Motorsports
    5325 Stowe Lane, Harrisburg, NC
    Car Owner: Rick Hendrick
    Mailing Address: P.O. Box 9, Harrisburg, NC 28075
    Driver: Jeff Gordon

25. Hendrick Motorsports
    5315 Stowe Lane, Harrisburg, NC
    Car Owner: Papa Joe Hendrick
    Mailing Address: see above #24
    Driver: Ricky Craven

26. Sadler Motorsports
    8013 Whitebark Terrace, Richmond, VA
    Driver: Hermie Sadler

27. David Blair Motorsports
    1950 Flintstone Drive, Statesville, NC
    Car Owner: David Blair
    Mailing Address: 1950 Flintstone Dr., Statesville, NC 28677
    Driver: Elton Sawyer

28. Robert Yates Racing
    115 Dwelle Street, Charlotte, NC
    Car Owner: Robert Yates
    Mailing Address: 115 Dwelle St., Charlotte, NC 28208
    Driver: Ernie Irvan

29. Diamond Ridge Motorsports
    5901 Orr Road, Charlotte, NC
    Car Owner: Gary Bechtel
    Mailing Address: 4201 Congress Street, Charlotte, NC 28209
    Driver: Robert Pressley

30. Bahari Racing
    208 Rolling Hills Road, Mooresville, NC (Lakeside Industrial Park)
    Car Owner: Chuck Rider
    Mailing Address: 208 Rolling Hills Rd., Mooresville, NC 28115
    Driver: Johnny Benson, Jr.

31. RCR Enterprises
    Industrial Drive, Welcome, NC
    Driver: Mike Skinner

33. Andy Petree Motorsports
    191 Airport Road, Arden, NC
    Car Owner: Andy Petree
    Mailing Address: P.O. Box 726, Arden, NC 28704
    Driver: Ken Schrader

36. MB2 Motorsports
    185 Armitage Rd., Mooresville, NC
    Driver: Derrike Cope

37. Kranefuss-Haas Racing
    163 Rolling Hills Road, Mooresville, NC (Lakeside Industrial Park)
    Car Owners: Michael Kranefuss and Carl Haas
    Mailing Address: 163 Rolling Hills, Rd., Mooresville, NC 28115
    Driver: Jeremy Mayfield

40. Team Sabco
    114 Meadow Hill Circle, Mooresville, NC
    Driver: Robbie Gordon

41. Larry Hedrick Motorsports
    114 Victory Lane, Statesville, NC
    Car Owner: Larry Hedrick
    Mailing Address: P.O. Box 511, Statesville, NC 28687
    Driver: Steve Grissom

42. Team Sabco
    114 Meadow Hill Circle, Mooresville, NC (Lakeside Industrial Park)
    Car Owner: Felix Sabates
    Mailing Address: 114 Meadow Hill Circle, Mooresville, NC 28115
    Driver: Joe Nemechek

43. Petty Enterprises
    311 Branson Mill Road, Randleman, NC
    Car Owner: Richard Petty
    Mailing Address: 311 Branson Mill Rd., Randleman, NC 27317
    Driver: Bobby Hamilton

44. Petty Enterprises 2
    7571 Flowes Store Rd., Concord, NC
    Driver: Kyle Petty

46. Team Sabco
    114 Meadow Hill Circle, Mooresville, NC
    Driver: Wally Dallenbach

71. Marcis Auto Racing
    71 Beale Road, Arden, NC
    Car Owner: Helen Marcis
    Mailing Address: P.O. Box 645, Skyland, NC 28776
    Driver: Dave Marcis

75. Butch Mock Motorsports
    217 Rolling Hills Road, Mooresville, NC (Lakeside Industrial Park)
    Car Owner: Butch Mock
    Mailing Address: 217 Rolling Hills Rd., Mooresville, NC 28115
    Driver: Rick Mast

77. Jasper Motorsports
    110 Knob Hill Road, Mooresville, NC (Lakeside Industrial Park)
    Car Owners: Doug Bawel, Mark Harrah, Mark Wallace, Bobby Hillin, Jr.
    Mailing Address: 110 Knob Hill Rd., Mooresville, NC 28115
    Driver: Bobby Hillin, Jr.

78. Diamond Rio Motorsports
    6006 Ball Park Road, Thomasville, NC
    Car Owners: Jim Wilson and Steve Lane
    Mailing Address: 6006 Ball Park Rd., Thomasville, NC 27360
    Driver: Billy Standridge

81. Filmar Racing
    2730 Zion Church Road, Concord, NC
    Car Owner: Filbert Martocci
    Mailing Address: 2730 Zion Church Rd., Concord, NC 28025
    Driver: Kenny Wallace

86. Ridling Motorsports
    159 Bevan Dr., Mooresville, NC
    Driver: Kevin Lepage

87. Nemco Motorsports
    7 South Iredell Industrial Road, Mooresville, NC
    Car Owner: Joe Nemechek
    Mailing Address: P.O. Box 177, Mooresville, NC 28115
    Driver: Joe Nemechek

88. Robert Yates Racing
    115 Dwelle Street, Charlotte, NC
    Car Owner: Robert Yates
    Mailing Address: 115 Dwelle St., Charlotte, NC 28208
    Driver: Dale Jarrett

90. Donlavey Racing
    5011 Old Midlothian Pike, Richmond, VA
    Car Owner: Junie Donlavey
    Mailing Address: 5011 Old Midlothian Pike, Richmond, VA 23224
    Driver: Dick Trickle

91. LJ Racing, Incorporated
    4372 Providence Rd., Maiden, NC
    Driver: Mike Wallace

94. Elliott/Hardy Racing
    310 Airport Road, Hickory, NC
    Car Owners: Bill Elliott and Charles Hardy
    Mailing Address: P.O. Box 456, Hickory, NC 28603
    Driver: Bill Elliott
    NOTE: This shop is within the Hickory Airport. It is inaccessable unless
    you have an appointment and can be escorted across the airfield to the
    shop building.

95. Sadler Racing
    54 Parris Ave., Nashville, TN
    Driver: Gary Bradberry

96. American Equipment Racing
    7701-C N. Tryon St., Charlotte, NC
    Driver: David Green

97. Mark Rypien Motorsports
    177 Knob Hill Rd., Mooresville, NC
    Driver: Chad Little

98. Cale Yarborough Motorsports
    9617 Dixie River Road, Charlotte, NC
    Car Owner: Cale Yarborough
    Mailing Address: 9617 Dixie River Rd., Charlotte, NC 28208
    Driver: John Andretti

99. Roush Racing
    122 Knob Hill Road, Mooresville, NC (Lakeside Industrial Park)
    Car Owner: Jack Roush
    Mailing Address: 122 Knob Hill Rd., Mooresville, NC 28115
    Driver: Jeff Burton

Appendix K

Fifty Current NASCAR-Related Web Sites

The following sites are accurate as of mid-November of 1996. The author takes no responsibility for their accuracy or content matter. Web sites often change with little or no warning, so be prepared to make adjustments to addresses as necessary.

American Racing Scene
http://www.racecar.com/Index.html

Bill Davis Racing Home Page
http://ourworld.compuserve.com/homepage

Budweiser
http://www.Budweiser.com

Chad Little Home Page
http://www.chadlittle.com

Charlotte Motor Speedway
http://www.raceshop.com

Daytona Speedweeks & International Speedway Calendar
http://www.charm.net/~Ibc/daytona/nascar.html

Dupont Lubricants Web
http://www.Lubricants.dupont.com/lubricants/home.html

ESPN SportsZone (main page with access to racing)
http://ESPNET.SportsZone.com

Ford Worldwide Connection Home Page
http://www.ford.com/

Joe Gibbs Racing Online
http://www.git.net/jgr/

GM Goodwrench
http://guide-p.infoseek.com/Title?qt=GM+Goodwrench&col+ww&sv=N1

GM Pro Shop Limited Edition Collectibles
http://www.gmproshop.com/collectibles/Index.html

Hayes Modems
http://www.hayes.com

Hooters Restaurants Home Page
http://www.hooters.com

Interstate Batteries
http://www.interstatebatteries.com

Jeff Gordon Home Page
http://www.jeffgordon.com

Kodak Films Home Page
http://www.kodak.com

Kyle Petty
http://www.petty.com

Las Vegas Motor Speedway
http://www.derekdaly.com/lvms.html

Lowe's Incorporated (connection to Team Lowe's)
http://www.lowes.com

Martinsville Speedway NASCAR Racing
http://www.martinsvillespeedway.com

McDonald's Corporation
http://www.mcdonalds.com

Michael Waltrip page (unofficial)
http://www.angelfire.com/pages1/micwal 21/index.html

MNI: NASCAR Index
http://www.motorsport.com/series/NASCAR.html

Mobil 1 NASCAR Forum
http://www.Mobil.com/mobil_1/racing/NASCAR/NASCAR.htm/

NASCAR Online
http://www.NASCAR.com

New Hampshire International Speedway
http://www.nhis.com

Newsgroup: rec.autos.sport.nascar
news:rec.autos.sport.nascar

Pennzoil Home Page
http://www.pennzoil.com

Penske Racing South Home Page
http://www.rustywallace.com/prs.html

Prodigy
http://www.prodigy.com

Quad-Cities International Raceway Park
http://www.qcirp.com

RACESHOP
http://www.raceshop.com

RaceWeb
http://www.io.org/~raceweb/Isindex.html

REV Speedway Fan Club (multiple fan club sites)
http://www.revspeedway.com

Ricky Rudd's Official Home Page
http://www.rickyrudd.com

Speed Net
http://www.starnews.com/speednet/directory.html

Speed Net Index of Winston Cup & Busch Drivers
http://www.StarNews.com/speednet/drivers/driver_Index.html

Speedworld
http://www.speedworld.net

Sports Line USA Auto Racing Page
http://www.sportsline.com/u/racing/auto/Index.html

Spyder's NASCAR Racing Page
http://home.gvl.net/~spyder/nascar.html

Talladega Superspeedway
http://www.webex.com/racedega.html

Team Penske
http://www.teampenske.com

Texaco
http://www.texaco.com/

Tide Racing Team (via Tide Home Page)
http://www.clothesline.com

Dick Trickle Web Site
http://www.ca/tim.com/shoemaker/driver

UNOCAL Racing Gasolines Home Page
http://www.76racing.com

Valvoline
http://www.Valvoline.com

Watkins Glen International Raceway
http://www.theglen.com

Western Auto
http://westernauto.com/

Appendix L

Restaurants with Racing Themes

The following list is by no means complete. These are some of the restaurants I discovered while doing research for this book. Additions to this list for use in future editions of this book may be sent to the author at: Department of American Thought and Language, Michigan State University, 235 Ernst Bessey Hall, East Lansing, MI 48824-1033.

Montana's
    Hickory, NC

Sandwich Construction Company
    University City Boulevard
    Charlotte, NC

Stock Car Cafe
    (owned by Sandwich Construction Co.)
    20208 Knox Road (I-77 North off exit 28)
    Cornelius, NC
    also in Atlanta, GA
    also in Bristol, TN

Lancaster's
    Mooresville, NC

Harry Gant's Steakhouse
    Taylorsville, NC

Kenny Wallace Motorsports Grill
    Interstate 4 and Kirkman Road
    (opposite Universal Studios)
    Orlando, FL

Race Rock
    Detroit, MI
    also in Orlando, FL
        International Drive (near Sea World)
        Pit Road
        Route I-285 South two miles off exit 89
    also in Atlanta, GA
        (between Road Atlanta and Atlanta Motor Speedway)

Sagebrush
    Statesville, NC

Big Daddy's Oyster Bar
    Lake Norman
    Cornelius, NC

Quaker Steak and Lube
    101 Chestnut
    Sharon, PA

The Lube's Hot Rod Cafe
    101 Chestnut
    Sharon, PA

Quaker Steak and Wings
    1800 East State Street
    Hermitage, PA

Appendix M

Stock Car Driving Schools

The following information supplies addresses and telephone numbers for an assortment of driving schools that use stock cars. The author and/or publisher is not responsible for incorrect or changed information. This list has been adapted from "High Performance Driving Schools." Compiled and written by Robin Hartford and published in *Stock Car Racing's Race Fan Special*, Spring 1996. Reproduced by permission of *Stock Car Racing* magazine.

American Spectator Stock Car Driving School
RR Box 138
Enfield, NH 03748
1-800-722-3606 or (603) 632-5243

Buck Baker Racing School
1613 Runnymede Lane
Charlotte, NC 28211
1-800-529-BUCK or (704) 366-6224

Drivetech Racing School
7300 Scout Avenue, Unit B
Bell Gardens, CA 90201
1-800-678-8864 or (310) 806-0306

Fast Track High Performance Driving School
P.O. Box 160
5540 Morehead Road
Harrisburg, NC 28075-0160
(704) 455-1700

Finishline Racing School
3113 South Ridgewood Avenue
Edgewater, FL 32141
(904) 427-8522

Richard Petty Driving Experience
6022 Victory Lane
Harrisburg, NC 28075
1-800-BE-PETTY or (704) 455-9443

Racing Adventures
P.O. Box 3960
Seminole, FL 34645
1-800-961-RACE
e-mail: GE1208@AOL.COM

Southard's Racing School
P.O. Box 1810
New Smyrna Beach, FL 32170
1-800-422-9449 or (904) 428-3307

If interested, please contact these schools for details regarding prices, required driving experience, scheduling, and information on types of cars and tracks used.

Notes

Chapter 1

1. A "yellow shirt" is an official at the Indianapolis Motor Speedway. Their duties include crowd control, gate clearance, and infield parking.

2. These television ratings are for race broadcasts only. Ratings for NASCAR-oriented programs (*This Week in NASCAR, Inside NASCAR, Speedweek, RPM 2 Night*) were not figured into the total number of viewers.

3. Many thanks to Dr. Michael Marsden, one of my graduate school professors who used this analysis to "read" the sport of golf. In golf, the course is meant to use the natural landscape as the venue for the game, yet we manipulate nature by building such man-made hazards as sand traps, grass bunkers, and ponds.

Chapter 2

1. CART stands for "Championship Auto Racing Teams." In December of 1996, a court ruled that CART could not use "IndyCar" as an official name.

2. Ironically, Al Unser, Jr., two-time Indy 500 champion and son of four-time 500 winner Al Unser, Sr., sided with CART once the rift developed in 1995.

3. Robby Gordon is no relation to 1995 Winston Cup Champion Jeff Gordon. In August of 1996, Robby Gordon announced his intentions to leave Walker Racing for a Winston Cup ride with Felix Sabates.

4. "Supporting" divisions for Winston Cup events today include the NASCAR Busch Grand National division and the ARCA (Automobile Racing Club of America) Supercar Series. These races are often run on Saturday afternoon prior to the final Winston Cup practice session.

Chapter 5

1. There are conflicting dates and details with regard to specifics about Barney Oldfield's accomplishments while with Ford. Some of the details cited in this section are given different dates by other reputable sources.

2. Perhaps there is something symbolic in the fact that Barney Oldfield outraced a locomotive in this film, as though the automobile, by 1913, had exceeded the railroad in terms of American importance.

3. Gordon has made commercials for Chevrolet, Coca-Cola, Quaker State motor oil, and Nutmeg sports apparel. His face has also appeared on numerous Kellogg's cereal boxes, like many other drivers as part of their affiliation with NASCAR.

4. The Mechanic of the Race Award includes a check, along with a shot at winning the Mechanic of the Year Award, which is presented at the annual NASCAR Awards Banquet in New York City. An additional cash prize is given at that time.

Chapter 6

1. Dwight Gooden suffered from drug problems while pitching for several major league baseball teams. Lawrence Phillips was arrested for drunk driving and disorderly conduct just prior to his rookie season with the St. Louis Rams in 1996. While playing football at the University of Nebraska, Phillips was arrested for beating his ex-girlfriend.

2. This move came in handy when moonshine runners found a road blocked and needed to head in the opposite direction quickly. See the glossary for a detailed definition of this historic driving move.

3. For specific information about Hippodromes, including sketches, see John M. Humphrey's *Roman Circuses: Arenas for Chariot Racing*.

Chapter 7

1. Richie Evans is regarded as the finest Modified driver of all time, even though he was killed in a wreck at Martinsville in 1989.

2. Ironically, Lowe's announced shortly after this event that they were going to leave Brett's team and sponsor a second car owned by Richard Childress Racing. Their new driver is Mike Skinner.

3. Rockingham has since remodeled these stalls, enclosing them from the elements.

Chapter 8

1. Earnhardt and Jarrett also drive for multi-car teams. Jarrett is teamed with Ernie Irvan out of the shops of Robert Yates Racing, while Earnhardt will be teamed with Mike Skinner out of Richard Childress Racing beginning in 1997.

2. While the federal government has focused its attention on tobacco companies, little has been done about the involvement of breweries in professional sports. Associating drinking with a sport that involves driving seems more dangerous than the association between tobacco firms and NASCAR.

3. This firm released NASCAR Racing 2 and NASCAR Racing for Mac in November 1996 with some new features, including access to 16 Winston Cup Series speedways ("NASCAR Expands," *NASCAR Online*, 15 Oct. 1996).

Glossary

AAA. The American Automobile Association.

ARCA. The Automobile Racing Club of America.

ASCRA. The American Stock Car Racing Association.

The "Alabama Gang." A group of NASCAR drivers from Hueytown, Alabama. The group includes Bobby and Donnie Allison, Red Farmer, Hut Stricklin, the late Davey Allison, the late Neil Bonnett, and the late Clifford Allison.

Automobile Dealer Franchise Act of 1956. From U.S. Code Number 1222 (Authorization of suits against manufacturers; amount of recovery; defenses). The Act reads as follows: "An automobile dealer may bring suit against any automobile manufacturer engaged in commerce, in any district court of the United States in the district in which said manufacturer resides, or is found, or has an agent, without respect to the amount in controversy, and shall recover the damages by him sustained and the cost of suit by reason of the failure of said automobile manufacturer from and after August 8, 1956, to act in good faith in performing or complying with any of the terms or provisions of the franchise, or in terminating, canceling, or not renewing the franchise with said dealer: Provided, That in any such suit the manufacturer shall not be barred from asserting in defense of any such action the failure of the dealer to act in good faith."

bootlegger's turn. This move is executed by turning the front wheels sharply while putting the gas pedal to the floor. The idea is to spin the rear of the car around a pivot point (created by the front tires) and make a 180-degree change of direction. This was used by bootleggers to avoid road blocks. Credit for this move is often given to Junior Johnson.

Busch Grand National Racing. This is the NASCAR division often considered one step below the Winston Cup Series. The cars are roughly the same, except that BGN cars produce a bit less horsepower. This division often runs as a supporting event to Winston Cup races, usually on Saturday afternoons.

car owner. The person who possesses ownership of a racing team. It is their job to supply and oversee the team's facilities, equipment, personnel, and financial support. The car owner hires (and fires) crew chiefs, drivers, pit crewmen, and shop staff and often negotiates sponsorship deals.

CART. Championship Auto Racing Teams.

Craftsman Truck Series. A division of NASCAR that uses pickup truck bodies formed from sheet metal on stock car chassis. This series was created to capitalize on the large number of pick-up truck owners in North America. Craftsman is a brand name of tools sold by the Sears and Roebuck Company, which sponsors the entire schedule of races.

crew chief. This is the team member who runs the team while at the speedway. The crew chief supervises the race car's preparation for practice, qualifying, and the race itself. Crew chiefs orchestrate pit stops, help make adjustments to the car, and assist with strategy regarding the car's performance.

flags. There are several flags used in stock car racing to control the action in races. These flags are interpreted as follows:

• **green flag** = signals the start of the race; drivers accelerate to racing speed. Also used to restart races after caution periods.

• **yellow flag** = tells drivers to slow down because of unsafe racing conditions.

• **red flag** = used to stop the race because of hazardous racing conditions.

• **blue flag with yellow stripe** = notifies a driver to make room for faster traffic.

• **black flag** = notifies a driver to report to the pits immediately for some reason. In NASCAR, if the driver fails to report after three laps, scoring for the car will stop.

• **white flag** = signals field that they are beginning their final lap.

• **checkered flag** = signals the end of the race; first car to receive this flag wins.

Formula One racing. A type of racing done mainly in Europe using highly technological cars. The races are held on road courses throughout the world, and one event is held on the streets of Monte Carlo in Monaco. This is a very expensive form of racing because of its emphasis on technology, which includes computer technology and space-age materials used to manufacture the cars.

FPA. The Federation of Professional Athletes.

fuel cell. A 22-gallon bladder (encased in metal) used as a gasoline tank on stock cars. The bladder keeps fuel from spilling in an accident, and the top of the cell (where it is filled) contains metal balls that keep fuel from spilling if the car turns upside down. These became manditory equipment on stock cars in 1967.

GNAB. The Grand National Advisory Board. A governing body founded in 1961 to administer various aspects of NASCAR Grand National competition. Very similar to the NSCC that oversees Winston Cup appeals today.

go-cart. A small four-wheeled vehicle powered by a gasoline engine. There are many varieties of these machines used for racing. Because of their size, simplicity, and relatively low cost, they are often used as a first step toward a race car driving career.

IMCA. The International Motor Contest Association. Founded in 1915 to organize and represent racing's "outlaw" element. The IMCA hosted events for
drivers suspended by the AAA on tracks blacklisted by the AAA. Less
experienced drivers were often allowed to race in IMCA events.

IRL. The Indy Racing League, created by Indianapolis Motor Speedway
President Tony George in 1995 to counter CART's attention to road
courses and foreign-born drivers. The IPL attempts to make an
"American" series of open-wheel speedway racing like that of USAC
during the 1960s and 1970s.

ISC. The International Speedway Corporation. This is the branch of NASCAR
that oversees Daytona International Raceway, Darlington Raceway,
Talladega Superspeedway, and Watkins Glen International. This branch
also oversees Daytona USA, a racing-based interactive theme attraction
outside the Daytona International Raceway.

lift. To raise your foot off of the accelerator.

loose. A term that refers to a race car's handling characteristics. This term
means a car whose back end wants to come around (or break loose) while
making a turn. This condition is sometimes called "oversteer."

Modified. A type of race car sanctioned by NASCAR that loosely resembles an
ordinary car, but is actually changed and improved for safety and performance. One of the first NASCAR divisions utilized modified production
cars, especially because of a shortage in new production-type cars during
World War II. Today's NASCAR Modifieds are open-wheeled, short-
wheel-based cars with large engines. These cars are especially common
throughout the Northeast and New England. This is how Geoff Bodine,
Brett Bodine, and Jimmy Spencer gained experience as race car drivers.

NARC. National Auto Racing Club.

NARL National Auto Racing League.

NASCAR. The National Association of Stock Car Automobile Racing. Founded
by William H.G. France in 1947.

Nash car. The name some people in 1947 felt might create confusion with
NASCAR. Nash was a small independent manufacturer that eventually
was overpowered by the postwar strength of the Big Three—Ford, GM,
and Chrysler. In 1954, Nash joined forces with Hudson to create American
Motors.

NCSCC. The National Championship Stock Car Circuit. Founded and operated
by William H.G. France prior to his creation of NASCAR.

NSCC. The National Stock Car Commission. This governing body addresses
appeals to NASCAR by Winston Cup competitors who have been accused
of and/or cited with violating NASCAR rules. This body was created by
NASCAR itself, which causes some racers to question its actions.

NSCRA. The National Stock Car Racing Association.

proletariat (or prole) sport. According to Eldon Snyder and Elmer Spreitzer, *Social Aspects of Sport,* these are events that attract a proletariat or blue-collar audience because of their emphasis on speed and power over grace or finesse and their use of proletariat artifacts like cars or motorcycles. Prole sports often have athletes that audiences can identify with and, in some cases, the audience can actually become a participant.

push. A term that refers to a race car's handling characteristics. This term means a car that wants to go straight into a corner after the front wheels have been turned. Sometimes called "understeer."

restrictor plate. A thin piece of metal placed between a stock car's carburetor and intake manifold in order to limit the amount of fuel and air mixture being fed to the engine. This is done to reduce horsepower and speed. NASCAR requires these plates at Daytona and Talladega, two of the fastest speedways on the Winston Cup circuit.

SCCA. The Sports Car Club of America.

stock. A standard or production-type vehicle or part. Not modified in any way. This is how the original NASCAR "Strictly Stock" Division competed. No changes could be made with the exception of basic safety modifications (removing of hub caps and mufflers, taping over headlamps). Today the term refers to the basic shape of a Winston Cup or Busch Grand National race car. They look like a "stock" automobile, yet are anything but that beneath their sheet metal.

SVSCRA. The Southern Vintage Stock Car Racing Association.

USAC. The United States Automobile Club.

USCRA. The United Stock Car Racing Association.

wedge. An adjustment that increases or decreases pressure on the springs at the rear corners of a stock car. By turning screw jacks at the rear of the car with a wrench, the weight on the rear springs can be manipulated in order to make the car handle better and run faster. This is how teams correct race cars that are either pushing or loose.

Whiskey Rebellion. An armed uprising in 1794 by settlers along the Western frontier of Pennsylvania (near what is today Pittsburgh) to protest the federal government's charging of excise taxes on homemade alcohol.

Bibliography

"Action to Debut a New Line of NASCAR Toys." *Speedworld.* Online. Netscape. World Wide Web. 7 Nov. 1996. Available: http://www.speedworld.net

Adams, James R. *Chief: The Pride Is Back.* Kinston, NC: Sheer Joy Publishing, 1988.

"Alabama Speedway Called Unsafe, Drivers Pull Out." *New York Times* 14 Sept. 1969: 13.

Alan Kulwicki: Champion of Dreams. Videocassette. Prod. DSL Communications. NASCAR Video, 1993. 30 min.

Alger, Horatio, Jr. *Ragged Dick and Struggling Upward.* New York: Penguin, 1985.

Allison Legacy Race Cars, Incorporated. Salisbury, NC: N.d. N.p.

Altheide, David L., and Robert P. Snow. "Sport Versus the Mass Media." *Urban Life* July 1978: 189-204.

"Atlanta to Host Second Champion's Breakfast." *NASCAR Online.* Online. Netscape. World Wide Web. 15 Oct. 1996. Available: http://www.nascar.com

Babich, Lawrence J. and Harvey M. Zucker, comp. *Sports Films: A Complete Reference.* Jefferson, NC: McFarland, 1989.

"Bahre Offers to Purchase Fall Race Date from Smith." *Winston Cup Scene* 25 April 1996: 54.

Baker, William J., and John M. Carrol, ed. *Sports in Modern America.* St. Louis: River City, 1981.

Ball, D.W. and J.W. Loy, ed. *Sport and the Social Order.* Reading: Addison-Wesley, 1975.

Ballard, Steve. "Bruton Smith: Auto Racing's Big Wheel." *USA Today* 5 Nov. 1996: C1+.

——. "Gordon Win Increases Points Lead." *USA Today* 30 Sept. 1996: C1.

"Banjo Matthews, the Passing of a Legend." *NASCAR Online.* Online. Netscape. World Wide Web. 2 Oct. 1996. Available: http://www.nascar.com

Barendse, Michael A. "Individualism, Technology, and Sport: The Speedway Nexus." *Journal of Sport and Social Issues* Winter/Spring 1983: 15-23.

Barney Oldfield's Race for a Life. Dir. Mack Sennett. With Mabel Normand, Barney Oldfield, and Ford Sterling. Keystone, 1913.

Barthes, Roland. *Mythologies.* New York: Hill and Wang, 1972.

235

Beckow, Steven M. "Culture, History, and Artifact." *Material Culture Studies in America*. Ed. Thomas J. Schlereth. Nashville, TN: American Association for State and Local History, 1982. 114-23.

Benedict, Ruth. *Patterns of Culture*. Boston: Houghton, 1934.

Benson, Johnny. "A Letter From Johnny Benson." *NASCAR Online*. Online. Netscape. World Wide Web. 6 Nov. 1996. Available: http://www.nascar. com

Benson, Michael. *Dale Earnhardt*. New York: Chelsea House, 1996.

Berger, Arthur Asa. *Pop Culture*. Dayton: Pflaum/Standard, 1973.

Berggren, Dick. "An Interview with Bill France." *Stock Car Racing* Mar. 1996: 70-80.

——. "Big Government Takes Us On." *Stock Car Racing* Nov. 1996: 16+.

——. "Rick Hendrick." *Stock Car Racing* Dec. 1990: 64-75.

——. "Rob." *Stock Car Racing* Jan. 1991: 13+.

——. "30 Years." *Stock Car Racing* May 1996: 56-69.

——. "Winston Cup Is Coming to Town." *Stock Car Racing* Sept. 1996: 16-33.

"Better Late Than Never: Marlin's First Catch Is a Biggie: A Narrow Victory in the Daytona 500." *Toledo Blade* 21 Feb. 1994: 15+.

Birrell, Susan. "The Rituals of Sports." *Social Forces* Dec. 1981: 354-76.

Black, James T. "The South's Fastest Sport." *Southern Living* May 1990: 12-14.

Blake, Ben W. "Hendrick Carved NASCAR Niche." *Richmond Times-Dispatch* 2 July 1996: E6.

Blonde Comet. Dir. William Beaudine. With Virginia Vale, Vince Barnett, and Barney Oldfield. Producers Releasing Corp., 1941.

Blunk, Frank M. "Eleven Car Crash Mars 100-Mile Daytona Trials Won by Johnson and Dieringer." *New York Times* 13 Feb. 1965: 16.

——. "Lorenzen Wins Daytona Stock Car Race Shortened by Rain to 332.5 Miles." *New York Times* 15 Feb. 1965: 36.

——. "Stock Car Fans Gather in South." *New York Times* 12 Feb. 1965: 23.

"Bobby Is Fast at Talladega." *National Speed Sport News* 27 Aug. 1969: 3.

"Bodine to Race Gold Thunderbird." *NASCAR Online*. Online. Netscape. World Wide Web. 25 Sept. 1996. Available: http://www.nascar.com

Bolton, Clyde, with Mike Bolton. *Remembering Davey: Portrait of an American Hero*. Birmingham: *Birmingham News,* 1993.

Bond, John R. "Miscellaneous Ramblings." *Road and Track* Dec. 1964: 19.

"Bonnett, Childress to Team at Talladega." *Winston Cup Scene* 15 July 1993: 38.

"Bonnett Killed in Daytona Crash: Veteran Driver was Attempting Comeback From Severe Accident in 1990." *Toledo Blade* 12 Feb. 1994: 21+.

Boorstin, Daniel J. *The Americans: The National Experience*. New York: Vintage, 1965.

"Borg-Warner Joins NASCAR's Aftermarket Program." *NASCAR Online.* Online. Netscape. World Wide Web. 29 Oct. 1996. Available: http://www. nascar.com

Bourcier, Bones. "Bruton Smith Bares His Teeth." *Stock Car Racing* Aug. 1996: 44-62.

——. "Dale Earnhardt." *Stock Car Racing Race Fan Special* Spring 1996: 12-27.

——. "Getting Personal With Jeff Gordon." *Stock Car Racing* Apr. 1995: 30-45.

——. "Jeff Gordon's Growing Scrapbook." *Stock Car Racing Race Fan Special* Spring 1996: 36-50.

——. "Jeff Gordon's Problem." *Stock Car Racing* Mar. 1996: 20-32.

——. "Kyle Petty." *Stock Car Racing* Aug. 1993: 36+.

——. "Mark Martin Lightens Up." *Stock Car Racing* Sept. 1995: 20-36.

——. "The Marlins of Mahon Road." *Stock Car Racing* June 1996: 20-39.

——. "Pressure to Perform: Stress in the NASCAR Garage Area." *Stock Car Racing* July 1996: 116-25.

"Boycotters Will Return." *Toledo Blade* 15 Sept. 1969: 17.

Brantlinger, Patrick. *Crusoe's Footprints: Cultural Studies in Britain and America.* New York: Routledge, 1990.

"Brickhouse Seizes Chance." *Toledo Blade* 15 Sept. 1969: 17.

"Brickhouse Wins 500 at the New Talladega Speedway." *New York Times* 15 Sept. 1969: 66.

"Brickyard Brickbats." *Forbes* 11 Apr. 1994: 20.

Brown, Allan E., ed. *The History of the American Speedway: Past and Present.* Marne, MI: Slideways, 1984.

Browne, Ray B., Marshall Fishwick, and Kevin Browne, eds. *Dominant Symbols in Popular Culture.* Bowling Green, OH: Bowling Green State University Popular Press, 1990.

——. *Heroes of Popular Culture.* Bowling Green, OH: Bowling Green State University Popular Press, 1972.

Butterworth, W.E. *The High Wind: The Story of NASCAR Racing.* New York: Norton, 1971.

Byrnes, Nanette. "Rolling Billboards." *Financial World* 12 Apr. 1994: 46-56.

Calhoun, Donald W. *Sport, Culture, and Personality.* 2nd ed. Champaign, IL: Human Kinetics, 1987.

"Call It Texas International Raceway." *NASCAR Online.* Online. Netscape. World Wide Web. 17 Sept. 1996. Available: http://www.nascar.com

"Camel Ads Ignite Debate." *USA Today* 21 Feb. 1994: 1B.

Carr, Patrick. "The Outlaws Revolution Revisited." *Country Music* July / August 1996: 30-34.

Case, Carole. *Down the Backstretch: Racing and the American Dream.* Philadelphia: Temple UP, 1991.

Cawelti, John G. "Regionalism and Popular Culture: From Social Force to Symbolism." *Dominant Symbols in Popular Culture.* Ed. Ray Browne, Marshall Fishwick, and Kevin Browne. Bowling Green, OH: Bowling Green State University Popular Press, 1990. 96-111.

Cawthon, Raad. "Beer's on Earnhardt as Fans Swarm Wrecked Chevy." *Atlanta Journal Constitution* 22 May 1994: E10.

——. "Honor Among Thieves Is Out in NASCAR." *Atlanta Journal Constitution* 19 Feb. 1995: E6.

——. "NASCAR Puts Dent in New York City." *Atlanta Journal Constitution* 4 Dec. 1993: C3.

——. "Rudd Gets Probation, $10,000 Fine." *Atlanta Journal Constitution* 11 Nov. 1994: B3.

——. "Why NASCAR Is Such a Rush." *Atlanta Journal Constitution* 12 Feb. 1993: H1+.

——. "Winless Elliott Still Most Popular Driver." *Atlanta Journal Constitution* 3 Dec. 1993: B9.

"CBS Extends Daytona 500 Broadcast Deal Through 2001." *NASCAR Online.* Online. Netscape. World Wide Web. 25 Sept. 1996. Available: http://www.nascar.com

Chapin, Kim. "Curtis Lives!" *Sports Illustrated* 26 Feb. 1968: 48-60.

——. *Fast as White Lightning: The Story of Stock Car Racing.* New York: Dial, 1981.

Chengelis, Angelique. "NASCAR Makes Changes to Slow Down Race Speeds." *Detroit News* 10 Mar. 1995: 6F.

——. "Wallace's Victory a Gas." *Detroit News* 24 June 1996: C1.

"Chevy, Ford Continue Squabble Over Changes." *Toledo Blade* 28 April 1995: 25.

"Chicken Snake's 13th." *Toledo Blade* 21 Feb. 1994: 19.

"Childress Having Hard Time Finding Crew Chief." *Speedworld.* Online. Netscape. World Wide Web. 7 Nov. 1996. Available: http://www.speed-world.net

Clarke, Liz. "Will Attacks on Tobacco Slow NASCAR's Show?" *Charlotte Observer* 21 May 1994: A1+.

Coble, Don. "NASCAR: Lots of Dough Just to Go." *USA Today* 14 Feb. 1992: 7F.

Collector's World. Charlotte, NC: NA-TEX, 1992.

Collier, Peter, and David Horowitz. *The Fords: An American Epic.* New York: Summit Books, 1987.

Combs, James. "The Political Meaning of Popular Symbolic Activity." *Dominant Symbols in Popular Culture.* Ed. Ray Browne, Marshall Fishwick, and Kevin Browne. Bowling Green, OH: Bowling Green State University Popular Press, 1990. 30-38.

"A Conversation with Dale Earnhardt." *NASCAR Online.* Online. Netscape. World Wide Web. 20 Sept. 1996. Available: http://www.nascar.com

Cooper, Andrea. "Charlotte Business Report: Charlotte Motor Speedway Unveils Plans for Major Expansion." *North Carolina* May 1993: 72.

Cotsonika, Nicholas J. "It's Jarrett by a Bumper." *Detroit Free Press* 19 Aug. 1996: D1+.

Craft, John. *The Anatomy and Development of the Stock Car.* Osceola, WI: Motorbooks International, 1993.

——. *Vintage and Historic Stock Cars.* Osceola, WI: Motorbooks International, 1994.

Cramer, J., L. Rado, and J. Walker. "Athletic Heroes and Heroines: The Role of the Press in Their Creation." *Journal of Sport Behavior* Dec. 1981: 175-85.

Crepeau, R.C. "Sport, Heroes, and Myth." *Journal of Sport and Social Issues* Spring/Summer 1981: 23-31.

Crowe, Steve. "The King and The Comeback." *Detroit Free Press* 22 June 1996: B1+.

——. "Marlin Wins 500-Miler; Craven Gets Gift of Life." *Detroit Free Press* 29 April 1996: 5D.

——. "NASCAR Blows It, and Irvan Pays." *Detroit Free Press* 29 April 1996: 5D.

Culbertson, Todd. "Stock Car Races and Politics." *The American Enterprise* May/June 1990: 94-96.

"Dana Corporation and NASCAR Team Up." *NASCAR Online.* Online. Netscape. World Wide Web. 2 Nov. 1996. Available: http://www.nascar.com

"Darrell Waltrip Motorsports Hires Bickle." *NASCAR Online.* Online. Netscape. World Wide Web. 25 Sept. 1996. Available: http://www.nascar.com

"A Day in the Ivy League." *Speedworld.* Online. Netscape. World Wide Web. 1996. Available: http://www.speedworld.net

Days of Thunder. Dir. Tony Scott. With Tom Cruise, Robert Duvall, Randy Quaid, and Nicole Kidman. Paramount, 1990.

"Daytona's Gonna Be Smokin'." print advertisement. R.J. Reynolds Tobacco Co., 1994. *Winston Cup Scene* 13 Jan. 1994: back cover.

Denzin, Norman K. *Interpretive Interactionism.* Newbury Park: Sage, 1989.

DeVita, Philip R., and James D. Armstrong, eds. *Distant Mirrors: America As a Foreign Culture.* Belmont, CA: Wadsworth, 1993.

"Diamond Tower Terrace to Be Built at Charlotte." *Speedworld.* Online. Netscape. World Wide Web. 1996. Available: http://www.speedworld.net

"Dodge's Brickhouse Wins Strike-Marred '500' at Talladega." *National Speed Sport News* 17 Sept. 1969: 3+.

"Dover Downs Going Public." *NASCAR Online.* Online. Netscape. World Wide Web. 7 Oct. 1996. Available: http://www.nascar.com

"Dover Set to Add 73,000 Seats." *NASCAR Online.* Online. Netscape. World Wide Web. 28 Oct. 1996. Available: http://www.nascar.com

"Drivers, HASBRO Set for Toy Line." *NASCAR Online.* Online. Netscape. World Wide Web. 27 Oct. 1996. Available: http://www.nascar.com

Dunn, Clif H. "Country Stars Storm the Daytona 500." *Country Weekly* 21 March 1995: 30-34.

Dunn, Jim. "Golden Boy: The Fred Lorenzen Story." *Stock Car Racing* July 1996: 30-52.

"Dunnaway Wins Stock Car Race." *New York Times* 20 June 1949: 24.

DuPree, David. "Warriors' Webber Inks $74.4 M Deal." *USA Today* 24 Feb. 1994: 2B.

"Earnhardt, Elliott Close in Most Popular Driver Vote." *NASCAR Online.* Online. Netscape. World Wide Web. 5 Oct. 1996. Available: http://www. nascar.com

Easley, Greg. "King Richard, the Happy-Hearted." *Bubba Magazine* Summer 1993: 14-20.

Economaki, Chris. "From the Editor's Notebook." *National Speed Sport News* 11 Jan. 1995: 4+.

——. "From the Editor's Notebook." *National Speed Sport News* 17 Sept. 1969: 4+.

——. "Reynolds Tobacco in NASCAR: $100,000 Fund, 'Winston 500' Set." *National Speed Sport News* 16 Dec. 1970: 3+.

Economaki, Chris, and Leonard Laye. "Controversial '70 Entry Blanks Signed by PDA at 11th Hour." *National Speed Sport News* 7 Jan. 1970: 3+.

Egan, Peter. "Gone South." *Road and Track* Nov. 1991: 114-20.

"Elliott Leads Charge of Veterans Racing Trucks at Las Vegas." *NASCAR Online.* Online. Netscape. World Wide Web. 31 Oct. 1996. Available: http://www.nascar.com

"End of an Era." *Speedworld.* Online. Netscape. World Wide Web. 1996. Available: http://www.speedworld.net

Engel, Lyle Kenyon. *Racing to Win Wood Brothers Style.* New York: Arco, 1974.

——. *The Complete Book of NASCAR Stock Car Racing.* New York: Four Winds, 1974.

Falls, Joe. "Driver's 0-for-397 Record Is Tempered by $4.7 Million in Earnings and a 'Great Day' at MIS." *Detroit News* 24 June 1996: C1.

The Fan's Guide to Racing Shops: 1996 Edition. Charlotte, NC: Digital Desktop, 1996.

Fast Track High Performance Driving School. Harrisburg, NC: N.d. N.p.

Fenster, J.M. "Indy." *American Heritage* 43.3 (1992): 66-81.

Fetterman, David M. *Ethnography: Step by Step.* Newbury Park: Sage, 1989.

Fielden, Greg. *Forty Years of Stock Car Racing.* 5 vols. Pinehurst, SC: Galfield. 1990-94.

———. *High Speed at Low Tide.* Surfside Beach, SC: Galfield, 1993.

———. *Rumblin' Ragtops: The History of NASCAR's Fabulous Convertible Division and Speedway Division.* Pinehurst, SC: Galfield, 1990.

Fielden, Larry [Greg Fielden]. *Tim Flock: Race Driver.* Pinehurst, NC: Galfield, 1991.

"Field Set for Japan." *Speedworld.* Online. Netscape. World Wide Web. 1996. Available: http://www.speedworld.net

Finch, Christopher. *Highways to Heaven: The Auto Biography of America.* New York: HarperCollins, 1992.

Fireball 500. Dir. William Asher. With Frankie Avalon, Annette Funicello, and Fabian. American-International, 1966.

Fishwick, Marshall W. "Symbols: America's 'Natural Facts.'" *Dominant Symbols in Popular Culture.* Ed. Ray Browne, Marshall Fishwick, and Kevin Browne. Bowling Green: Bowling Green State University Popular Press, 1990.

———, and Ray B. Browne, eds. *Icons of Popular Culture.* Bowling Green, OH: Bowling Green State University Popular Press, 1970.

Flink, James J. *The Automobile Age.* Cambridge: MIT Press, 1988.

———. *The Car Culture.* Cambridge: MIT Press, 1975.

Flint, Jerry. "Auto Makers Gingerly Accelerate Promotion of Speed, Horsepower." *Wall Street Journal* 5 Mar. 1962: 1.

"Former Racer Robinson Paired with WTBS." *NASCAR Online.* Online. Netscape. World Wide Web. 2 Oct. 1996. Available: http://www.nascar. com

Foy, Jessica. "Johnson, Junior." *Encyclopedia of Southern Culture.* Ed. Charles Reagan Wilson and William Ferris. 4 vols. New York: Anchor Books, 1989.

Foyt, A.J. ,with William Neely. *A.J.* New York: Times Books, 1983.

Frank, Steven. *The Allisons: America's First Family of Stock-car Racing.* New York: Chelsea House, 1996.

Friedman, Alan, ed. *Sports Marketing: Inside Information.* Chicago: Team Marketing Report, 1991.

Friedman, Maurice. *The Confirmation of Otherness in Family, Community, and Society.* New York: Pilgrim Press, 1983.

"From the NASCAR of the Past to NASCAR of the Future." *Speedworld.* Online. Netscape. World Wide Web. 1996. Available: http://www.speed-world.net

From Thunder Road to Victory Lane: The NASCAR Story, vol. 1, 1947 to 1958. Videocassette. Prod. Creative Sports, 1993. 75 min.

"FTC Proposes Warnings with Tobacco Logos." *Toledo Blade* 29 Oct. 1993: 3.

Fuller, Don. "The Psyche of Champions." *Motor Trend* July 1988: 82+.

Fusco, Andy. "The Olds 88: NASCAR's First Supercar." *Stock Car Racing* June 1989: 40-49.

Gabbard, Alex. *Return to Thunder Road: The Story Behind the Legend.* Lenoir City, TN: Gabbard, 1992.

Gaillard, Frye, with Kyle Petty. *Kyle at 200 M.P.H.* New York: St. Martin's, 1993.

Gans, Herbert J. *Popular Culture and High Culture: An Analysis and Evaluation of Taste.* New York: Basic, 1974.

Geertz, Clifford. *The Interpretation of Cultures.* New York: Basic, 1973.

Georgano, Nick. *The American Automobile: A Centenary, 1893-1983.* New York: Smithmark, 1992.

"Gibbs, Labonte Switch to Pontiac for '97 Season." *NASCAR Online.* Online. Netscape. World Wide Web. 16 Oct. 1996. Available: http://www.nascar. com

Girdler, Allan. *Stock Car Racers: The History and Folklore of NASCAR's Premier Series.* Osceola, WI: Motorbooks International, 1988.

Glick, Shav. "France: Benevolent Dictator." *Los Angeles Times* 12 June 1992: C2.

——. "Still in Harm's Way: Method to Prevent Accidents Involving Pit Crews Eludes Auto Racing." *Los Angeles Times* 28 Nov. 1990: C1+.

Goldfield, David R. *Promised Land: The South Since 1945.* Arlington Heights, IL: Harlan Davidson, 1987.

Golenbock, Peter. *American Zoom: Stock Car Racing—From the Dirt Tracks to Daytona.* New York: Macmillan, 1993.

"Good ole Races." *The Economist* 4 June 1994: 94.

"Goodyear Report Says: Attendance Up 500,000 in '93." *National Speed Sport News* 28 Jan. 1994: 8+.

"Gordon Finishes First in North Wilkesboro's Last." *NASCAR Online.* Online. Netscape. World Wide Web. 29 Sept. 1996. Available: http://www.nascar. com

Grable, Ron. "A Pair of Pontiacs at Talladega." *Motor Trend* Jan. 1989: 96+.

Granatelli, Andy. "Rap 'n 'pinion." *Motor Trend* May 1970: 18.

Granger, Gene. "Baseball Dreams Shattered by Injury, Derrike Cope Turns to Stock Cars." *Budweiser at the Glen Race Program* 10 Aug. 1986: 98-99.

——. "A Critical Look at NASCAR." *Auto Racing Digest* Mar. 1974: 22-26.

Grant, Robert W. *The Psychology of Sport: Facing One's True Opponent.* London: McFarland, 1988.

Greased Lightning. Dir. Michael Schultz. With Richard Pryor, Beau Bridges, and Cleavon Little. Warner Brothers, 1977.

Green, David. "No Gain, No Loss for Irvan." *Winston Cup Scene* 18 Aug. 1994: 10.

——. "TV Rights Competition Reaches a Comfort Zone." *Winston Cup Scene* 27 Jan. 1994: 6.

Green, Ron. *From Tobacco Road to Amen Corner: On Sports and Life.* Asheboro, NC: Down Home Press, 1990.

Griffin, Larry. "Sign of the Cross." *Car and Driver* May 1990: 169-81.

Grizzard, Lewis. *I Haven't Understood Anything Since 1962 and Other Nekkid Truths.* New York: Villard, 1992.

Gross, Ken. "Racer Tim Richmond Set Records Aplenty, but His Lovers Now Fear that AIDS Will Be His Real Legacy." *People* 12 Dec. 1989: 75-81.

Grubba, Dale. "Knowing Alan." *Stock Car Racing* July 1993: 64-72.

Gunnell, John A., ed. *Race Car Flashback: A Celebration of America's Affair with Auto Racing from 1900-1980s.* Iola, WI: Krause, 1994.

Guttmann, Allen. *From Ritual to Record: The Nature of Modern Sports.* New York: Columbia UP, 1978.

——. *A Whole New Ball Game: An Interpretation of American Sports.* Chapel Hill: U of North Carolina P, 1988.

——. *Sports Spectators.* New York: Columbia UP, 1986.

Hager, Dave. "'Thunder' Row." *Entertainment Weekly* 10 Aug. 1990: 50-53.

Handelman, Don. *Models and Mirrors: Towards an Anthropology of Public Events.* Cambridge: Cambridge UP, 1990.

Handzel, Will. "The Brickyard 400: A Race to Remember." *Hot Rod* Aug. 1994: 88-91.

Hargreaves, John. *Sport, Power, and Culture: A Social and Historical Analysis of Popular Sports in Britain.* New York: St. Martin's, 1986.

Harris, H.A. *Sport in Greece and Rome.* Ithaca: Cornell UP, 1972.

Harris, Marvin. *Our Kind: Who We Are, Where We Came From, Where We Are Going.* New York: HarperCollins, 1989.

Harris, Mike. "Labontes Sweep Race and Championship at Atlanta Track." *RACESHOP.* Online. Netscape. World Wide Web. 10 Nov. 1996. Available: http://www.raceshop.com

——. "Marlin Comes From Behind for Winston Select Victory." *USA Today* 29 April 1996: 3C.

Hartford, Robin. "Collectibles and Souvenirs." *Stock Car Racing* Nov. 1996: 96-100.

——. "High Performance Driving Schools." *Stock Car Racing Race Fan Special* Spring 1996: 28-33.

——. "Racing Toward a College Degree." *Stock Car Racing* Sept. 1995: 46-49.

——. "Texas Motor Speedway." *Stock Car Racing* June 1996: 122-23.

"Help for Dealers." *Time* 13 Feb. 1956: 80-81.

Hembree, Mike. "Building a Better Mousetrap." *Winston Cup Scene* 14 Sept. 1995: 27-29.

——. "Dream Teams." *Beckett Racing Monthly* May 1996: 24-29.

——. "Owner-Driver." *Winston Cup Scene* 22 Feb. 1996: 44-45.

Hemphill, Paul. *The Good Old Boys.* New York: Simon & Schuster, 1974.

Hickman, Herman. "Curtis Turner." *American Racing Classics* Apr. 1992: 28-37.

Hinton, Ed. "Attitude For Sale." *Sports Illustrated* 6 Feb. 1995: 68-76.

——. "The King." *Sports Illustrated* 19 Oct. 1992: 66-72.

Hmiel, Steve. "The Price of Success." *Stock Car Racing* Jan. 1991: 10.

"Hoffa Asks Teamsters for Power to Set Up New Labor Federation." *Wall Street Journal* 5 July 1961: 8.

Holman, Blan. "The ABC's of NASCAR: A Rookie's Guide to High-Speed Land Travel." *Bubba Magazine* Summer 1993: 21-25.

Horovitz, Bruce. "Fine-Tuning an Image: New Breed of Sponsors Race to NASCAR." *USA Today* 5 April 1996: B1+.

Howell, Mark D. "Barney Oldfield and His Golden Submarine." *Car Collector and Car Classics* May 1996: 34-42.

Huff, Richard M. *Behind the Wall: A Season on the NASCAR Circuit.* Chicago: Bonus Books, 1992.

Humphrey, John M. *Roman Circuses: Arenas for Chariot Racing.* Berkeley: U of California P, 1986.

Hunnicutt, Benjamin K. "Sports." *Encyclopedia of Southern Culture.* Ed. Charles Reagan Wilson and William Ferris. 4 vols. New York: Anchor, 1989.

"Inconsistent Enforcement." *Winston Cup Scene* 15 July 1993: 4.

Ingham, A.G. "Occupational Subcultures in the Work World of Sport." *Sport and the Social Order.* Ed. D.W. Ball and J.W. Loy. Reading: Addison-Wesley, 1975. 337-89.

Ingram, Jonathan. "The Boys are Back." *Stock Car Racing* Jan. 1995: 24-42.

——. "No Place Like Home." *Beckett Racing Monthly* Jan. 1995: 18-23.

——. "Rick Hendrick: Man on the Fast Track." *Motor Trend* Aug. 1989: 116-22.

"Japan May Get Two Exhibition Races in 1998, Schedule May Expand." *Speedworld.* Online. Netscape. World Wide Web. 1996. Available: http://www.speedworld.net

"Japanese Drivers." *Stock Car Racing* Nov. 1996: 146.

Jaspersen, Mike. "Signs of the Time." *Beckett Racing Monthly* Jan. 1995: 66.

Jeanes, William. "When Big Bill France Moved on Motown." *Car and Driver* Oct. 1991: 119-26.

Jenkins, Dan. "Drive, She Said." *Playboy* July 1989: 27.

Johnson, David M. "Stock Car Racing." *Encyclopedia of Southern Culture.* Ed. Charles Reagan Wilson and William Ferris. 4 vols. New York: Anchor, 1989.

Johnson, Junior. "Interview: Junior Johnson." *Winston Cup Illustrated* Oct. 1991: 8+.

Jones, Robert F. "It's a Go at the Glen." *Sports Illustrated* 22 Aug. 1988: 36-37.

Kanaley, Reid. "Driving Like a NASCAR Pro on a 'Virtual' Racing Circuit." *Philadelphia Inquirer* 15 Aug. 1996: F1+.

Kate, Nancy Ten. "Make It an Event." *American Demographics* Nov. 1992: 40-44.

Kefauver, Estes, with Irene Till. *In a Few Hands: Monopoly Power in America.* New York: Pantheon, 1965.

Kelly, Bob. "A New Beginning." *American Racing Classics* Apr. 1992: 6-19.

Kidd, Al. "Trends in Auto Racing." *Motor Trend* July 1956: 26+.

Kimes, Beverly Rae. "The Dawn of Speed." *American Heritage* 38.7 (1987): 92-101.

Kirby, Jack T. *Media-Made Dixie: The South in the American Imagination.* Athens: U of Georgia P, 1986.

Kleber, Marion. "Dale Jarrett's Struggle." *Stock Car Racing* Jan. 1991: 76-82.

Knotts, Bob. "Shifting Into the Fast Lane." *Inside Sports* Mar. 1996: 48-58.

Kolodny, Annette. *The Lay of the Land: Metaphor as Experience and History in American Life and Letters.* Chapel Hill: U of North Carolina P, 1975. 28.

Kuebelbeck, Amy. "Hooters: Invitation to Harassment?" *Toledo Blade* 18 July 1993: G2.

"Kyle Petty, Mattel Join Petty Enterprises." *NASCAR Online.* Online. Netscape. World Wide Web. 25 Oct. 1996. Available: http://www.nascar.com

"Labonte Brothers Win Big!" *Speedworld.* Online. Netscape. World Wide Web. 11 Nov. 1996. Available: http://speedworld.net

The Last American Hero. Dir. Lamont Johnson. With Jeff Bridges, Valerie Perrine, Gary Busey, and Ned Beatty. 20th Century Fox, 1973.

Lawrence, Elizabeth Atwood. *Rodeo: An Anthropologist Looks at the Wild and the Tame.* Chicago: U of Chicago P, 1984.

Laye, Leonard. "Inconclusive Charlotte." *Motor Trend* Dec. 1969: 70-72.

——. "1970 Racing Preview: NASCAR." *Motor Trend* March 1970: 46-47.

——. "Talladega's Troubled Baptism." *Motor Trend* Nov. 1969: 34-36.

"Lee Roy Yarbrough Leading Annual Race Drivers' Contest." *New York Times* 14 Sept. 1969: 13.

Legends: The Statesmen of the Racing World. Videocassette. Prod. DSL Communications, Inc. NASCAR Video, 1993. 30 min.

Lewis, David L., and Laurence Goldstein, ed. *The Automobile and American Culture.* Ann Arbor: U of Michigan P, 1983.

"Life Goes on After Death at Daytona." *Toledo Blade* 13 Feb. 1994, B3.

Linde, Debbie. "Sawdust in Their Shoes: Black Performers in American Circuses." *American Visions* April/May 1992: 12-19.

Lipsitz, George. *Time Passages: Collective Memory and American Popular Culture.* Minneapolis: U. of Minnesota P., 1990.

"A Little Sake with His 'Shine." *Autoweek* 7 Oct. 1996: 55.

Luther, Bill. "Labonte-ful! Terry, Bobby Both Winners." *ESPNET Sports Zone: Auto Racing.* Online. Netscape. World Wide Web. 10 Nov. 1996. Available: http://www.ESPNET.SportsZone.com/car

MacAloon, John J., ed. *Rite, Drama, Festival, Spectacle: Rehearsals Toward a Theory of Cultural Performance.* Philadelphia: Institute for the Study of Human Issues, 1984.

The Making of Days of Thunder. With Dr. Jerry Punch. Paramount and ESPN Enterprises, Inc., 1990.

Mandel, Leon. *Driven: The American Four-Wheeled Love Affair.* New York: Stein and Day, 1977.

Manning, Frank E., ed. *The Celebration of Society: Perspectives on Contemporary Cultural Performance.* Bowling Green, OH: Bowling Green State University Popular Press, 1983.

Marquez, Edrie J. *Amazing AMC Muscle: Complete Development and Racing History of the Cars from American Motors.* Osceola, WI: Motorbooks International, 1988.

Marsh, Peter, and Peter Collett. *Driving Passion: The Psychology of the Car.* Boston: Faber, 1986.

Marx, Leo. *The Machine in the Garden: Technology and the Pastoral Ideal in America.* New York: Oxford UP, 1964.

Mayer, Steve. "Charlotte-Atlanta Offering Prospectus Lays Bare Financial Aspect of Tracks." *National Speed Sport News* 11 Jan. 1995: 2+.

McCracken, Grant. *Culture and Consumption: New Approaches to the Symbolic Character of Consumer Goods and Activities.* Bloomington: Indiana UP, 1988.

McCrary, Bill. "Rap 'n 'pinion." *Motor Trend* Feb. 1970: 18.

McCredie, Gary. "The First NASCAR Race." *American Racing Classics* Apr. 1992: 118-27.

Mitchell, Cynthia. "Mello Yello Dressed Up for the Teen-age Crowd." *Atlanta Journal Constitution* 12 Nov. 1994: C1.

"Monopoly." *Stock Car Racing* Sept. 1995: 140.

Moody, John. *The Truth About the Trusts: A Description and Analysis of the American Trust Movement.* New York: Greenwood, 1968.

"Moog Joins NASCAR Aftermarket Program." *NASCAR Online.* Online. Netscape. World Wide Web. 22 Oct. 1996. Available: http://www.nascar. com

Moonshine Highway. Dir. Andy Armstrong. With Kyle MacLachlan, Randy Quaid, and Maria Del Mar. Paramount, 1996.

Moriarty, Frank. "Back on Track." *Philadelphia Weekly* 5 June 1996: 21-26.

Mortimer, Jeylan T., Jon Lorence, and Donald S. Kumka. *Work, Family, and Personality: Transition to Adulthood.* Norwood, NJ: Ablex Publishing Corp., 1986.

Moses, Sam. "Ready to Trade Some Paint." *Sports Illustrated* 3 July 1989: 43-48.

——. "Taking the Wrong Track." *Sports Illustrated* 25 July 1988: 72.

——. "Vroooom With a View." *Sports Illustrated* 20 Aug. 1990: 26-27.

"Motor Trend Interview: Lawrence H. LoPatin." *Motor Trend* Sept. 1969: 87-92.

Mott, Evelyn Clarke. *A Day at the Races with Austin and Kyle Petty.* New York: Random House, 1993.

Mottram, Eric. *Blood on the Nash Ambassador: Investigations in American Culture.* London: Hutchinson Radius, 1983.

Muhleman, Max. "1965 Stock Car Predictions." *Motor Trend* Jan. 1965: 52-57.

——. "Stock Car Foresight and Hindsight." *Motor Trend* Mar. 1964: 70-73.

——. "Stock Talk." *Motor Trend* Apr. 1964: 94-95.

——. "Stock Talk." *Motor Trend* June 1964: 94-95.

——. "Stock Talk." *Motor Trend* Aug. 1964: 88.

——. "Stock Talk." *Motor Trend* Dec. 1964: 90-91.

Nachbar, Jack, and Kevin Lause, eds. *Popular Culture: An Introductory Text.* Bowling Green, OH: Bowling Green State University Popular Press, 1992.

Nagy, Bob. "Motorsport: NASCAR's Inch of Prevention." *Motor Trend* May 1988: 151-54.

"NASCAR Alters Grand Nat'l Specs; Step in Right Direction Says PDA." *National Speed Sport News* 12 Aug. 1970: 3+.

"NASCAR Announces Final Driver List for Japan." *NASCAR Online.* Online. Netscape. World Wide Web. 9 Nov. 1996. Available: http://www.nascar.com

"NASCAR Announces Modifications." *NASCAR Online.* Online. Netscape. World Wide Web. 30 Sept. 1996. Available: http://www.nascar.com

"NASCAR Approves 'Fancy' Engines." *New York Times* 13 Feb. 1965: 16.

"NASCAR Asks 'Good Faith' Pledge." *National Speed Sport News* 24 Sept. 1969: 3+.

"NASCAR Believes, Then So Do We." *Winston Cup Scene* 28 July 1994: 4.

"NASCAR Cafe Hits Music City." *NASCAR Online.* Online. Netscape. World Wide Web. 23 July 1996. Available: http://www.nascar.com

"NASCAR Confirms 1997 Rules Changes." *NASCAR Online.* Online. Netscape. World Wide Web. 11 Sept. 1996. Available: http://www.nascar.com

"NASCAR Drives into Automotive Aftermarket." *NASCAR Online.* Online. Netscape. World Wide Web. 2 Oct. 1996. Available: http://www.nascar.com

"NASCAR Expands in Video Game Market." *NASCAR Online.* Online. Netscape. World Wide Web. 15 Oct. 1996. Available: http://www.nascar. com

"NASCAR Fines Gordon's Crew a Record $60,000." *Toledo Blade* 31 May 1995: 25.

"NASCAR Garage Opens its Doors." *NASCAR Online.* Online. Netscape. World Wide Web. 7 Nov. 1996. Available: http://www.nascar.com

"NASCAR Notes: Winston Cup Losing Piece of its Soul." *ESPNET Sports Zone: Auto Racing.* Online. Netscape. 1996. Available: http://ESPNET. SportsZone.com/car

"NASCAR on the Move." *Stock Car Racing* May 1996: 172.

"NASCAR Products Provide Quality and Performance." *NASCAR Online.* Online. Netscape. World Wide Web. 2 Oct. 1996. Available: http://www. nascar.com

"NASCAR Races into Toy Vehicle Market." *NASCAR Online.* Online. Netscape. World Wide Web. 7 Aug. 1996. Available: http://www. nascar.com

"NASCAR Right Up the Alley of America's Bowlers." *NASCAR Online.* Online. Netscape. World Wide Web. 7 Aug. 1996. Available: http://www. nascar.com

"NASCAR Set to Drive into Automotive Aftermarket." *NASCAR Online.* Online. Netscape. World Wide Web. 2 Oct. 1996. Available: http://www. nascar.com

"NASCAR Stiffens Rules." *New York Times* 15 Oct. 1983: 30.

"NASCAR, Suzuka Circuit Announce Final Field." *NASCAR Online.* Online. Netscape. World Wide Web. 13 Sept. 1996. Available: http://www. nascar.com

Nelson, Mariah Burton. *Are We Winning Yet?: How Women are Changing Sports and Sports are Changing Women.* New York: Random House, 1991.

Nerpel, Charles. "The Editor's Auto-Graphs." *Motor Trend* Jan. 1965: 10.

———. "The Editor's Auto-Graphs." *Motor Trend* Feb. 1965: 10.

Neuborne, Ellen. "Uproar Adds to Joe Camel's Image." *USA Today* 24 Feb. 1994: 2B.

Nixon, Howard L. *Sport and the American Dream* New York: Leisure Press, 1984.

"No Stock Answers." *Sports Illustrated* 29 Aug. 1994: 16.

Nolan, William F. *Barney Oldfield: The Life and Times of America's Legendary Speed King.* New York: Putnam, 1961.

Noverr, Douglas A., and Lawrence E. Ziewacz. *The Games They Played: Sports in American History, 1865-1980.* Chicago: Nelson-Hall, 1983.

The Official Directory for the NASCAR Winston Cup Series 1996. N.p.: BellSouth Advertising and Publishing Corporation, 1996.

The Official NASCAR 1994 Preview and Press Guide. Charlotte, NC: UMI Publications, 1994.

The Official NASCAR 1995 Preview and Press Guide. Charlotte, NC: UMI Publications, 1995.

The Official NASCAR 1996 Preview and Press Guide. Charlotte, NC: UMI Publications, 1996.

The Official NASCAR 1987 Yearbook and Press Guide. Charlotte, NC: UMI Publications, 1987.

The Official Pocket Price Guide for Die-Cast Racing Collectables. Crossville, AL: Pocket Guide, 1994.

Oldfield, Barney. *Barney Oldfield's Book for the Motorist.* New York: Small, Maynard, 1919.

O'Shei,Tim. "Cardboard Creation." *Beckett Racing Monthly* Jan. 1995: 28-33.

Owens, Jeff. "Allison Just Misses Victory." *Winston Cup Scene* 15 July 1993: 11.

Owens, Thomas S. "Manufacturing Miniatures." *Beckett Racing Monthly* Jan. 1995: 70-74.

Ownby, Ted. *Subduing Satan: Religion, Recreation, and Manhood in the Rural South, 1865-1920.* Chapel Hill, NC: U of North Carolina P, 1990.

"PDA Drivers Must Post Bonds Before Next Race." *National Speed Sport News* 17 Sept. 1969: 3+.

Parkes, Henry Bamford. *The American Experience.* New York: Random House, 1959.

"Penske Announces PSL's at California Speedway." *NASCAR Online.* Online. Netscape. World Wide Web. 28 Oct. 1996. Available: http://www. nascar.com

Peterson, Karen S. "The Love of Thrills May Lie in the Genes." *USA Today* 22 Feb. 1994: 4D.

"Petty Fined $35,000 for Rule Violations." *New York Times* 10 Oct. 1983: C7.

Petty, Kyle. "How I Spent My Winter Vacation." *Atlanta Journal Constitution* 19 Feb. 1995: E6.

——. "Sponsor Demands Often Can Conflict With Racing Needs." *Atlanta Journal Constitution* 22 May 1994: E10.

Petty, Richard. "Franchise the League." *Stock Car Racing* Jan. 1995: 15.

——. *King of the Road.* New York: Macmillan, 1977.

——. "Rap 'n 'pinion." *Motor Trend* March 1970: 18.

Petty, Richard, with William Neely. *King Richard I: The Autobiography of America's Greatest Auto Racer.* New York: Macmillan, 1986.

Phillips, Benny. "Ernie Irvan." *Stock Car Racing* Jan. 1995: 22.

——. "Feel the Power." *Stock Car Racing* Nov. 1996: 10.

——. "Flossie Johnson's Career as a Car Owner." *Stock Car Racing* Oct. 1991: 10.

——. "Harry Hyde." *Stock Car Racing* Sept. 1996: 130-31.

——. "Junior Johnson Moves On." *Stock Car Racing* March 1996: 60-68.

——. "Neil Blurs into Memory." *Stock Car Racing* May 1994: 7.

Phillips, John, III. "The Dynamo of Dynamometers." *Car and Driver* April 1990: 155-74.

Pillsbury, Richard. "Carolina Thunder: A Geography of Southern Stock Car Racing." *Fast Food, Stock Cars, and Rock 'n' Roll: Place and Space in American Pop Culture.* Ed. George O. Carney. Lanham, MD: Rowman and Littlefield, 1995. 229-38.

——. "A Mythology at the Brink: Stock Car Racing in the American South." *Fast Food, Stock Cars, and Rock 'n' Roll: Place and Space in American Pop Culture.* Ed. George O. Carney. Lanham, MD: Rowman and Littlefield, 1995. 239-48.

"Pontiac by a Nose?" *Road and Track* Aug. 1994: 144.

Pope, Thomas. "Racing's Bottom Line Is Selling the Product." *Winston Cup Illustrated* July 1996: 10.

Post, Robert C. *High Performance: The Culture and Technology of Drag Racing, 1950-1990.* Baltimore: Johns Hopkins UP, 1994.

Potter, David C. *People of Plenty.* Chicago: U of Chicago P, 1954.

Potter, Jerry. "Junior Says New Rules Are the Pits." *USA Today* 15 Feb. 1991: 4E.

Pozzetta, George E., ed. *Assimilation, Acculturation, and Social Mobility.* New York: Garland, 1991. Vol. 13 of *American Immigration and Ethnicity: 20 vols.*

Price, Karsen Palmer. "In Honor of Jefferson and Good ol' Paul Revere." *Winston Cup Illustrated* Apr. 1996: 12.

Pursell, Carroll W., Jr. "The History of Technology and the Study of Material Culture." *Material Culture: A Research Guide.* Ed. Thomas J. Schlereth. Lawrence: UP of Kansas, 1985. 113-26.

"Quaker Joins the NASCAR Aftermarket Parts Program." *NASCAR Online.* Online. Netscape. World Wide Web. 7 Nov. 1996. Available: http://www.nascar.com

"The Race to History at Talladega." *Southern Living* Jan. 1989: 22.

"Racing Camp for Kids to be Held at Atlanta." *Speedworld.* Online. Netscape. World Wide Web. 1996. Available: http://www.speedworld.net

Racing Legends: 1956 Darlington, 1957 Daytona. Videocassette. Prod. United American Video, 1990. 50 min.

"Racing Restaurants." *Winston Cup Illustrated* July 1996: 54-60.

Real, M.R. "Super Bowl: Mythic Spectacle." *Journal of Communication* Winter 1975: 31-43.

Reasoner, Harry, comm. "King Richard." *Sixty Minutes.* CBS Television. 17 Dec. 1989.

Red Line 7000. Dir. Howard Hawks. With James Caan, Laura Devon, and Gail Hire. Paramount, 1965.

Reed, John Shelton. *One South: An Ethnic Approach to Regional Culture.* Baton Rouge: Louisiana State UP, 1982.

——. *Southern Folk, Plain and Fancy: Native White Social Types.* Athens, GA: U of Georgia P, 1986.

——. *Whistling Dixie: Dispatches From the South.* Columbia: U of Missouri P, 1990.

Richard Petty Driving Experience. Harrisburg, NC: N.d. N.p.

Richter, Les. "Rap 'n 'pinion." *Motor Trend* Jan. 1970: 16+.

"Rick Mast Chat Session." *NASCAR Online.* Online. Netscape. World Wide Web. 17 Sept. 1996. Available: http://www.nascar.com

Rider, Phil. "Racin' Down the Information Superhighway: Computers and Race Fans Are Connecting." *Stock Car Racing* July 1995: 120-21.

"RJR: No Conflict of Interest." *Winston Cup Scene* 27 Jan. 1994: 33.

"Robby Gordon Headed to NASCAR." *Speedworld.* Online. Netscape. World Wide Web. 1996. Available: http://www.speedworld.net

Roberts, John M., and David F. Kundrat. "Variation in Expressive Balances and Competence for Sports Car Rally Teams." *Urban Life* July 1978: 231-51.

Roberts, Tom. "One More Call." *Stock Car Racing* July 1993: 52-63.

Robertson, Ian. *Sociology.* New York: Worth Publishers, 1987.

Robinson, Bill. "Daytona 500." *Motor Trend* May 1965: 52-57.

Rockland, Michael Aaron. "American Mobility." *Dominant Symbols in Popular Culture.* Ed. Ray B. Browne, Marshall Fishwick, and Kevin Browne. Bowling Green: OH: Bowling Green State University Popular Press, 1990. 59-74.

Rosenberg, E. "Sports as Work: Characteristics and Career Patterns." *Sociological Symposium* Spring 1980: 39-61.

Rubin, Mike. "The Big Show." *Spin* May 1996: 48-54.

"Rush Races Camaro to Victory in Talladega's 'Bama 400 GT." *National Speed Sport News* 17 Sept. 1969: 2+.

"Rush Takes First Race at New Alabama Track." *Toledo Blade* 14 Sept. 1969: G2.

Sage, George H., ed. *Sport and American Society: Selected Readings.* 3rd ed. Reading: Addison-Wesley, 1980.

Sanoff, Alvin P. "A Family of Floorboarders." *U.S. News and World Report* 12 Dec. 1988: 85.

Scharff, Virginia. *Taking the Wheel: Women and the Coming of the Motor Age.* New York: Free Press, 1991.

Schlereth, Thomas J., ed. *Cultural History and Material Culture: Everyday Life, Landscapes, Museums.* Ann Arbor: UMI Research, 1990.

———. *Material Cultural Studies in America.* Nashville: American Association for State and Local History, 1982.

"Schrader Suspension Is Lifted." *Detroit News* 7 July 1993: 6F.

Scura, Dorothy M., ed. *Conversations with Tom Wolfe.* Jackson, MS: UP of Mississippi, 1990.

Shaffir, William B., and Robert A. Stebbins, ed. *Experiencing Fieldwork: An Inside View of Qualitative Research.* Newbury Park: Sage, 1991.

Sharp, Linda. "Faithful Fan Shares in NASCAR Win." *Atlanta Journal Constitution* 3 Dec. 1993: S2.

Shaw, Donna. "Behind the Wheels." *Philadelphia Inquirer* 15 Aug. 1996: F1+.

Shenon, Philip. "The World: Asia's Having One Huge Nicotine Fit." From *New York Times* 15 May 1994, 4, p.1. *CHANCE News 3.07.* Online. Netscape. World Wide Web. 22 Oct. 1996. Available: http://www.geom.umn.edu/docs/snell/chance/Chance.html

Shuman, A.B. "Foyt Wins/Jones Wins Eighth Annual *Motor Trend* 500." *Motor Trend* Mar. 1970: 74+.

Shurmaitis, Dawn. "NASCAR's All-new Models." *Wilkes-Barre Times Leader* 17 July 1996: 3A.

Shuster, Rachel. "Robinson Faces Extra Hurdles to Keeping Career on Track." *USA Today* 3 Feb. 1994: 2C.

Six Pack. Dir. Daniel Petrie. With Kenny Rogers, Diane Lane, and Erin Gray. 20th Century Fox, 1982.

Slaughter, Thomas P. *The Whiskey Rebellion: Frontier Epilogue to the American Revolution.* New York: Oxford UP, 1986.

Slotkin, Richard. *The Fatal Environment: The Myth of the Frontier in the Age of Industrialization, 1800-1890.* Middletown: Wesleyan UP, 1985.

Smith, Gary J. "The Sport Hero: An Endangered Species." *Quest* Jan. 1973: 59-70.

Smith, Henry Nash. *Virgin Land: The American West as Symbol and Myth.* New York: Vintage, 1957.

Smith, Stephen A. *Myth, Media, and the Southern Mind.* Fayetteville: U of Arkansas P, 1985.

Sneddon, Rob. "Glimpses." *Stock Car Racing* July 1993: 29-47.

Snider, Mike. "Ads Cited for Teen Smoking." *USA Today* 24 Feb. 1994: 2B.

Snyder, Eldon E., and Elmer A. Spreitzer. *Social Aspects of Sport,* 3rd ed. Englewood Cliffs: Prentice, 1989.

Snyder, John. "NASCAR Numerology." *Stock Car Racing* Feb. 1995: 64-70.

Sowers, Richard. "The Continuing American Hero: NASCAR's Junior Johnson Wins as Car Builder, Too." *Sporting News* 23 Oct. 1989: 38.

"Spam May Be Leaving Melling Racing as Sponsor in 1997." *Speedworld.* Online. Netscape. World Wide Web. 1996. Available: http://www.speedworld.net

The Speed Kings. Dir. Mack Sennett. With Mabel Normand, Roscoe Arbuckle, Earl Cooper, Teddy Tetzlaft, and Barney Oldfield. Keystone, 1913.

Speedway. Dir. Norman Taurog. With Elvis Presley, Nancy Sinatra, Bill Bixby, and Gale Gordon. Metro Goldwyn Meyer, 1968.

"Speedway Motorsports Joins Quad-Cities Project." *NASCAR Online.* Online. Netscape. World Wide Web. 17 Oct. 1996. Available: http://www.nascar. com

Spence, Steve. "The Plumb Fast Turn Plug Crazy." *Car and Driver* Aug. 1992: 104-09.

——. "Touring: A Tale of Two Kings." *Car and Driver* Aug. 1992: 164.

Spencer, Reid and Candi Spencer. "Racing Collectables: New Collectables and Souvenirs for the 1994 Racing Season." *Winston Cup Scene* 20 Jan. 1994: A1-A16.

"Sponsor News and Notes." *NASCAR Online.* Online. Netscape. World Wide Web. 9 Nov. 1996. Available: http://www.nascar.com

"Spotlight on Detroit: Forecasts, Facts and Rumors." *Motor Trend* Feb. 1965: 6.

Steinbreder, John. "Will the Buyout Mean Bye-Bye?" *Sports Illustrated* 12 Dec. 1988: 18.

Stern, Jane, and Michael Stern. *Encyclopedia of Pop Culture.* New York: HarperCollins, 1992.

Stilley, Al. "The Indianapolis 500." *Stock Car Racing* Sept. 1995: 78-82.

Stinson, Tom. "Which Came First, Racing or the Corporate Sponsor?" *NASCAR Online.* Online. Netscape. World Wide Web. 14 Aug. 1996. Available: http://www.nascar.com

Stone, Gregory P. "Sport as a Community Representation." *Handbook of Social Science of Sport.* Ed. G. Lincoln and G.H. Sage. Champaign, IL: Stipes, 1981. 214-45.

Stroker Ace. Dir. Hal Needham. With Burt Reynolds, Ned Beatty, Jim Nabors, and Loni Anderson. Universal, 1983.

Sumner, Jim L. *A History of Sports in North Carolina.* Raleigh: Division of Archives and History, North Carolina Department of Cultural Resources, 1990.

Susman, Warren. *Culture As History: The Transformation of American Society in the Twentieth Century.* New York: Pantheon, 1984.

Swan, Tony. "Motorsports: Red, White and Blue Racing." *Popular Mechanics* Feb. 1989: 38-39.

"Talladega: The Principals and the Principles." *Motor Trend* Nov. 1969: 37+.

"Teams and Drivers Join the Aftermarket Program." *NASCAR Online.* Online. Netscape. World Wide Web. 7 Nov. 1996. Available: http://www.nascar. com

Teinowitz, Ira. "Ads a Casualty in Cig Price War." *Advertising Age* 6 Sept. 1993: 2.

——. "Miller's Race Cars Change Their Look." *Advertising Age* Feb. 1988: 46.

"Texas Gets '97 Date, NHIS Adds Second Race." *NASCAR Online.* Online. Netscape. World Wide Web. 11 July 1996. Available: http://www.nascar. com

"Texas Motor Speedway May Get two Winston Cup Dates in 1997." *Speedworld.* Online. Netscape. World Wide Web. 1996. Available: http://www. speedworld.net

Thigpen, David E. "Real-Life Days of Thunder." *Time* 30 July 1990: 55.

Thomy, Al. *Bill Elliott: The Fastest Man Alive.* Atlanta: Peachtree Publishers, 1988.

Thunder in Carolina. Dir. Paul Helmick. With Rory Calhoun, Alan Hale, and Connie Hines. Howco, 1960.

Thunder Road. Dir. Arthur Ripley. With Robert Mitchum, Gene Barry, and Keely Smith. DRM Productions, 1958.

Tichi, Cecelia. *Shifting Gears: Technology, Literature, Culture in Modernist America.* Chapel Hill: U of North Carolina P, 1987.

"Tobacco Sponsorship Threatened." *Speedworld.* Online. Netscape. World Wide Web. 1996. Available: http://www.speedworld.net

"Top Drivers Quit Talladega 500." *Toledo Blade* 14 Sept. 1969: G2.

"Top NASCAR Names Form Drivers' Ass'n." *National Speed Sport News* 27 Aug. 1969: 3+.

Turner, Victor. *The Anthropology of Performance.* New York: PAJ Publications, 1986.

Tuschak, Beth. "Bonnett Was Driven to Return to Racing." *USA Today* 14 Feb. 1994: 6C.

——. "Champion, Owner Put It in Reverse." *USA Today* 7 Sept. 1994: C10.

——. "Ford to Stand Pat Despite GM Cutbacks." *USA Today* 10 July 1991: C10.

——. "Marlin Family Win Was a Long Time Coming: After 279 Tries, Coo Coo's Son Gets Win No. 1." *USA Today* 21 Feb. 1994: 3C.

——. "Marlin Learned Winning Message." *USA Today* 21 Feb. 1994: 3C.

——. "Marlin Triumphs at Daytona." *USA Today* 21 Feb. 1994: 1C.

——. "NASCAR Drivers Talk Tax Write-Offs." *USA Today* 28 April 1993: C9.

——. "Scanners in Fans' Hands Cause Talk." *USA Today* 14 Feb. 1992: 3F.

——. "Sons Casting Shadows All Their Own." *USA Today* 12 Feb. 1993: 3E.

"Twelve Week Ban for Johnson." *Washington Post* 21 May 1991: E5.

"Two Hundred MPH Pit Stop." *Stock Car Racing* Dec. 1990: 100-01.

"Unlicensed NASCAR Merchandise Seized." *Speedworld.* Online. Netscape. World Wide Web. 1996. Available: http://www.speedworld.net

"Unocal 76, NASCAR Join Forces in Automotive Aftermarket." *NASCAR Online.* Online. Netscape. World Wide Web. 5 Oct. 1996. Available: http:// www.nascar.com

"Update on Tobacco Sponsorship in Auto Racing." *Speedworld.* Online. Netscape. World Wide Web. 1996. Available: http://www.speedworld.net

Vehorn, Frank. *A Farewell to the King.* Asheboro, NC: Down Home Press, 1992.

——. *The Intimidator: The Dale Earnhardt Story, An Unauthorized Biography.* Asheboro, NC: Down Home Press, 1991.

"A Very Unusual Sponsorship." *Speedworld.* Online. Netscape. World Wide Web. 1996. Available: http://www.speedworld.net

Waid, Steve. "A Future for an Old Track?" *NASCAR Winston Cup Scene* 1 Aug. 1996: 4.

——. "Indiana's Own Makes Motorsports History." *Winston Cup Scene* 11 Aug. 1994: 8-9.

——. "James Hylton." *American Racing Classics* April 1992: 54-63.

——. "Jarrett Does It Again." *Winston Cup Scene* 22 Feb. 1996: 8-10.

——. "Labontes End Season in Style." *NASCAR Online.* Online. Netscape. World Wide Web. 11 Nov. 1996. Available: http://www.nascar.com

——. "What the Move Represents." *Winston Cup Scene* 27 Jan. 1994: 4.

Wecter, Dixon. *The Hero in America: A Chronicle of Hero-Worship.* Ann Arbor: U of Michigan P, 1963.

Whalen, Jeanne. "Cigarette Interest Flags in Racing." *Advertising Age* 6 Dec. 1993: 28.

"While Auto Industry Booms—Dealers Say They're in Trouble." *U.S. News and World Report* 25 Nov. 1955: 26-28.

White, Ben. *Circle of Triumph: The Bobby Allison Story.* Concord, NC: Griggs, 1993.

——. "Fred Lorenzen." *American Racing Classics* April 1992: 46-53.

Wilkinson, Sylvia. *Dirt Tracks to Glory: The Early Days of Stock Car Racing as Told by the Participants.* Chapel Hill: Algonquin, 1983.

——. *The Stainless Steel Carrot: An Auto Racing Odyssey.* Boston: Houghton Mifflin, 1973.

Williams, Chareau. "Crash Kills NASCAR Veteran: Bonnett Dies During Daytona 500 Practice." *Chicago Tribune* 12 Feb. 1994, sec. 3: 3.

Williams, Deb. "National Stock Car Commission Lifts Suspension." *Winston Cup Scene* 15 July 1993: 28-30.

——. "RJR Becomes Team Sponsor: 'Smokin' Joe's Racing' Will Be Camel's Label." *Winston Cup Scene* 4 Nov. 1993: 21+.

Wise, Suzanne. *Social Issues in Contemporary Sport: A Resource Guide.* New York: Garland, 1994.

Wolfe, Tom. *The Kandy-Kolored Tangerine-Flake Streamline Baby.* New York: Farrar, Straus, and Giroux, 1965.

——. "The Last American Hero Is Junior Johnson." *Esquire* Mar. 1965: 68+.

Woolford, Dave. "Inside Track." *Toledo Blade* 19 Sept. 1969: 29.

——. "Racing Is in Their Blood: Driving Attracts Sons to Copy What Father Did on Wheels." *Toledo Blade* 19 June 1994: B1+.

Wylie, Frank. "Rap 'n 'pinion." *Motor Trend* Nov. 1969: 18+.

Yarborough, Cale, with William Neely. *Cale: The Hazardous Life and Times of America's Greatest Stock Car Driver.* New York: Times Books, 1986.

Yates, Brock. "The $8500 Race Car." *Car and Driver* Aug. 1992: 149-56.

——. *The Great Drivers: Profiles of America's Fastest Heroes.* Nashville, TN: Opryland USA Inc., 1984.

Yiannakis, A. "Birth Order and Preference for Dangerous Sports Among Males." *Research Quarterly* 47.1 (1976): 62-67.

Zeske, Mark. "Defining a Champion." *Beckett Racing Monthly* Jan. 1995: 34-39.

Index

AAA, 21, 23

ABC, 4

AC-Delco 400, 193

AC-Delco 500, 162, 165

Aero Commander 500, 89

"Alabama Gang," 64, 65

Alabama International Motor Speedway, 39, 40, 43.
See also Talladega Superspeedway.

Alberts, Trev, 191

Alger, Horatio, 111, 129

Allison, Bobby, x, 39-40, 46, 48, 52-
55, 57-58, 61, 64, 65, 196

Allison Brothers Race Cars, Inc., 196

Allison, Clifford, 64, 66

Allison, Davey, xi, 58-61, 64-66, 160,
164

Allison, Donnie, x, 39-40, 58, 196

Allison, Judy, 65

American 500, 89

American Legion, 51

American Racing, 45

American Revolution, 187

American Zoom, 161

Andretti, Mario, 39

Arawak, 113

ARCA, 59, 61, 64, 155, 156

Armour Canned Meats, 95

Arrow ("Red Devil"), 82

ASCRA, 22

Atlanta 500, 37

Atlanta Motor Speedway, 181, 182,
195

Automobile Dealer Franchise Act, 44

"Awesome Bill from Dawsonville,"
127

AYSO, 50

B & R Engines, 26, 27

Baja 1000, 115

Bahre, Dick, 141

Baker, Buddy, 39, 42, 46

Baker, Buck, 42

Baker, E. G. "Cannonball," 17, 43

Ballard, Walter, 106

Barfield, Ron, 155-56

*Barney Oldfield's Book for the
Motorist*, 84

Barney Oldfield's Race for a Life, 85

BDR Motorsports, xii

Beam, Alex, 170, 175

Beebe, Leo C., 36

Behrman, Barbara, 93

Benson, Johnny Jr., 49, 174

Berggren, Dick, 185, 187

Bernstein, Kenny, xi, 168

Bestwick, Allen, 169

Birrane, Martin, 26-27

Biscoe, Billy, 171-72

Blonde Comet, 85

Blitzen Benz, 84

Bobby Allison Motorsports, 176

Bobby Allison Racing, 58

Bodine, Brett, xi, 3, 66, 70, 149, 151-
55, 168

Bodine, Geoff, 3, 66, 99, 149, 179

Bodine, Todd, 66

Bonnett, David, 65

Bonnett, Neil, 27, 60-61, 63, 65, 164, 178
Boone, Daniel, 111
Bourcier, Bones, 59, 125
Bowden, Henry L., 84
Bown, Chuck, 66
Bown, Jim, 66
Brewer, Tim, 26
Brickyard, The, 3, 18-19, 20, 125
Brickyard 400, 3, 14, 91, 124, 125
Broadway, 85
Brickhouse, Richard, 43
Bristol International Raceway, 180, 195
Brooks, Dick, 62
Broward Speedway, 22
Bruckheimer, Jerry, 7
Budweiser, 26, 161, 167, 171
Buffalo Bill, 111
Buick, 22, 30
Burger King, 189
Burton, Jeff, 66, 174, 181
Burton, Ward, 66, 71
Busch Clash, 161, 184
Busch Grand National, 64, 138, 156, 168, 174, 185
Busch North, 156
Byron, Red, 30, 115

California Speedway, 116
Camel, 160, 165, 187-88
Carr, Patrick, 130
CART, 18-20
Carter, Travis, 162, 165-69, 187-89
Cartoon Network, The, 100, 189
Cash, Johnny, 128
Catalyst Communications, xii
CBS, x, 66
CBS News, 88, 93
Celebration of Society, The, 131
Charlotte Motor Speedway, 23, 26, 30-32, 115, 124, 131, 175-77, 180, 195

Cherokee Speedway, 170, 171
Chevrolet, 11, 24, 26, 37, 44, 53, 88, 92, 98, 130, 149, 156, 159, 170, 176, 182, 194, 195-96
Chicago Cubs, 68
Childress, Richard, 129, 130
Christian, Sara, 94
Chrysler, 35-36, 46-47
Circuit City, 168
Citgo, 69
Civil War, 111
Clemson University, 189, 191-92
Clinton, President William, 186-87
Close Call Phone Card, xii, xiii
CMS Industrial Park, 176
Coca-Cola, 94
Colorado, University of, 191
Columbus, Christopher, 113
Cooper, Earl, 85
Cooper, Tom, 82-83
Constitution of the United States of America, 120
Cope, Derrike, 68-69
Craft, John, 35
Craven, Ricky, 161, 183, 196
Cross, Nim, 192
Cruise, Tom, 7, 195
Cub Scouts, 151
Curb, Mike, 62

Dallenbach (family), 19
Darlington Raceway, 39, 115, 149
Darwal Racing, 175
Days of Thunder, 7, 195
Daytona 500, x, 35-36, 56, 59, 63, 65-66, 91, 161, 188, 195
Daytona International Speedway, x, 43, 46, 54, 65, 96, 110, 115, 124, 134, 148, 154, 164, 168, 188-89
Daytona USA, 193
Denzen, Norman, 178
Diamond Rio, 189

Dinner Bell, 95
Dodge, 43, 175
Doolin, Lucas, 6
Doubleday, Abner, 124
Dover Downs Intl. Speedway, 151
Dunnaway, Glenn, 118
Dupont, 92, 98, 159
Duryea Brothers, 82
Duvall, Robert, 7

Earnhardt, Dale, 8, 11, 14, 26, 66,
  115, 126-31, 133, 156, 161, 166,
  171, 180, 181
Earnhardt, Ralph, 66, 126
"Easter Egg," 179
Eastman Kodak, 94
Economaki, Chris, 45
Elders, Joycelyn, 187
Ellington, Hoss, xi
Elliott, Bill, 72, 95, 127, 155-56, 160,
  164, 167, 171-72
Elliott, Cindy, 164, 167
Ellis, Tommy, 26
Empire Management Group, 191
Empire, Roman, 119, 134
Entertainment Weekly, 8
ESPN, 7, 14, 17, 86, 105, 177
Esquire, 116
European Sports Car, 22
Evans, Richie, 149
Evernham, Ray, 92-93, 183, 190
"Excitement, Mr.," 127

Farmer, Red, 65
Fast Track High Performance Driving
  School, The, 195
Fatal Environment, The, 122
Federation of Professional Athletes,
  32, 34-35, 37, 39, 48, 89
Fiat, 85
Fielden, Greg, 15, 24, 32-33, 42
Firestone, 40

Fisher-Price, 153
Fittipaldi, Emerson, 19
Flock, Bob, 179
Flock, Fonty, 115, 179
Flock, Tim, 5, 23, 31-34, 46, 115
Folger's Coffee, 90
Food and Drug Administration, 186-
  87
Ford, xii, 25-26, 35-36, 39, 44, 62, 67,
  77, 91, 93, 99, 110, 115, 118, 129,
  143, 151-53, 155-56, 162-63, 165,
  167-75, 79, 187-89, 191, 193-96
Ford, Henry, 21, 82-84, 86, 96, 169
Ford Motor Company, 26, 36, 173
Formula One, 19, 155
Fortune 500, ix, x, xi, 7, 135, 182
Fox, Stan, 19
Foyt, A. J., 19, 63
France, William H. G. "Big Bill," ix,
  14-19, 21-23, 28-35, 37-48
France, William Jr., 15, 48, 116, 185
Frontier Communications, xii

Gabbard, Alex, 121
Gant, Harry, 7, 88, 127, 170
Geertz, Clifford, 109, 110
General Foods, 94
General Motors, 35-37
Geoff Bodine Racing, 94, 176
George, Homer, 83-85, 111-12
George, Tony, 18-19
Georgeson, Benny, 22
Giles, Felix "The Nighthawk," 115
Gillette, 95
Girdler, Allan, 15, 17
Glotzbach, Charlie, 39-40, 43
GM Goodwrench, 11, 127, 156
Golden State Warriors, 51
Golenbock, Peter, 62, 161
Good Morning America, 92
Gooden, Dwight, 114
Goody's Headache Award, 95

Goody's headache powders, 95
Goodyear, 40-41
Goodyear Racing Eagle, 158
Gordian, John, 115
Gordon, Brooke, 164
Gordon, Jeff, 2-3, 14, 76-77, 92-93, 98, 124-26, 130-31, 140, 159, 164, 181, 183, 190
Gordon, Robby, 19, 174
Grand National, 4, 30-31, 34-39, 41-42, 44-47, 54-55, 58, 65, 67, 115, 124, 148-49, 156, 162
Grand National Advisory Board, 25, 34-35, 38
Grand Touring, 42, 45
Greased Lightning, 115
Green, David, 156
Green, Jeff, 156
Grey, Zane, 181
Grigg, Gordon, 191
Guthrie, Janet, 94
Guttman, Allen, 123

Hager, Dave, 8
"Handsome Harry," 89, 127
Hanes 500, 158
Hamilton, Bobby, 63, 88, 181, 193
Hamilton, Pete, 39
Hardy, Charles, 155
Harlem Globetrotters, 4
Hartford, Robin, 161
Harvey, Herb, 147
Hayes Modems, 189
Head, Jim, xii
Hedrick, Larry, 196
Heinz, 93, 95
"Hemi," 35-36
Hendrick, Joe, 24-27
Hendrick Motorsports, 26
Hendrick, Rick, xi, 7, 26-27, 90, 183
Hialeah Speedway, 53-54
Hickman, Herman, 30

"High Riser," 35-36
Hillin, Bobby, Jr., 26, 174
Hiner, Glen H., 154
Hinton, Ed, 131, 133
Hippodrome, 134
Hmiel, Steve, 93
Hoffa, Jimmy, 31
Hogge, Harry, 7
Holly Farms 400, 180
Hollywood, 7, 116
Holman, John, 30, 67
Householder, Ronny, 36
Hudson, 194
Hyde, Harry, 7-8, 195
Hylton, James, 39

"Iceman, the," 182
IMCA, 32
Indianapolis Colts, 191
Indianapolis 500, 3, 18-19, 54, 94, 115, 155
Indianapolis Motor Speedway, 3, 18, 124-25, 134
Indy Racing League, 18-19
Inman, Dale, 63
International Speedway Corp., 46, 94
Internet, 4, 192
Interstate Batteries, 182, 189
"Intimidator, the," 127
"Ironhead," 127
Irvan, Ernie, 3, 127, 164
Irvan, Kim, 164
Ivy League, 93

Janis, Elsie, 85
Jarrett, Dale, 66, 91, 181, 193
Jarrett, Glen, 66, 105, 193
Jarrett, Ned, 34, 66, 171
Jefferson, Thomas, 119
"Joe Camel," 166, 187-89
Joe Gibbs Racing, 189
John Deere, 92

Johnson, Flossie, 26
Johnson, Robert Glenn ("Junior"), xi,
    xii, 5, 25-27, 35, 55, 73, 114-17,
    121-22, 126, 167-68, 171-74, 182
Jordan, Michael, 114
Junior Johnson and Assoc., 171, 174

Kellogg's, 94
Kellogg's Corn Flakes, 182
Kennedy, Lesa, 94
Kessel, Dean, 153-54
Keystone Studios, 85
"Kid, The," 124, 181
"King Richard," 62, 127
Kinser, Steve, 168
Kirk, Tammy Jo, 94
Knuckles, Joey, 106
Kodak, 66
Kodiak, 24
Kolodny, Annette, 123
Kulwicki, Alan, 7, 68, 164, 176
Kulwicki, Gerry, 68

Labonte, Bobby, 66, 181-82
Labonte, Terry, xi, 66, 130-31, 181-82
Lakeside Industrial Park, 104, 138,
    162, 174
Langley, Elmo, 39
Larry Hedrick Racing, 196
Las Vegas Motor Speedway, 195
Last American Hero, The, 73, 116,
    122
Late Model Sportsman, 68, 148
Late Night with David Letterman,
    183
Latford, Bob, 185
Legacy cars, 143, 195-96
Legends cars, 195-96
Letterman, David, 92
Lincoln, Abraham, 111
Lindbergh, Charles, 113
Little, Chad, 91-92

Little League, 50-51
"Lone Eagle," 113
LoPatin, Larry, 45-46
Lorenzen, Fred, 30, 35, 67
Lovable intimate apparel, 94
Lowe's Home Improvement Ware-
    house, xii, 153-54
Lund, Tiny, 63
Luzerne County Community College,
    189

Macvicar, Andy, 162, 167
Madison Avenue, ix, x, xi, 27, 91,
    141, 197
"Man in Black, the," 128, 131
Manning, Frank E., 131, 133
Marlin, Clifton "Coo Coo," 65-66
Marlin, Sterling, 65-66, 106, 171
Martin, Mark, 25-26, 77, 93, 163, 181,
    183
Martinsville Speedway, 149, 158,
    180-81
Mason-Dixon Line, 67, 135
Mast, Rick, 110, 174, 179, 184
Mattel, Inc. "Hot Wheels," 64
Mayfield, Jeremy, 174
Maxwell House, 171
Mazda, 143, 196
McCrary, W. R., 40
McDonald's Corp., 72, 94, 168, 189
McIntosh, Burr, 81
McReynolds, Larry, xi
Mechanic of the Race, 92
Melling, Harry, 191
Mercury Outboard Motor Co., 54
Miami Vice, 90
Michigan International Speedway, 18,
    37, 65, 154, 156, 158, 161, 164,
    168-69
Michigan, University of, 51, 191
Mickey Mouse, 125
Miller Brewing Co., 92, 161

Miller High Life 500, 23
Mitchell, Eddie, 22
Mitchum, Robert, 6
Model T Ford, 56
Modifieds, 2, 20-23, 29, 126, 148-50, 168-69, 179, 195
Moise, Patty, 94
Montana's Steak House, 177
Moody, John, 29
Moody, Ralph, 67
Moonshine Highway, 117-18
Moore, Bud, xi, 129
Moroso, Rob, 89-90
Most Popular Driver, 34, 72, 88, 175
Motor Racing Network, 13
Motor Racing Outreach, 164
Motorsports Hall of Fame and Museum, 168, 170
MTD Yard Machines, 153-54
Muldoon, Jed, 118
Murphy, David Lee, 189
Myers, John, xiii

NAPA 500, 181
NARL, 22
NASCAR Cafe, 177
NASCAR Craftsman Truck Series, 94, 115, 155-56, 185
NASCAR Racing, 192-93
"Nash" car, 17
National Anthem, 132-33, 139
National Grand Prix Roadster, 22
National Speed Sport News, 42, 46
National Stock Car Commission, 24-26, 34
N. C. Auto Racing Hall of Fame, 138, 174
NCSCC, 16-17
Nebraska, University of, 191
Nelson, Gary, 185, 190
Nelson, Willie, 129-30
Nemechek, Joe, 74

Neuborne, Ellen, 166
New Hampshire International Speedway, 65
New Holland farm equipment, 156
New York Times, 97
New York Yankees, 114
NFL Properties, 189
NHRA Winston drag racing circuit, xiii, 158, 160, 168
"999," 21, 82-83, 84, 169
Normand, Mabel, 85
North Carolina Motor Speedway, xi, 89.
    See also Rockingham.
North Wilkesboro Speedway, 179, 180-83
Nova, 58
NSCRA, 22-23
NWCS, 95

Oakley, Annie, 111
Oldfield, Berna Eli "Barney," 21, 67, 83-86, 95, 107, 111-14, 124, 169
Oldsmobile, 67, 122
Order of the German Eagle, 113
Orr, Rodney, 164
Otto, Ed, 17, 33
Owens-Corning, 151, 153-54
Ozley, John, 58

Papyrus Design Group, Inc., 192
Park, Steve, 156
Parsons, Benny, 66
Parsons, Phil, 66
PASS Sports, 168
Passino, Jacque, 67
Patton, Arthur, 53
Patton, General George, 53
PE 2, 64
Pearson, David, 39, 63, 127
Penn State, 191
Penske, Roger, 18, 198

People of Plenty, 87
Pepsi 400, 24
Persian War, 133
Petty, Adam Kyler, 60, 64
Petty, Austin, 64
Petty Engineering, 58
Petty Enterprises, 55, 60-64, 78, 175
Petty, Judson, 56
Petty, Kyle, 14, 56, 58-64, 66, 106, 180
Petty, Lee, 14, 30, 54-58, 61-62, 64,
    66, 115, 175, 179
Petty, Maurice, 54-55, 62
Petty, Pattie, 60
Petty, Richard, x, 11, 23-24, 35, 37,
    39, 41-42, 46-47, 54-64, 66-67, 88,
    97, 127, 131, 161, 172, 175, 181
Philadelphia Inquirer, 192
Philip Morris, 186
Phillips, Benny, 10
Phillips, Lawrence, 114
Pickens, William Hickman "Will,"
    112-13, 124
Pinewood Derby, 151-52
Plan 2000, 176
Plymouth, 54, 175
Pocono International Raceway, 60,
    64-65, 71, 75-77, 79, 98, 101, 105,
    140, 147, 151, 156-57, 171, 176
Polachek, Larry, 148-49
Pontiac, 62-64, 78, 88, 128, 149, 181,
    189
Potter, David M., 87
Princeton University, 93, 190
Proctor and Gamble, 88, 90, 94
Prodigy, 189
Producers Releasing Corp., 85
Professional Drivers Assoc., 37-48
Prohibition, 121, 131, 187
Pro Stock Motorcycle, xiii
Pryor, Richard, 115
Punch, Jerry, 7
Pyne, George, 194

Quad-Cities International Raceway
    Park, 116, 185
Quaid, Randy, 7
Quaker State, 168
Quality Care, 193
Quality Care Ford Credit, 91
Quality Metal Products, 148-49, 155
QVC, 99, 176, 179

Rabin, William R., 31
"Race City, U.S.A.," 174
"Racers Edge, The," 194
Racing for Kids, 156
"Rainbow Warriors," 2, 98, 183
Ralstin, Dick, 40
Raybestos, 176
Reasoner, Harry, 88, 93, 96
Rebel 300, 30
Remington Arms, 110, 152, 179
Remington Arms Racing, 110, 152,
    179
Ribbs, Willy T., 115
Rick Hendrick Racing, 175
Richard Petty Driving Experience,
    185, 195
Richeson, Donna, xi
Richeson, Donnie, xi
Richmond, Tim, 7-8, 89-90, 131
Riverside 500, 47
R. J. Reynold's Tobacco Co., ix, 14,
    48, 95, 101, 156-57, 159-60, 165-66,
    170, 185-89
Roadster, 21
Robert Yates Racing, 106
Roberts, Glenn "Fireball," 31-32, 55
Robertson, Ian, 87
Robertson, T. Wayne, 14, 165-66, 168
Robertson, Toby, xiii
Robinson, Shawna, 94
Rockingham, 168, 180, 193.
    See also N. C. Motor Speedway.
Rookie of the Year, 91, 196

Roper, Jim, 119
Roush, Jack, 25-26
Rudd, Ricky, 52, 115, 174, 183
Rush, Ken, 42
Ruth, Babe, 114
Ruttman (family), 19

Sabates, Felix, 63
Sabco Racing, 63-64
Sagebrush, The, 176
Samples, Ed, 23
Sandwich Construction Company,
  The, 136, 176-77
SCCA, 151
Schrader, Ken, 14-15, 24-27, 161
Scott, Tighe, 106
Scott, Wendell, 115-16
Sears, Roebuck & Co., 95
Seeling, Angelle, xiii
Sega, 193
Sennett, Mack, 85
Sevier, John, 121
Shalala, Donna, 186
Shangri-La Speedway, 148-49, 168-69
Shepherd, Morgan, 62, 152
Shuman, Buddy, 23
Sierra On-Line, Inc., 192
"Silver Fox, the," 127
Simon, Dick, 18
Simpson, Don, 7
Simpson World, 104, 174
600 Racing, Inc., 195
Skoal Bandit, 88-89, 161, 170
Slaughter, Thomas P., 119-20
Slender You Health Spa, 94
Slim Jim All Pro Series, 94
Slotkin, Richard, 122
Smokin' Joe's Team, 103, 160, 162,
  165-70, 187-89
Smith, Henry Nash, 123
Smith, O. Bruton, 30
Snyder, Eldon, 81

Social Aspect of Sport, 81
Sociology, 87
Southeast wood treating, 153
Southern 500, 39, 67
SPEC car, 196
Speed Kings, The, 85
Speed, Lake, 52, 75, 191
Speedvision, 105
Speedway Club, 175
Speedweeks, 36, 154, 188
Spencer, Ed, 66
Spencer, Jimmy, 66, 127, 166, 168-70
Sports Illustrated, 133
Sports Image, 161
Sports Marketing Enterprises, xii, 14,
  153
Spreitzer, Elmer, 81
St. Louis Rams, 114
Stavola Brothers, 168
Stern, Jane, 5
Stern, Michael, 5
Stetson hats, 130
Stock Car Cafe, 137, 177
Stock Car Racing magazine, 4, 59, 130
STP, 11, 60-64, 88, 181, 194
Stranahan Auditorium, 152
Streamline Hotel, 16
Stricklin, Hut, 165, 168, 188
Strictly Stock, 2, 16, 20-22, 29-30, 94,
  118, 179, 195
Strug, Carrie, 122
Stutz, 85
Suzuka, 184-85
SVSCRA, 170
"Swervin' Irvan," 127
Sylvania lighting fixtures, 153-54

Talladega 500, 39-40, 42-44
Talladega Superspeedway, 46, 65,
  161, 165, 168, 183, 194.
  See also Alabama International
  Motor Speedway.

Tate, Mark, xiii
TBS, 86, 130
Teague, Marshall, 17, 23
Team Ireland, 26
Team Lowe's, 151-54
Teamsters, 30-32, 38, 46, 48, 89
Tennessee, University of, 191
Tetzlaft, Teddy, 85
Texas Motor Speedway, 184, 198
"Texas Terry," 181
"This Week in NASCAR," 168
Thomas, Herb, 14
Thomas, Speedy, 23
Thunder Road, 6, 117
Tide, 88
Tide Machine, 88
Tide Racing Team, 115
TNN, 92, 105, 193
Tony Packo's, 152
Toyota, 195
Trickle, Cole, 7-8
Trickle, Dick, 105, 193
Tri-County Speedway, 125-26
Turner, Curtis, 5, 23, 30-35, 37-39,
    46-47, 89-91, 115-16, 126, 131, 171
Tuschak, Beth, 94
Tuthill, Bill, 17
Twentieth Century Fox, 117
Tyson Foods, 91-92

UAW-GM Quality 500, 181
UAW-GM Teamwork 500, 79, 105,
    140, 156-57
Underalls pantyhose, 94
United Way, 151-52
Unocal, 182, 193
Unocal Race Stoppers, 94
Unocal World Pit Crew Champion-
    ship, 158, 162
Unser (family), 19, 54
U.S. 500, 18
USAC, 32, 36, 39, 67

U.S.A. Today, 94, 154, 166, 176
USCRA, 22
U.S. News & World Report, 161
U.S. Tobacco, 89, 162

Valspar Paints, 153
Valvoline, 77, 93, 163
Van Camps, 95
Vanderbilt Cup, The, 85
Vanderbilt, William K., 84
Vehorn, Frank, 57
Vogt, Jerome "Red," 17
Vukovich (family), 19

Waid, Steve, 13, 124
Waldorf-Astoria, 14
Walker, Derrick, 19
Wallace, Kenny, 66, 164
Wallace, Mike, 66
Wallace, Rusty, 3, 7-8, 66, 161, 174
Walt Disney World, 125-26
Waltrip, Darrell, x, 15, 24, 66, 79, 88,
    130, 155, 164, 175, 180
Waltrip, Michael, 66, 69
Waltrip, Stevie, 164
Warner, "Pop," 50
Washington, George, 120
Watkins Glen International Speedway,
    46, 154, 185
Weatherly, Joe, 55
Webber, Chris, 51
Wecter, Dixon, 113, 127, 129
Western Auto Parts America, 79, 175
Westmoreland, Hubert, 118
Wheeler, H. A. "Humpy," 131, 133
Wheeler, Patty, 94
Whiskey Rebellion, 8, 119-21, 187
White, Rex, 34
Whitman College, 68
"Wide World of Sports," 4
Williams, Deb, 24, 94, 166, 177
Williams, Richard "Chip"

Wilson, "Hooch," 118

"Winners," 60

Winston, 95, 157

Winston Cup Online, 190

Winston Cup Scene, 13, 24, 94, 124, 166, 177

Winston Cup Tire Challenge, 102, 158

Winston Million, 95

Winston, Miss, 94, 140, 158

Winston Simulator, 103, 160

Winston, The, 26, 161

Winston Trackhouse, 101, 157-58, 160

Winston West, 185

Winton, Alexander, 21, 82

Winton "Bullet," 21, 83

Wisconsin, University of, 6.

Wolfe, Tom, 116, 121

Wood Brothers, 62-63

Wood, Leonard, 62

World Karting Assoc., 75

World 600, xi, 30, 115

World Sports Enterprises, 94

World War II, 12, 55

World Wide Web, 4, 192

Wrangler Blue Jeans, 128-30

Yamaha FJ motorcycle engine, 195

Yankee 600, 37

Yarborough, Cale, x, 39, 41-42, 63

Yarborough, LeeRoy, 39

Yates, Brock, 16

Yates, Robert, xi, 65, 194